Dubai
VISITORS' GUIDE

explore

there's more to life...
ask**explorer**.com

GOLF & SHOOTING CLUB
SHARJAH

PRACTICE TARGET SHOOTING WITH REAL GUNS & REAL BULLETS

A COMPLETE SHOOTING COURSE WITH COURSE CERTIFICATE

INDOOR SHOOTING & ARCHARY RANGE - OUTDOOR AIR RIFLE SHOOTING RANGE - GARDEN ARCHERY RANGE

For more information, please call 050 524 8777

P.O. Box 12, Sharjah, UAE, Tel: +971 6 5487777, Fax: +971 6 5382305
Email: shooting@golfandshootingshj.com, URL:
www.golfandshootingshj.com

SHARJAH PAINTBALL PARK

BUBBLE SOCCER

24 Hrs. OPEN on Thursday and weekends

Bubble Soccer now available at Sharjah Golf And Shooting Club

FOR BOOKINGS
050 203 2288

BIGGEST PAINTBALL PARK IN THE MIDDLE EAST
1 INDOOR & 3 OUTDOOR FIELDS
CORPORATE EVENTS, TEAM BUILDING, BIRTHDAYS AND FUN DAYS OUT

GOLF & SHOOTING CLUB
SHARJAH

Tel: +971 6 548 7777
Email: paintball@golfandshootingshj.com
URL: www.paintballuae.com
f Sharjah Paintball Park

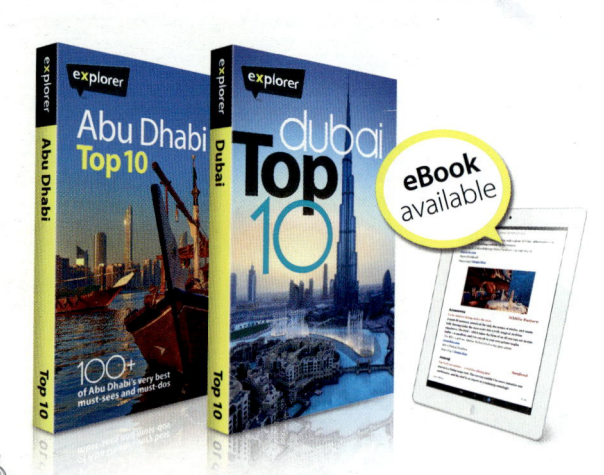

GOVERNMENT OF DUBAI

DUBAI MUNICIPALITY

An experience of a lifetime | DOLPHIN PLANET

Join the most lovable creatures of the ocean at Dolphin Planet. From poolside dolphin interactions to deep water adventures, swimmers get a unique experience to meet these incredible mammals; all under the supervision of our expert trainers.

Remember, advance booking is essential. See you soon!

Dubai.Dolphinarium @dolphinariumdxb
#lovedubaidolphinarium, Call +971 4 336 9773
or 800 DOLPHIN (3657446) Creek Park, Gate 1, Dubai.
Book tickets online at **dubaidolphinarium.ae**

DUBAI DOLPHINARIUM

Mackenzie Art

ART · MURALS · TROMPE L'OEIL · DECORATION

ENHANCE YOUR ENVIRONMENT

Manhattan Mural – Ramada Hotel, Doha

Dome Mural in Spa, Dubai

Exterior Wall garden mural

Abstract Painting

Gold Mural – Prayer Room

Trompe L'Oeil Mural Design

Mural Design

Gold Leaf Panel

Trompe L'Oeil Arches – Palace, Abu Dhabi

Trompe L'Oeil Foun

"From small to tall – we paint it all!"
Interior, exterior, walls and canvases – we provide personalised paintings for your homes, offices and projects

THE ULTIMATE FORMULA FOR FUN
SCAN TO DOWNLOAD OUR VIRTUAL REALITY APP
Add more rides with more time spent in the water, subtract waiting in line and multiply it all by the perfect location. Now that's what we call the ultimate formula for fun! Hurry and come out to Wild Wadi for a day of unbeatable fun with family and friends.
Buy your ticket online today on wildwadi.com
Wild Wadi
WATERPARK
Jumeirah

COMPLETE
YOUR SPORTS KIT

WITH THE ALL NEW **SPORT360.COM**

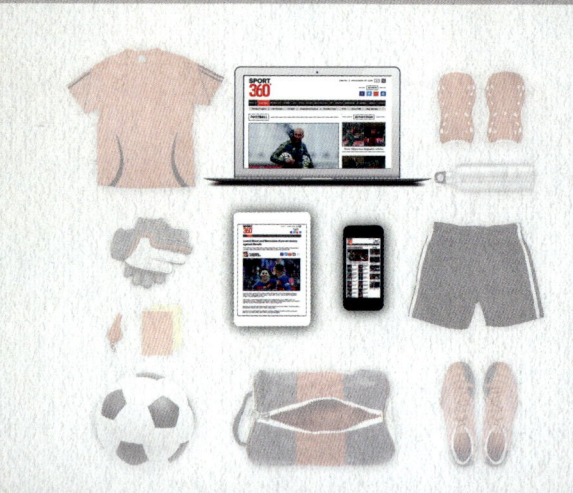

- NEWS
- ANALYSIS
- INTERVIEWS
- VIDEOS
- FAN RATINGS
- EVENTS CALENDAR

SPORT 360

BETTER CARE IS NOW CLOSER TO YOUR HEART

AMERICAN HOSPITAL CLINICS DUBAI MEDIA CITY

The new American Hospital Clinics based in Dubai Media City offers close and convenient access to high quality primary care for adults and children, with Western board certified specialists for patients in the nearby residential areas as well as access to the American Hospital Dubai's full range of specialty services and diagnostics at the main hospital campus.

The American Hospital's new Dubai Media City Clinics is based on the ground floor of the Business Central Towers, Sheikh Zayed Road.

For appointments, please call +971 4 377 5500 or visit www.ahdubai.com

Infinite fun for everyone

**Dolphin & Seal Shows
Illusion Shows
Swim with Dolphins
Exotic Bird Shows**

DUBAI

نحو مستقبل مستدام للحبارى

A SUSTAINABLE FUTURE FOR THE
HOUBARA BUSTARD

www.houbarafund.org

International Fund For Houbara Conservation

Dubai Visitors' Guide
Copyright © Explorer Group Ltd 2016
1st Published 2006

Published by Explorer Publishing & Distribution L.L.C.
PO Box 34275
Dubai, United Arab Emirates
+971 4 340 8805
info@ask**explorer**.com
ask**explorer**.com

Text, maps and photographs © Explorer Group Ltd 2006 – 2016

All rights reserved. No part of this publication may be reproduced, stored in a retrieval system, or transmitted in any form or by any means, electronic, mechanical, photocopying, recording or otherwise, without the prior written permission of the copyright owner Explorer Group Ltd.

To buy additional copies of this or any other of Explorer's award-winning titles visit ask**explorer**.com/shop. Special discounts are available for bulk purchases.

ISBN 978-1-78596-023-9

National Media Council Printing Approval No. 211

Welcome...

Welcome to the ninth edition of the *Dubai Visitors' Guide*. Brimming with insider tips on everything from cultural hotspots to 'in' eateries and the best boutiques, this mini marvel has all you need to make the most out of your time in this fascinating desert metropolis.

Dubai is a dynamic city with an iconic skyline and a host of top attractions. From sandy beaches to the world's tallest tower, man-made islands to mega-malls, the City of Gold is just waiting to be discovered. Written entirely by local residents, the following pages have been passionately created by the same team that brought you the *Dubai Residents' Guide*. Packed with useful information, our guides are updated every year to help you make the most of your trip.

For more information about Dubai and the rest of the region, plus to find out what's happening when you're in town, log onto askexplorer.com – the UAE's one-stop source for everything there is to know about Dubai and beyond.

There's more to life...
The Explorer Team

f 🐦 ▶ g+ 📷 in ℗ / **askexplorer**

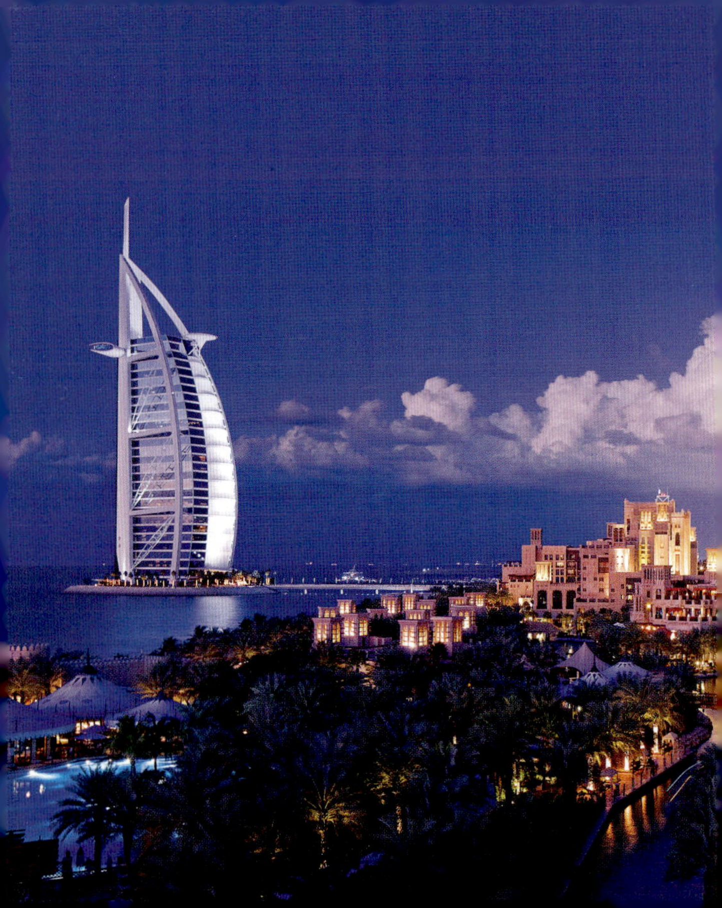

Contents

Essentials — 2
- Welcome To Dubai — 4
- Culture & Heritage — 6
- Modern Dubai — 14
- Dubai Checklist — 18
- Best Of Dubai — 30
- Visiting Dubai — 34
- Local Knowledge — 38
- Media & Further Reading — 46
- Public Holidays & Annual Events — 48
- Getting Around — 52
- Places To Stay — 62

Exploring — 74
- Explore Dubai — 76
- At A Glance — 78
- Old Dubai: Around The Creek & Beyond — 82
- Al Qouz — 92
- Downtown & Sheikh Zayed Road — 98
- New Dubai: JBR & Marsa Dubai — 106
- Festival City & Garhoud — 110
- Jumeira: Beachside Life — 114
- Nakhlat Jumeira & Al Sufouh — 120
- Outside The City & Dubailand — 126
- Further Out — 130
- Tours & Sightseeing — 138

Sports & Spas — 142
- Active Dubai — 144
- Sports & Activities — 146
- Spas — 164

Shopping — 176
- Do Buy — 178
- Where To Go For... — 182
- Souks & Markets — 188
- Shopping Malls — 196
- Department Stores — 210

Going Out — 216
- Dine, Drink, Dance — 218
- Entertainment — 222
- Area Directory — 226
- Cuisine Finder — 238
- Restaurants & Cafes — 246
- Bars, Pubs & Clubs — 310

Index — 330

askexplorer.com

Essentials

Welcome To Dubai	4
Culture & Heritage	6
Modern Dubai	14
Dubai Checklist	18
Best Of Dubai	30
Visiting Dubai	34
Local Knowledge	38
Media & Further Reading	46
Public Holidays & Annual Events	48
Getting Around	52
Places To Stay	62

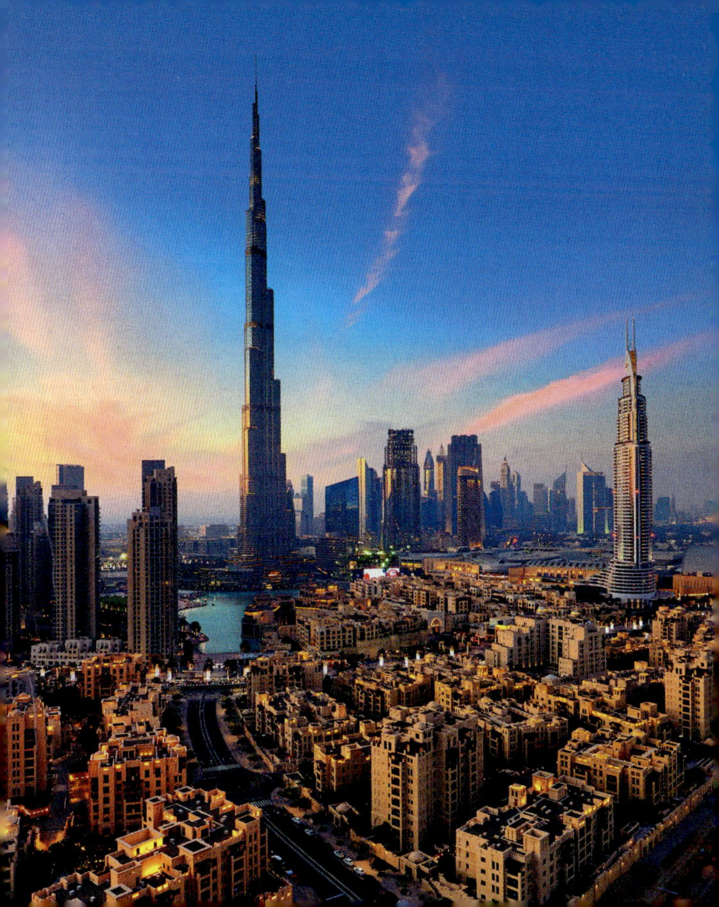

WELCOME TO DUBAI

Welcome to a city of stark contrasts; of sand dunes and skyscrapers, camels and fast cars, museums and malls. Welcome to Dubai.

Whatever your reason for touching down in this desert metropolis, it's hard not to be captivated by its growth and unshakeable ambition. The world's tallest building is already here, and a slew of architectural masterpieces and whole new communities are not far behind. Yet underneath the shiny surface there is more to Dubai than cranes and five-star cliches – you'll find Emiratis, expats and sunburnt tourists, all exploring this surprisingly multilayered city.

There is a wide scope of activities, cuisines and adventures to be had, many at prices that you wouldn't expect from the 'seven-star' headlines. Try dining in Arabic street cafes, browsing the souks and haggling for souvenirs to get a sense of local tradition, or sample Dubai's plethora of malls, upmarket hotels and fine-dining restaurants for a taste of its luxury reputation.

Outside the city are a whole new set of landscapes and a more traditional way of life. Seemingly endless vistas of untouched sand dunes are just waiting to be explored, so pile into that Land Cruiser and take a tour. Further out, the east coast of the UAE is a haven for divers and snorkellers, and the delights of Oman's rugged Musandam peninsula are only an hour or so north.

Over the next few pages, descriptions of the local culture and history will provide context to your trip. Following this is the vital information you'll need to get here and stay in style, plus advice on what to do when you first arrive. Things you really shouldn't miss are elaborated on in our handy Dubai Checklist. The Exploring chapter divides the city up, highlighting each area's best bits, such as museums, galleries and heritage sites. In Sports & Spas, you'll find out what the city has to offer for sports fans, keen golfers and those who simply prefer to be pampered. Shopping is your detailed guide to malls, boutiques and souks, and Going Out will help you manoeuvre your way through Dubai's increasingly impressive maze of restaurants, bars, pubs and clubs.

Essentials

CULTURE & HERITAGE

Rapid change and multiculturalism hasn't stopped the UAE embracing a proud heritage.

Early History

Dubai's history can be traced back over 4,000 years to the Bronze Age. It has long been a centre of trade for the region, partly because its creek (Khor Dubai) provides a sheltered harbour. The remains of a settlement in Jumeira, dating to the early centuries of the Islamic era, which began in the 7th century AD, provide evidence of those trading links. Today's modern city can chart its growth back to the arrival of the ruling Al Maktoum family in 1833 and by the late 19th century, it was the most important port on the UAE's Arabian Gulf coastline.

The Trucial States

By the 1800s, the town had developed considerably, supported by the income from pearling, which brought in important trade and revenue. In 1820, Dubai and the other emirates signed treaties with the British that eventually led to a guaranteeing of peace at sea, and, in consequence, to a boom in the pearling industry. Officially known as a 'maritime truce', this led to the area being called the Trucial States (or Trucial Coast), the name remaining until the United Arab Emirates (UAE) was born in 1971.

Growing Trade

In the late 1800s Dubai's ruler, Sheikh Maktoum bin Hasher Al Maktoum, granted tax concessions to foreign traders, encouraging many to switch their operations from Iran and Sharjah to Dubai. By 1903, a British shipping line had been persuaded to use Dubai as its main port in the area, giving traders direct links with British India and other key ports. Dubai's importance as a trading hub was further enhanced by Sheikh Rashid bin Saeed Al Maktoum, father of the current ruler, who ordered the creek to be dredged to provide access for larger vessels. The city came to specialise in the import and re-export of goods, mainly gold to India, and trade became the foundation of the emirate's wealthy progression.

Forming The Federation

The British announced their withdrawal from the region in 1968 and the emirates began to prepare for a new era. The ruling sheikhs – in particular Sheikh Zayed bin Sultan Al Nahyan and the ruler of Dubai, His Highness Sheikh Rashid bin Saeed Al Maktoum – realised that by joining forces they would have a stronger voice in both the wider Middle East region and globally. When negotiations began, the aim was to create a single state consisting of Bahrain, Qatar and the Trucial States, but eventually Bahrain and Qatar chose to go it alone. The Trucial States remained committed to forming an alliance and, on 2 December 1971, the federation of the United Arab Emirates was created.

A New Country Is Born

In 1971, the new state of the UAE comprised the emirates of Dubai, Abu Dhabi, Ajman, Fujairah, Sharjah, Umm Al Quwain and, in 1972, Ras Al Khaimah. Each emirate is named after its main town. Under the agreement, the individual emirates each retained a degree of autonomy.

The leaders of the new federation elected the ruler of Abu Dhabi, His Highness Sheikh Zayed bin Sultan Al Nahyan, to be their president, a position he held until he passed away on 2 November 2004. His eldest son, Sheikh Khalifa bin Zayed Al Nahyan, was then elected to take over the presidency. Sheikh Zayed is still enormously revered in the UAE and the country has continued to witness astonishing growth under the leadership of his son, Sheikh Khalifa. With his continued focus on the development of the UAE's infrastructure, economic health and cultural contributions, the country has gone from strength to strength, furthering its international relations, safeguarding its environment and promoting its heritage.

The Discovery Of Oil

The formation of the UAE came after the discovery of huge oil reserves in Abu Dhabi in 1958. The emirate has an incredible 6% of the world's known oil reserves. This discovery dramatically transformed the economy.

In 1966, Dubai, which was already a relatively wealthy trading centre, also discovered oil. Dubai's ruler at the time, the late Sheikh Rashid bin Saeed Al Maktoum, ensured that the emirate's oil revenues were used to develop an economic and social infrastructure, which is the basis of today's modern society. His work was continued through the reign of his son and successor, Sheikh Maktoum bin Rashid Al Maktoum and by the present ruler, His Highness Sheikh Mohammed bin Rashid Al Maktoum.

Culture & Heritage

The UAE's culture is tolerant and welcoming, and visitors are sure to be charmed by the genuine friendliness and hospitality of the people. Dubai is a melting pot of nationalities and cultures and the city's effort to become modern and cosmopolitan is proof of an open-minded and liberal outlook. There's a healthy balance between western influences and eastern traditions. The rapid economic development of the last 44 years has, in many ways, changed life in the UAE beyond recognition. However, despite rapid development and increased exposure to foreign influences, indigenous traditions and culture are alive and thriving.

The people of Dubai enthusiastically promote cultural and sporting events that are representative of their past, such as falconry, camel racing and traditional dhow sailing. Arabic poetry, dances, songs and traditional art are encouraged, and weddings and celebrations are still colourful occasions with feasting and Arabic music.

Food & Drink

Traditional Arabic coffee (kahwa) is served on many occasions and, if offered, it is gracious to accept because coffee plays a special role as a symbolic expression of welcome. Even the pot itself, with its characteristic shape and long spout, has come to depict Arabic hospitality. Freshly ground and flavoured with cardamom, Arabic coffee comes in tiny cups with no handles. The cup should be taken with the right hand. The server will stand by with the pot and fill the cups when empty. It's normal to accept one or two servings, then signal you have had enough by shaking the cup gently from side to side.

Local Cuisine

Dubai's restaurant scene has a truly global flavour, with most of the world's major national cuisines represented, and many of the fast food outlets too. Eating out is very popular, but people tend to go out late so restaurants are often quiet in the early evenings. Modern Arabic cuisine reflects a blend of Moroccan, Tunisian, Iranian and Egyptian cooking styles, with a significant Lebanese influence.

From pavement stands serving mouth-watering shawarma (lamb or chicken sliced from a spit) and falafel (mashed and fried chickpea balls) sandwiches to the more elaborate khouzi (whole roast lamb served on a bed of rice, mixed with nuts), it's all here.

Pork is not part of the Arabic menu and the consumption of it is taboo to a Muslim. Many restaurants don't serve it, though you can find it on the menu in some of the larger hotels and it is also available in some supermarkets.

Religion

Islam, the official religion in the UAE, is widely practised. The religion is based on five pillars (Faith, Prayer, Charity, Fasting and Pilgrimage) and Muslims are called upon to pray five times a day, with these times varying according to the position of the sun. It is worth keeping in mind that Islam is more than just a religion; it is the basis for a complete way of life that all Muslims adhere to.

There are plenty of mosques dotted around the city and, while most people pray in them when possible, most offices and public buildings have rooms set aside for prayers. Also, it's not unusual to see people kneeling by the side of the road if they are not near a mosque at prayer times. It is considered impolite to stare at

Essentials

Culture & Heritage

askexplorer.com

people praying or to walk over prayer mats. The abundance of mosques means that the call to prayer can be heard five times a day from the loudspeakers of the many different minarets. Friday is the Islamic holy day when many businesses are closed until mid-afternoon, in accordance with state and Islamic law.

During the holy month of Ramadan, Muslims are obliged to fast during daylight hours. Non-Muslims should not eat, drink or smoke in public areas during the fasting hours. You should also dress more conservatively. At sunset, the fast is broken with the Iftar feast. All over the city, Ramadan tents are filled each evening with people of all nationalities and religions enjoying traditional Arabic hospitality. The timing of Ramadan is not fixed in terms of the western calendar, but each year it occurs approximately 11 days earlier than the previous year, with the start date depending on the sighting of the moon. Parks and shops open and shut later and many are closed during the day. Entertainment such as live music is stopped, and cinemas limit daytime screenings. At the end of

> **Cross Culture**
> The Sheikh Mohammed bin Rashid Centre for Cultural Understanding was established to help bridge the gaps between cultures and give visitors and residents a clearer appreciation of the Emirati way of life. The centre organises tours of Jumeirah Mosque, one of the few mosques in the UAE that is open to non-Muslims. Visit cultures.ae to find out more.

Ramadan is a three-day holiday, when the new moon is spotted. This holiday is called Eid Al Fitr, meaning the feast of the breaking of the fast. It is the year's main religious event, like Diwali for Hindus and Christmas for Christians, and you will notice a distinct festive atmosphere around the country.

National Dress

Emiratis wear their traditional dress in public. For men, this is the dishdash(a) or khandura – a white, full length shirt-dress, worn with a white or red checked headdress, known as a gutra. This is secured with a black cord (agal). Sheikhs and important businessmen may also wear a thin black or gold robe, or bisht, over their dishdasha at important events, which is like an equivalent to a dinner jacket.

In public, women wear the abaya – a long, loose black robe that covers their normal clothes – plus a head scarf called the sheyla. Abayas are often far from plain, with intricate embroidery and beadwork along the wrists and hemline. Sheylas are also becoming more elaborate and a statement of individuality, particularly among the young. Not all women cover their face in public. Of those who do, some wear a thin black veil and others, generally older women, wear a burkha – a leather mask which covers the nose, brow and cheekbones.

Underneath the abaya, the older women traditionally wear a long tunic over loose trousers, called a sirwall. These are often heavily embroidered and fitted at the wrists and ankles.

Younger women are just as fashion conscious as in other countries and often wear designer labels with trendy accessories underneath their abayas.

MODERN DUBAI

The City of Gold has transformed into a thriving metropolis with an iconic skyline and ambitious future plans.

Dubai's rise to prominence has taken place at an astounding pace. Since the discovery of oil in the 1960s, the city has transformed beyond recognition. The rate of development over the past decade or so has been particularly noteworthy, with a stream of billion-dollar developments that have transformed Dubai into a regional metropolis with its eyes firmly fixed on the future. New projects continue to be announced. It is appropriate then, that Dubai won the right to host the Expo 2020, which is also helping the emirate to realise its goal of attracting 20 million tourists by 2020. Both transport and infrastructure projects are now full steam ahead.

People & Economy

There are an estimated 200 nationalities living in Dubai and the population has multiplied over the past few decades. According to a national census, the population in 1968 was 58,971 – in 2016, Dubai Statistics Center put it at almost 2.5 million.

Expat arrivals, robust economic expansion and high birth rates have continued to push up the total number, with the vast majority of growth coming from foreign workers moving to the country from all over the world. This has resulted in a diverse population. Aside from the huge number of Indians settling in the UAE,

Emirati nationals still make up the largest ethnic group and have considerable influence.

Dubai's economy has been successfully diversifying away from petrochemicals for the last few decades. Today, the main contributors to the economy include trade, transport, real estate, tourism and finance.

Tourism

The UAE is well ahead of many other countries in the Middle East in terms of travel and tourism. Boosting tourism plays a central part in the government's economic diversification plan and is a major force behind the array of record-breaking infrastructure and hospitality developments of recent times. Dubai is perhaps the most famous tourist destination in the UAE, with hundreds of hotels and attractions such as the man-made Palm Jumeirah island, the Burj Al Arab hotel and an ever-growing marina area. Meanwhile, in the Downtown area records are set: the Burj Khalifa, the world's tallest building, towers over the world's largest dancing fountain and nearby is the world's largest mall by total area, The Dubai Mall. Inside, visitors can even visit one of the world's largest sweet shops.

The development of these high-end tourist amenities and visitor attractions, in conjunction with an aggressive overseas marketing campaign, means that Dubai's popularity as a holiday destination continues to increase. It is striving to reach its target of 20 million visitors a year by 2020 – a goal that will surely be boosted following the emirate's winning bid to host the Dubai Expo 2020.

Visitor numbers to Dubai increased by 7.5% in 2015, with the city welcoming more than 14.3 million visitors according to the online statistics portal Statista.

Passengers through Dubai International Airport – now ranked the world's busiest in terms of international traffic – reached 78,000,500 in 2015 according to Dubai Airports, up 10.7% from 2014. The airport is projected to receive 89 million passengers in 2016 and has increased its capacity from 75 million to 90 million passengers with the development of the newly opened $1.2 billion Concourse D.

Al Maktoum International Airport opened in 2010, in the south of Dubai, near Jabal Ali industrial area. It opened for passenger services in the second half of 2013, and is expected eventually to become the world's largest airport, with a capacity of 160 million passengers and 12 million tonnes of cargo per year.

New Developments

There's barely a week that goes by when something from the UAE doesn't claim to be the world's tallest, fastest or most expensive. It's actually a smart way to get the country on the map. The Palm Jumeirah and the iconic Burj Khalifa are two examples of developments that have come to symbolise Dubai, and the world's longest driverless metro provides an alternative way to get around, as does the Dubai tram. There are ongoing metro expansion plans, including three brand new routes, as part of the infrastructure being built for the Dubai Expo 2020.

Further mega projects include the construction of a canal from Business Bay to the sea on the Jumeira coast, which will create an abundance of waterside living and leisure spaces. Dubailand outside the city will shortly be a hotspot for theme parks, a number of which are due to open in the near future. More prestigious islands are also being constructed off the city's shoreline.

A celebratory light show on the Burj Al Arab after the city won the right to host Dubai Expo 2020

Essentials

Modern Dubai

askexplorer.com 17

Essentials

Dubai Checklist

01 Ski Dubai

This indoor slope at Mall of the Emirates has 22,500 sq m of snow. There are five runs, a nursery slope, jumps, penguins, and a snow park for kids to play in and even go tobogganing! Lessons are available, and there's a cafe halfway up the piste.

Essentials

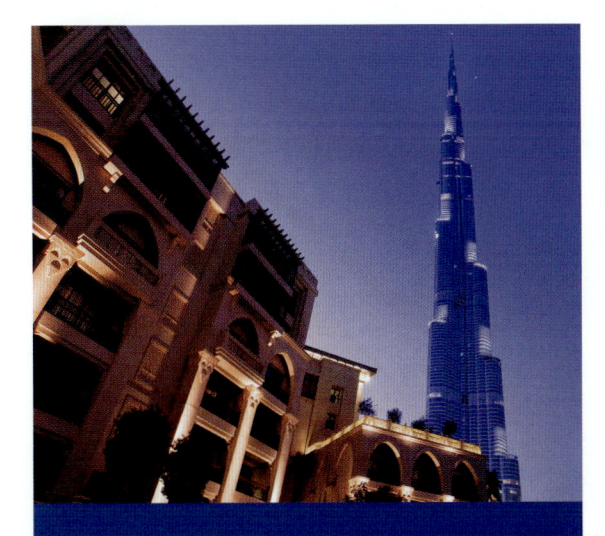

Dubai Checklist

02 At The Top, Burj Khalifa SKY

A visit to the world's tallest building is a must. Ride the super-fast elevator to the 148th floor's viewing deck, At The Top, Burj Khalifa SKY for breathtaking panoramic views of Dubai. Alternatively, book a table at At.mosphere – the world's highest restaurant.

Essentials

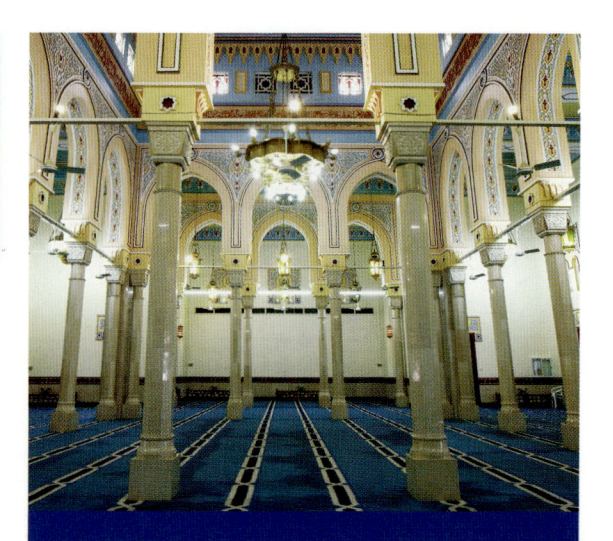

Dubai Checklist

03 Experience Local Culture

Take a tour of Jumeirah Mosque where you can learn about Islam and Emirati culture. The Sheikh Mohammed bin Rashid Centre for Cultural Understanding (cultures.ae) also demonstrates local hospitality through cultural meals in traditional Emirati style and heritage tours of the city.

04 Tackle The Dunes

A trip to the desert is a must during your stay in Dubai. Surfing over dunes in a car at impossible angles is great fun – as is a camel ride, sandboarding, falcon shows, and many of the other activities on offer. Tour operators are plentiful and professional, and safaris tend to include a barbecue.

Essentials

Dubai Checklist

05 Sample The Souks

Still an essential part of life for many people, Dubai's atmospheric souks are a welcome slice of tradition. Check out the spice souk, the colourful textile souk in Al Souk Al Kabeer, the fish market in Corniche Deira and the world-renowned gold souk.

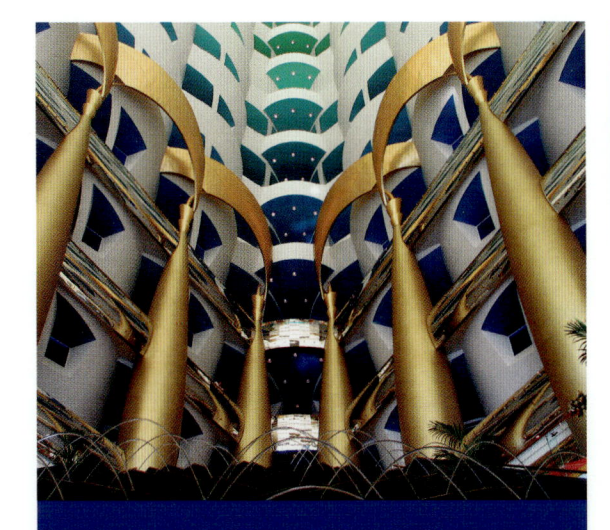

06 Burgeoning Buildings

Splash out on afternoon tea at the Skyview Bar at the iconic, sail-shaped Burj Al Arab hotel. Burj means 'tower', and the Burj Khalifa is the world's tallest building and as such a monument to Dubai's sky-high ambition. The skyline of Sheikh Zayed Road is also impressive for its tall towers.

Essentials

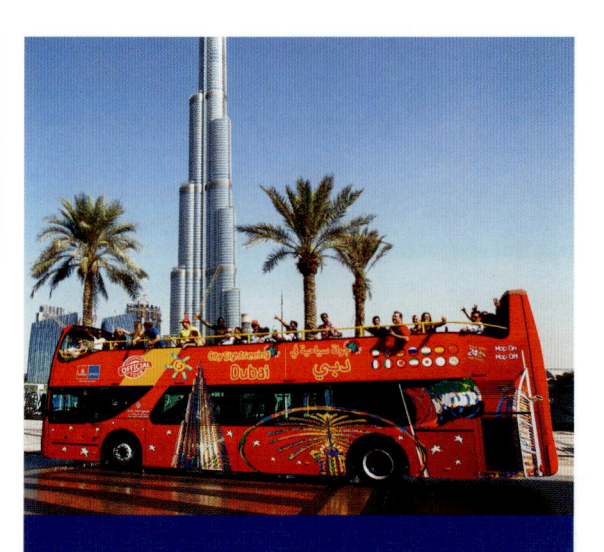

Dubai Checklist

07 Hop On A Sightseeing Bus

Combine sightseeing with transport to all major attractions with City Sightseeing Dubai's hop-on, hop-off bus tours, and learn some fascinating facts about the city along the way. Tickets also include free dhow cruises, entry to a number of the attractions along the way and discounts galore.

08 Hit The Malls

Dubai does shopping bigger and better than most. So whether it's to beat the heat or browse the boutiques, you won't be short of options. Read on for a full guide to the city's shopping hotspots, including one of the largest malls in the world, The Dubai Mall.

Essentials

Dubai Checklist

09 Explore Old Dubai

Wander along the narrow alleyways of the restored Al Fahidi Historical Neighbourhood and admire its traditional architecture and windtower houses. Explore the city's history at the Dubai Museum and learn about trades at the Heritage & Diving Villages on the banks of Dubai Creek.

10 Discover Downtown

Head downtown for trendy cafes, buzzing bars, chic restaurants and scintillating shopping opportunities at Souk Al Bahar and The Dubai Mall. The dancing Dubai Fountain is a delightful light, music and water spectacle not to be missed.

Essentials — Dubai Checklist

Essentials

Dubai Checklist

11 Paradise On The Palm

Live the high life on this man-made marvel. Experience the flamboyant Atlantis hotel with dinner at world-famous Nobu, swim with dolphins, walk through the watery world of the Lost Chambers Aquarium before taking the plunge at Aquaventure water park.

Essentials

Dubai Checklist

12 Life's A Beach

There's no shortage of sand in Dubai and with kilometres of aquamarine sea beckoning, spending time at the beach is a must. Relax on the golden sands at Sunset Beach or Kite Beach in Jumeira, or enjoy exclusive facilities at one of the city's many beachside hotels.

BEST OF DUBAI

For Adrenaline Junkies

Take a bird's-eye view of the growing metropolis while parasailing at one of the many beachside hotels or treat yourself to a skydive, indoors (theplaymania.com) or out (skydivedubai.com).

Dune bashing is a great way to clear the cobwebs and see some spectacular desert vistas. If you go with a tour group (arabianadventures.com), sand skiing or boarding might be on offer too. If you want to get behind the wheel, you'll find dune buggies and quad biking on the road to Hatta. If it's too hot for the desert, then head to Dubai Autodrome (dubaiautodrome.com) for a karting race around the 1.2km track or the 620m indoor circuit.

For real skiing, Ski Dubai (skidxb.com) at Mall of the Emirates has an indoor black run, giant ball run, and a 400m run is its longest.

To really get your pulse racing, why not take a dip with the sharks at Dubai Aquarium (thedubaiaquarium.com)? Novice and experienced divers can take the plunge with the aquarium's 33,000 inhabitants under the supervision of qualified instructors.

For Big Spenders

Dubai is a shopper's paradise offering everything from market stall haggling to haute couture. If labels are your thing, The Boulevard at Emirates Towers is home to several designers, but for anything you can't find there try the exclusive boutiques at BurJuman mall. Fashionistas will love the collections along Level Shoe District and Fashion Avenue at The Dubai Mall where they can rest their heels at the Armani Cafe post-purchase.

For Culture Buffs

Beneath its modern, glamorous exterior is the Dubai of old. Sample local cuisine in small eateries across Deira, hang out in shisha cafes, explore the souks, travel on an abra, visit the dhow wharfage on the Deira side of the creek, hunt for authentic souvenirs, and uncover history at Dubai Museum.

Meanwhile, the art and gallery scene is flourishing. Catch some exciting exhibitions at The Third Line and thejamjar; stay at XVA, a funky gallery and hotel in Al Fahidi Historical Neighbourhood; or visit the galleries at Alserkal Avenue in Al Qouz. For the lowdown on UAE culture, book a tour with Sheikh Mohammed bin Rashid Centre for Cultural Understanding.

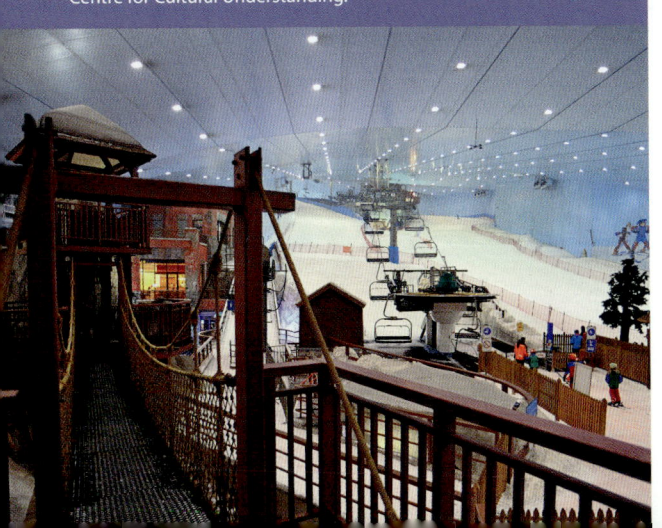

For Foodies

Dubai offers an eclectic mix of American fast-food staples, local street cafes and fine-dining hotel restaurants, but while in town it is the delicious Arabic food that should be top of your list. Try meaty shawarmas, vegetarian falafel, creamy hummus and fresh tabouleh, all washed down with the finest fresh juices.

For Water Babies

From relaxing at the hotel pool or one of the public beaches to diving, snorkelling, sailing and watersports, there are plenty of opportunities to cool off in the water. Make your own mind up in the battle of the water parks, choosing between Arabian-themed Wild Wadi and the Atlantis hotel's hair-raising Aquaventure.

For Architecture Admirers

An architect's playground, Dubai is home to many staggering feats of construction. From the sail-shaped Burj Al Arab to the world's tallest building, the Burj Khalifa, Norman Foster's Index Tower in DIFC, and the twisting Cayan Tower in Marsa Dubai, there are scores of skylines waiting to be photographed. Zaha Hadid's Signature Towers being built in Business Bay is an exciting addition for the near future.

For Party People

Sip cocktails to a Balearic soundtrack as the sun sinks into the Arabian Gulf at 360° or warm up at beach bar favourite Barasti. Trawl the stylish bars of Souk Al Bahar, then dance under the stars at open-sky nightclub Zero Gravity or strut your stuff with the designer set at White Dubai at Meydan. From the luxurious to the laidback, Dubai's nightlife offerings are surprisingly diverse.

Admire the architecture at Marsa Dubai

Essentials

Best Of Dubai

VISITING DUBAI

The UAE warmly welcomes visitors, but has a few rules and regulations that require extra attention. Read on for the vital information.

Getting There

Dubai International Airport (DXB) handled more than 78 million passengers in 2015. This makes it the world's busiest airport with flights to over 270 destinations. The newly opened $1.2 billion Concourse D has increased its capacity from 75 million to 90 million passengers. Terminal 1 handles major international airlines. Terminal 3 is exclusively used by Dubai's Emirates, while Terminal 2 is home to budget operator flydubai and other low-cost carriers, as well as charter flights. Terminal 3 has shopping, spas and chill-out gardens. The airport is clean and modern, and there's a huge duty free section in Terminals 1 and 3.

Al Maktoum International Airport (DWC) is located in the south of Dubai, not too far from the Dubai Expo 2020 site, and opened for passenger flights in 2013. It is expected eventually to be the world's largest airport, with a capacity of 160 million passengers and 12 million tonnes of cargo per year.

> **Airport Info**
> The main phone number for Dubai International Airport is 04 224 5555. For up-to-date flight information call 04 224 5555 and for baggage services, including lost property, call 04 224 5383.

Airport Transfer

If you booked your break through a hotel or travel agency, it's likely that pick-up from the airport will be included.

If not, the metro connects Dubai International Airport to destinations the length of Dubai directly from Terminals 1 and 3, or you could grab a cab. The taxi stand is straight in front of you as you leave the arrivals hall in all terminals. Taxis leaving from the airport charge an extra Dhs.25 so it costs around Dhs.50 for a

Airlines		
Air Arabia	06 558 0000	airarabia.com
Air France	800 23 823	airfrance.ae
American Airlines	04 316 6116	aa.com
British Airways	04 307 5555	britishairways.com
Emirates	600 555 555	emirates.com
Etihad Airways	02 407 2200	etihad.com
flydubai	04 231 1000	flydubai.com
Gulf Air	04 271 6207	gulfair.com
KLM Royal Dutch Airlines	800 556	klm.com
Lufthansa	04 216 2854	lufthansa.com
Oman Air	04 351 8080	omanair.com
Qatar Airways	04 231 9999	qatarairways.com
Royal Brunei Airlines	04 334 4884	flyroyalbrunei.com
Royal Jet	04 505 1777	royaljetgroup.com
Singapore Airlines	04 316 6888	singaporeair.com
South African Airways	04 397 0766	flysaa.com
United Airlines	800 0441 5492	united.com
Virgin Atlantic	04 406 0600	virgin-atlantic.com

journey to the hotels on Sheikh Zayed Road and the Burj Khalifa area or up to Dhs.90 to Marsa Dubai and the beach hotels of JBR.

An airport bus runs to and from the airport every 30 minutes, 24 hours a day. There are a number of loop routes: C1 runs to Satwa, while the 88 goes to Nakheel Metro Station. Log on to wojhati.rta.ae to plan your journey.

Visas & Customs

Requirements vary depending on your country of origin and it's wise to check the regulations before departure. GCC nationals (Bahrain, Kuwait, Qatar, Oman and Saudi Arabia) do not need a visa to enter Dubai. Citizens from many other countries get an automatic visa upon arrival at the airport which is valid for 30 days. For countries listed under the Schengen agreement, the

Visa On Arrival

Citizens of these countries receive an automatic 30 day visa on arrival in Dubai: Andorra, Australia, Brunei, Bulgaria, Canada, Croatia, Cyprus, Hong Kong, Ireland, Japan, Malaysia, Monaco, New Zealand, Romania, San Marino, Singapore, South Korea, United Kingdom, USA and Vatican City.

Schengen area countries eligible for a 90 day visa: Austria, Belgium, Czechia (Czech Republic), Denmark, Estonia, Finland, France, Germany, Greece, Hungary, Iceland, Italy, Latvia, Liechtenstein, Lithuania, Luxembourg, Malta, Netherlands, Norway, Poland, Portugal, Slovakia, Slovenia, Spain, Sweden and Switzerland.

visa on arrival has been extended to 90 days. Other nationalities may require a 30 day tourist visa, or 14 day special transit visa, sponsored by a local entity such as a hotel or tour operator, before entry. Some airlines can also apply for your visa, as can a family member resident in the UAE, as long as they meet the criteria.

Certain medications, including codeine, Temazepam and Prozac, are banned even though they are freely available in other countries. High-profile cases have highlighted the UAE's zero tolerance to drugs. Even a miniscule quantity in your possession could result in a lengthy jail term. Bags will also be scanned to ensure you have no offending magazines, DVDs or other forbidden items.

Dos & Don'ts

The UAE is one of the most tolerant and liberal states in the region, but as a guest in a Muslim country you should act accordingly. Lewd and drunken behaviour is not only disrespectful but can lead to arrest and detention. There is also zero tolerance to drinking alcohol and driving. Women should be aware that revealing clothing can attract unwanted attention, so very short dresses and strapless tops should be avoided outside of beach areas – though you will see short dresses and skimpy tops in nightclubs, along with those ubiquitous Dubai stilettos. Malls have put up signs making it clear that inappropriate clothing and public displays of affection are not allowed. It is courteous to ask permission before photographing people, particularly women. With prices for cigarettes low, smoking is very common. However, the law states that lighting up in malls and some restaurants is banned, so it's best to check the policy before striking up.

LOCAL KNOWLEDGE

Climate
Dubai has a subtropical and arid climate. Sunny blue skies and high temperatures can be expected most of the year. Rainfall is infrequent, averaging only 25 days per year, mainly in winter (December to March). Summer temperatures can hit a soaring 48°C (118°F) and with humidity well above 60% it can make for uncomfortable conditions from June to September. The most pleasant time to visit Dubai is during the cooler winter months when average temperatures range between 14°C and 30°C.

Time
The UAE is four hours ahead of UCT (Universal Coordinated Time – formerly known as GMT). There is no altering of clocks for daylight saving in the summer, so when Europe and North America lose an hour, the time in the UAE stays the same. Most offices and schools are closed on Fridays and Saturdays.

Electricity & Water
The electricity supply is 220/240 volts and 50 cycles. Most hotel rooms and villas use the three-pin plug that is used in the UK. Adaptors are widely available and only cost a few dirhams. Tap water is desalinated sea water and is perfectly safe to drink, although most people choose mineral water because it tastes

better. Bottled water is cheap, especially local brands such as Al Ain, Masafi and Arwa. Bottled water, both local and imported, is served in hotels and restaurants, but beware, imported water could cost many times the price of local water.

Money

Credit and debit cards are widely accepted around Dubai. Foreign currencies and travellers' cheques can be exchanged in licensed exchange offices, banks and hotels. Cash is preferred in the souks, markets and in smaller shops, and paying in cash will help your bargaining power. All banks operate ATMs accepting a range of cards and these can be found in the airport, shopping malls and most hotels, as well as at petrol stations.

The monetary unit is the dirham (Dhs.), which is divided into 100 fils. The currency is also referred to as AED (Arab Emirate Dirham). Notes come in denominations of Dhs.5 (brown), Dhs.10 (green), Dhs.20 (light blue), Dhs.50 (purple), Dhs.100 (pink), Dhs.200 (yellowy-brown), Dhs.500 (blue) and Dhs.1,000 (browny-purple). The dirham has been pegged to the US dollar since 1980, at a mid rate of $1 to Dhs.3.6725.

Tipping

Many places add a service charge onto the bill but no one really knows if this actually goes to the staff so many people add a little extra. The usual amount to tip is 10%. Many restaurant bills in hotels automatically come with 10% municipality tax and 10% service charge included, so check the total amount carefully. In a taxi it is standard, but not compulsory, to round up the fare to the nearest Dhs.5.

Language

Arabic is the official language of the UAE, although English, Hindi, Malayalam, Urdu and Tagalog are widely spoken. Arabic is the official business language, but English is commonly used and most road signs, shop signs and restaurant menus are in both languages. You can easily get by with English, but if you can throw in a couple of Arabic words here and there, you're likely to receive a smile.

Basic Arabic

General

Yes	na'am
No	la
Please	min fadlak (m)/min fadlik (f)
Thank you	shukran
Praise be to God	al-hamdu l-illah
God willing	in shaa'a l-laah

Greetings

Greeting (peace be upon you)	as-salaamu alaykom
Greeting (in reply)	wa alaykom is salaam
Good morning	sabah il-khayr
Good morning (in reply)	sabah in-nuwr
Good evening	masa il-khayr
Good evening (in reply)	masa in-nuwr
Hello	marhaba
Hello (in reply)	marhabtayn
How are you?	kayf haalak (m)/kayf haalik (f)
Fine, thank you	zayn, shukran (m)/zayna, shukran (f)

Essentials

Welcome	ahlan wa sahlan
Goodbye	ma is-salaama
My name is...	ismiy…
What is your name?	shuw ismak? (m) / shuw ismik? (f)

Questions

How many / much?	kam?
Where?	wayn?
When?	mataa?
Which?	ayy?
How?	kayf?
What?	shuw?
Why?	laysh?
Who?	miyn?

Numbers

Zero	sifr
One	waahad
Two	ithnayn
Three	thalatha
Four	arba'a
Five	khamsa
Six	sitta
Seven	saba'a
Eight	thamaanya
Nine	tiss'a
Ten	ashara

Accidents & Emergencies

Police	al shurtaa
Sorry	aasif (m) /aasifa (f)

Local Knowledge

Crime & Safety

Pickpocketing and crimes against tourists are a rarity in Dubai, and visitors can enjoy feeling safe and unthreatened in most places around town. A healthy degree of caution should still be exercised, however, and most hotels offer safes for keeping your valuables and travel documents locked away. Don't use an ATM if it looks like it may have been tampered with and inform your bank.

Police

Dubai Police's Department for Tourist Security is a helpful, friendly service should you run into any trouble during your stay. For assistance, call the toll free number (800 423) or visit the Dubai Police website, dubaipolice.gov.ae. There's a hotline for reporting problems on the beach, including sexual harassment or annoyance by quad bikes (04 266 1228). For other emergency services call 999 for police or ambulance and 997 for fire.

To avoid a great deal of hassle if your personal documents go missing, make sure you keep one photocopy with friends or family back home and one copy in your hotel safe. Dubai Police will advise you on a course of action in the case of a loss or theft. If taking a taxi, memorise the number on the door, then if you lose something, you can call the taxi company (see the last page of this book).

If you lose your passport, your next stop should be your embassy or consulate (see the pull-out map). With high accident rates, extra caution should be taken on Dubai's roads, whether navigating the streets on foot or in a vehicle. Use designated pedestrian crossings wherever possible (jaywalking is actually illegal), and make sure all cars are going to stop before you cross.

There is zero tolerance towards drink driving, even after one pint (there is no legal limit), and if you're caught you can expect a spell in prison. With thousands of low-fare taxis available, there is no excuse or need.

Accidents & Emergencies

If you witness an accident or need an ambulance in an emergency situation, the number to call is 999. For urgent medical care, there are several private hospitals with excellent A&E facilities.

The American Hospital Dubai (ahdubai.com) is among the biggest and most trusted – see the pull-out map for listings and contact details. Anyone can receive emergency treatment in government hospitals but note that charges apply to those without Dubai health cards. For general non-emergency medical care, most hospitals have a walk-in clinic where you can simply turn up for a consultation with a physicist; for example, Medcare (medcarehospital.com) has several clinics across Dubai.

People With Disabilities

Dubai is starting to consider the requirements of visitors with special needs more seriously although, in general, facilities are limited, particularly at older tourist attractions. When asking if a location has wheelchair access, make sure it really does – an escalator has been considered 'wheelchair access' in some instances.

That said, Dubai International Airport is well equipped for travellers with special needs, with automatic doors, large lifts and all counters accessible by wheelchair users, as well as several services such as porters, special transportation and quick check-in to avoid long queues. Dubai Roads & Transport Authority has a few specially modified taxis for journeys from the airport and around town, and all metro stations are designed to give easy access to wheelchair users. Metro stations also have tactile floor routes for visually impaired people. Most of the newer malls have wheelchair access and recently built five-star hotels should offer accessible rooms for visitors with special needs.

Telephone & Internet

Etisalat and du are the local mobile telecoms companies and have reciprocal agreements with most countries for roaming services, allowing visitors to use their mobile in the UAE.

Both Etisalat and du also offer short-term mobile lines and useful prepaid services aimed at tourists. Visitors can purchase a SIM card and local number pre-loaded with calling credit so you can make local calls at the local rate. Both Etisalat and du SIM cards are available at most malls and mobile phone shops.

International calls from local mobile lines are much cheaper than hotel rates and you can buy extra credit at most supermarkets, newsstands and gas stations.

A local SIM for your phone is useful in Dubai and means you can take advantage of all the mobile apps that make touring the city a smoother experience. Try Uber or Careem for an online GPS-enabled chauffeur service, Zomato for restaurants or ReserveOut to book a table. If you're not online, Explorer's Dubai offline map app allows visitors easily to navigate the city without the need for data. Available on iOS, search '*Explorer Dubai Map*' in the App Store.

Essentials

Local Knowledge

MEDIA & FURTHER READING

Newspapers & Magazines

There are several English language newspapers in Dubai. You will see free copies of *7Days* on display; this daily tabloid contains international news alongside cinema listings and gossip. *The National*, *Khaleej Times* and *Gulf News* are broadsheets that offer local and international current affairs with regular supplements. UK broadsheet *The Times* publishes an international edition, which is available daily in most supermarkets. Larger supermarkets and newsagents also stock copies of international newspapers from the *Financial Times* and *Wall Street Journal* to *Le Figaro* and *La Repubblica*. For magazines and lifestyle titles, there are plenty of local options, including a range of Middle Eastern editions of international titles that are produced in Dubai. These include *Harper's Bazaar*, *Time Out*, *OK!*, *Hello!* and *Grazia*.

Bookshops such as Kinokuniya and Borders stock a good selection, as do most larger supermarkets. Many of the major, international glossy magazines are also available in Dubai (although as they're imported from the US or Europe, you can expect to pay at least twice the normal cover price).

Television

Most hotel rooms will have satellite or cable, broadcasting a mix of local and international channels. You'll find MTV, major news stations and some BBC programming, in addition to the standard hotel room information loop. For a slice of local flavour, check out local stations City7, Dubai TV and Dubai One, all of which broadcast Arabic soap operas, talkshows and American sitcoms in addition to local news programmes.

Radio

Catering for Dubai's multinational inhabitants, there are stations broadcasting in English, French, Hindi, Malayalam and Urdu. Daily schedules can be found in newspapers. Of the English-speaking stations, there is a good range to choose from. Tune into Dubai 92 (92.0 FM) for chatty programmes with European music, or try Radio 1 (104.1 FM), Radio 2 (99.3 FM), Auto Radio (103.2 FM) and Virgin Radio (104.4 FM) for music, or Dubai Eye (103.8 FM) for talk radio and sport. All stations broadcast regular news and travel updates. Sadly, the BBC World Service ceased broadcasting in Dubai in 2010.

More Info?
To find out more about what's going on in Dubai, check out askexplorer. com, Explorer's community driven hub for news, events and local information. For the lowdown on all there is to experience across the whole country, grab a copy of *UAE & Oman Ultimate Explorer* or *UAE Daytripper*. If you fancy getting behind the wheel on the stunning sand dunes, Explorer's *UAE Off-Road* is essential reading. These titles and many more are available at askexplorer.com/shop.

PUBLIC HOLIDAYS & ANNUAL EVENTS

Public Holidays

The Islamic calendar starts from the year 622AD, the year of Prophet Muhammad's migration (Hijra) from Mecca to Al Madinah. Hence, the Islamic year is called the Hijri year and dates are followed by AH (AH stands for Anno Hegirae, meaning 'after the year of the Hijra'). As some holidays are based on the sighting of the moon and do not have fixed dates on the Hijri calendar, Islamic holidays are more often than not confirmed less than 24 hours in advance. The main Muslim festivals are Eid Al Fitr (the festival of the breaking of the fast), which marks the end of Ramadan, and Eid Al Adha (the festival of the sacrifice), which marks the end of the

Public Holidays	
Lailat Al Mi'raj	5 May 2016 (Moon)
Eid Al Fitr	6 July 2016 (Moon)
Arafat Day	10 Sept 2016 (Moon)
Eid Al Adha	11 Sept 2016 (Moon)
Islamic New Year's Day	2 Oct 2016 (Moon)
Commemoration Day	30 Nov 2016 (Fixed)
UAE National Day	2 Dec 2016 (Fixed)
Mawlid Al Nabee	11 Dec 2016 (Moon)
New Year	1 Jan 2017 (Fixed)

pilgrimage to Mecca). Mawlid Al Nabee is the holiday celebrating Prophet Muhammad's birthday, and Lailat Al Mi'raj celebrates the Prophet's ascension into heaven.

In general, public holidays are unlikely to disrupt a visit to Dubai, except that shops may open a bit later and on a few specific days, alcohol is not served. During Ramadan, food and beverages cannot be consumed in public during the day; however, in most tourist hotels, there are special areas which serve diners all day long. Smoking and chewing gum are also prohibited, and you should dress more conservatively than usual. These rules apply to Muslims and non-Muslims alike.

Annual Events

Throughout the year, Dubai hosts an impressive array of events, from the world's richest horse race and international tennis to well-respected jazz and film festivals. Thousands of international visitors arrive and tickets sell quickly.

Dubai Shopping Festival
January to February
Various Locations
dubaievents.ae

Dubai Shopping Festival is a great time to be in the city with bargains galore for shoppers and entertainers, prize draws and kids' shows held in participating malls.

Emirates Airline Dubai International Jazz Festival
February
Dubai Media City, Al Sufouh 2
dubaijazzfest.com

The jazz festival attracts a broad range of artists from all around the world to a chilled and pleasant setting in Dubai Media City.

Art Dubai

Madinat Jumeirah, Al Sufouh 1

March
artdubai.ae

This international art exhibition sees visits from dozens of international galleries, and runs alongside the Global Art Forum.

Dubai Canvas

Jumeirah Beach Residence, Marsa Dubai

March

This 3D art festival turns the streets of JBR into a large canvas, encouraging visitors to participate and interact with the exhibits.

Dubai Food Festival

Various locations

March
dubaifoodfestival.com

Fantastic for foodies, Dubai pulls out all the stops every March with food-themed events all over the city.

Dubai International Kite Fest

Jumeirah Beach

March
ikfdubai.com

During this three day festival of colour and laughter, the wildest and wackiest colourful kites are flown on the beach.

Dubai World Cup

Meydan Racecourse, Nadd Al Shiba 1

March
dubaiworldcup.com

The buzzing atmosphere at the richest horse race in the world makes it one of the year's big social occasions.

Al Marmoom Heritage Festival

Al Marmoom Camel Racetrack, Dubai-Al Ain Road

March

Held near the end of the racing season, this festival celebrates camels and features many traditional and cultural curiosities.

SIKKA Art Fair
Al Fahidi Historical Neighbourhood

March
artweek.ae

This free art fair features the work of UAE artists, including audio and video installations, painting, photography, sculpture and more.

Al Gaffal Dhow Race
Various locations

May

A UAE institution, this traditional dhow race commemorates the country's sailing heritage and celebrates the pearl divers of the past.

Modhesh World
Dubai World Trade Centre

June-August

Modhesh World provides entertainment and events for kids and families, and each year attracts about 500,000 visitors to join in.

Dubai Summer Surprises
Various locations

July to September
dubaievents.ae

Fun packed, family-orientated activities and big shopping discounts are held in malls across the city.

Dubai International Film Festival
Madinat Jumeirah, Al Sufouh 2

December
dubaifilmfest.com

DIFF is showcase of Hollywood, international and regional films with screenings in cinemas across the city.

Emirates Airline Dubai Rugby Sevens
The Sevens

December
dubairugby7s.com

The rivalry is friendly here as the top international and local Gulf teams battle it out. There are also prizes for best fancy dress.

GETTING AROUND

With the expanding metro system, air-conditioned buses and cheap taxis, travelling round Dubai is easier than you think.

You may have heard horror stories about arduous commutes, sticky strolls in the summer and terrifying taxi journeys, but it is surprisingly simple, and pretty cheap, to get around Dubai. Public transport took a real leap forward in 2009 with the launch of Dubai Metro. Cheap and plentiful taxis are still a popular method of transport, but don't overlook the even cheaper bus routes. It is possible to explore some areas on foot during the cooler winter months. If you prefer to be in control then hiring a car is a great way to get out of the city, but bear in mind the variable driving standards of many motorists. If you're keen to get off the road then take a trip on a traditional abra or modern water bus. Many people use them for daily trips and they offer a fresh perspective on the city.

Metro, Monorail & Tram

Dubai's driverless metro currently has two lines. The Red Line runs from Rashidiya to Dubai International Airport and down Sheikh Zayed Road – passing the financial district, Burj Khalifa, Al Barsha and Marsa Dubai – before terminating near Jabal Ali. The Green Line runs from Al Qusais on the Sharjah border to Jadaf. Blue, Gold and Purple Lines are planned to be running by 2030 and the current Red and Green Lines will be expanded further. You can check dubaimetro.eu for updates.

Arabian Gulf
N
Salah Al Din
Abu Baker Al Siddque
Abu Hail
Al Qiyadah
Stadium
Al Nahda
Dubai Airport Freezone
Al Qusais
Etisalat
Baniyas Square
Palm Deira
Al Ras
Al Ghubaiba
Al Fahidi
Union
BurJuman
Al Rigga
Deira City Centre
Terminal 1
Terminal 3
Emirates
Rashidiya
GGICO
ADCB
Al Jafiliya
World Trade Centre
Oud Metha
Dubai Healthcare City
Al Jadaf
Creek
Emirates Towers
Financial Centre
Burj Khalifa/Dubai Mall
Business Bay
Noor Bank
FGB
Mall of the Emirates
Sharaf DG
Dubai Internet City
Nakheel
DAMAC
Jumeirah Lakes Towers
Nakheel Harbour & Tower
Ibn Battuta
Energy
Danube
UAE Exchange
AL SUFOUH ST
Al Sufouh
Knowledge Village
Palm Jumeirah
Media City
Mina Seyahi
Marina Towers
Dubai Marina
JBR 1
JBR 2
Marina Mall
JLT
Dubai Internet City
SHK ZAYED RD
041602

Trains run from 5.30am (Red Line) or 5.50am (Green Line) to midnight Saturday to Wednesday, and until 1am on Thursdays and Fridays. Services begin at 10am on Fridays. The frequency is every 3.45 minutes during peak times, and every seven minutes during off-peak hours. Each train has a section for women and children only, which have recently been extended, and a first or 'gold' class cabin. It is important to note that passengers can be fined for riding in the wrong cabin. The fare structure operates as a pay-as-you-go system, in which you scan your prepaid Nol card in and out of stations. Also note that station names change regularly to reflect who sponsors them.

Commuters can also take advantage of du wi-fi at stations and on the trains themselves. Access cards are available for Dhs.20 per hour, or you can pay via credit card at a rate of Dhs.10 per hour.

There is a feeder bus system to transport passengers from stations to local destinations. The buses are free if boarded within 30 minutes of exiting the metro. Each station also has a taxi rank outside to help you reach destinations that aren't accessible by bus.

A monorail runs the length of Nakhlat Jumeira from the Gateway Towers station on the mainland to Atlantis hotel. Trains run daily from 10am to 10pm and cost Dhs.15 for a single fare or Dhs.25 for a return. Dubai Tram runs along Al Sufouh Road, linking Jumeira Beach Residence, Marsa Dubai and Jumeirah Lakes Towers to the Palm monorail and Knowledge Village.

Trams run from 6.30am to 1.30am Sunday to Thursday, and 9am to 1.30am on Fridays. They run every 10 minutes during peak times and every 12 minutes during off-peak times. For the four stations in Marsa Dubai, a new service has increased frequency to every six minutes.

Bus

There are over 100 bus routes servicing the main residential and commercial areas of Dubai. The buses and bus shelters are air conditioned, modern and clean, although they can be crowded at peak times. The main bus stations are near the gold souk in Deira and on Al Ghubaiba Road in Bur Dubai. Buses run at regular intervals until around midnight and a handful of Nightliner buses operate from 11.30pm until 6am. The front three rows of seats on all buses are reserved for women and children only. Cash is not accepted so you need to purchase a Nol card (see below) before boarding. Call the RTA (800 9090) or check the website (rta.ae) for comprehensive route plans, timetables and fares.

> **Hop-On, Hop-Off**
> Another great way to get around is on the City Sightseeing Dubai hop on, hop off bus tour (citysightseeing-dubai.com). Their 24, 48 and 72 hour tickets will take you to Dubai's top attractions. The buses cover 45 stops, and the frequency is every 20 to 30 minutes.

Nol Card

Nol cards are rechargeable travel cards which are used to pay for public transport, parking and some taxis. Single Metro journeys start at Dhs.1.80 for up to 3km, rising to Dhs.5.80 for travel across two or more zones. The red Nol card is a paper ticket aimed at tourists and occasional users. It can be charged for up to 10 journeys, but is only valid on one type of transport at a time – bus, metro or water bus. The silver Nol card costs Dhs.25, including Dhs.19 credit. It can be recharged up to Dhs.5,000 and can be used across all forms of transport and for street parking. This is a better option if you plan to use different types of public transport or travel extensively while in town. The gold card is identical to the silver, except that holders are charged first class prices (usually double the standard fare) and can travel in the gold class cabins of the metro. Nol cards can be purchased and topped up at metro and bus stations and at supermarkets including Carrefour and Spinneys.

Cycling

Although cyclists have not been well catered for in the past, the RTA is working to promote cycling in Dubai with its 850km Dubai Bicycle Master Plan. You cannot cycle on Dubai's highways and even riding within city neighbourhoods can be dangerous. Also, summer temperatures can reach 45°C, which makes riding around the city a very sweaty option. There are, however, a number of places where you can cycle for pleasure, including Jumeira St, Nadd Al Shiba, Al Qudra and most public parks.

Car Rental Agencies

Avis	800 2847	avis.ae
Budget Rent A Car	800 2722	budget-uae.com
Diamondlease Car Rental	800 37483	diamondlease.com
EuroStar Rent A Car	04 266 1117	eurostarrental.com
Hertz UAE	800 43789	hertzuae.com
National Car Rental	04 283 2020	national-ae.com
Thrifty Car Rental	800 4770	thriftyuae.com

نحو مستقبل مستدام للحبارى

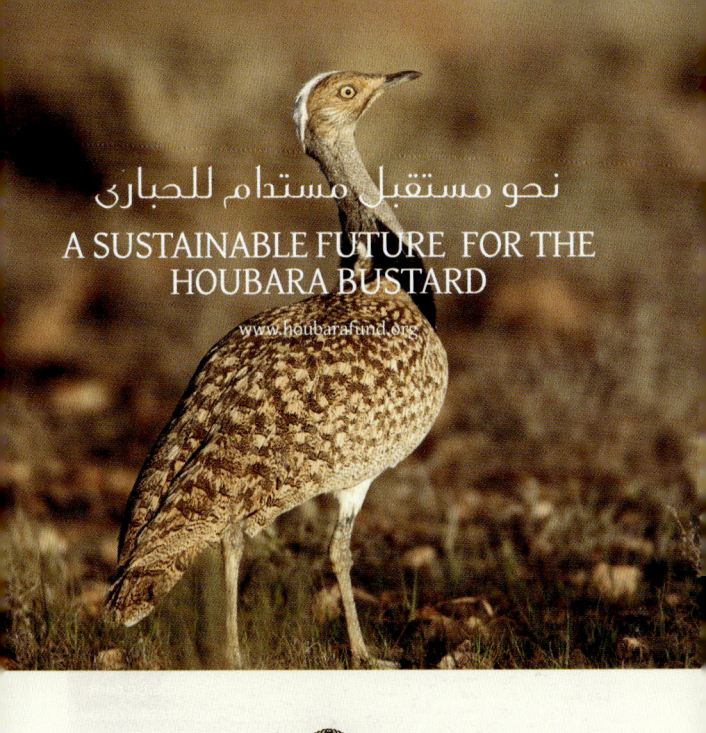

A SUSTAINABLE FUTURE FOR THE HOUBARA BUSTARD

www.houbarafund.org

المندوق الدولي للحفاظ على الحبارى
International Fund For Houbara Conservation

Driving & Car Hire

It's a brave individual who gets behind the wheel in Dubai. Drivers are erratic, roads are constantly changing and the traffic jams can be enduring. On the bright side, most cars are automatic, which makes city driving a lot easier. If you are a confident driver, you'll probably find that driving in Dubai looks much worse than it is in practice. Expect the unexpected, keep your distance and use your mirrors and indicators. Weekends, especially Fridays, are much clearer on the roads but during the week, traffic heading into Dubai from Deira in the morning and out in the evening can be horrendous. Driving is on the right-hand side of the road.

International car rental companies, plus a few local firms, can be found in Dubai. Prices range from Dhs.85 a day for smaller cars to well over Dhs.1,000 for limousines. Comprehensive insurance is essential; make sure that it includes personal accident coverage. To rent a car, you need a copy of your passport, a valid international driving licence and a credit card. The rental company may be able to help arrange international or temporary local licences for visitors.

Parking is plentiful at most malls and is free for at least the first three hours. Street parking spaces can be hard to find but cost just Dhs.2 for one hour and are free of charge between 1pm and 4pm. You can pay in cash or with a Nol card at ticket machines, or those with a local SIM can pay via SMS.

Taxi

Taxis remain a common way of getting around. There are seven companies operating nearly 8,000 metered cabs with a fixed fare structure. All cars are clean and modern, and the fares are cheaper than in most international cities. A fleet of 'ladies' taxis,'

Essentials

Getting Around

with distinctive pink roofs and female drivers, are meant for female passengers and families only. The minimum fare is Dhs.12 and the pick-up charge is Dhs.5 or Dhs.7 depending on whether or not you've made a booking, and Dhs.25 if you're picked up at the airport. It is also possible to hire a taxi for six or 12 hour periods. Taxis can be flagged down, or you can order one through Dubai Taxi (04 208 0808). This number is also useful for complaints and lost item enquiries. Chauffeur services Careem and Uber are also available.

Unlike some other cities, there's no 'knowledge' style exam for cabbies here, so it helps to carry a map or the phone number of your destination in case you hail a driver who's new to the city.

Walking

Most cities in the UAE are very car-orientated and not designed to encourage walking. Additionally, summer temperatures of more than 45°C are not conducive to a leisurely stroll. The winter months, however, make walking quite pleasant. Most streets are lined with pavements and there are pedestrian paths on either side of the creek, along the seafront in Deira and Jumeira, at The Walk at JBR, and around Marsa Dubai, as well as in the city's parks. In late 2014, the Dhs.100 million 14km Jumeira Corniche,

Street Strife
To make navigation more confusing, places may not always be referred to by their official name. For example, Jumeira St is often known as Beach Road, and Interchange 1 on Sheikh Zayed Road is often called Defence Roundabout.

running from Dubai Marine Resort (dxbmarine.com) to the Burj Al Arab, opened and includes designated running paths, scenic walkways, retail kiosks and toilets. Bucking the current trend, Burj Khalifa and Marsa Dubai are attractive communities designed with pedestrians in mind. Both are interesting places to walk around with plenty of cafes and shops to tempt you off the street.

Water Bus

Crossing the creek by a traditional abra is a common method of transport for many people living in Bur Dubai and Deira. For visitors, it's a must-do experience while in town. Abra stations have been upgraded recently, but the fares are still just Dhs.1.

Another fun addition to the creek is a fleet of air-conditioned water buses. These operate on two different routes crossing the creek, with fares set at Dhs.4 per one-way trip.

It's also possible to take a scenic cruise on RTA's new Dubai Ferry. The modern ferries whisk you on a scenic ride and the routes depart from Marsa Dubai and Al Ghubaiba. To keep up-to-date on all boating options on the creek and beyond, see rta.ae.

Further Out

If you want to explore the UAE during your stay then you'll need a driver or rental car. The east coast is known for its wonderful coastline and watersports, all within a two-hour drive. There is also a bus service to Abu Dhabi which runs hourly from Al Ghubaiba and Ibn Battuta bus stations. The journey takes two hours and costs Dhs.25. Contact the RTA on 800 9090 for more info.

PLACES TO STAY

Nowhere does five-star quite like Dubai, but while there's a vast array of luxury options to choose from, there's also something to suit every budget.

In addition to a high number of plush hotels, Dubai has plenty of mid-range hotels, self-catering villas, hotel apartments and even a youth hostel. Furthermore, a new hotel seems to spring up every few months, so you're never short of choice when it comes to deciding where to rest your head.

Most hotels are within 30 minutes of the airport and tend to be either on the beach, by the creek or on Sheikh Zayed Road. The coastal options will probably allow access to a private beach, but if you're in Dubai on business then proximity to the financial and business areas of DIFC and Trade Center is likely to be a priority. If you are in town to shop, then take your pick as malls are everywhere.

Popular hotels tend to be fully booked in the winter season, but summer visitors can often bag great discounts.

> **The VIP Set**
> With Roberto Cavalli's Cavalli Club (cavalliclub.com) at the Fairmont, an Armani Hotel at Burj Khalifa (armanihotels.com) and the Palazzo Versace (palazzoversace.ae) along the creek, there are plenty of places to show off your designer threads.

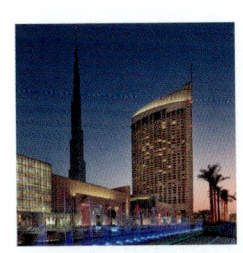

The Address Dubai Mall
theaddress.com
04 438 8888
Attached to The Dubai Mall and overlooking Burj Khalifa, this luxury hotel combines traditional Arabic hospitality with contemporary design. It also has a sister hotel at Dubai Marina (04 436 7777).
Map 2 B3 **Metro** Burj Khalifa/Dubai Mall

Anantara Dubai The Palm Resort & Spa
anantara.com
04 567 8888
This stunning hotel combines the hospitality of Thailand, the luxury of Arabia and the iconic over-water accommodation of the Maldives.
Map 1 D1 **Metro** Dubai Internet City

Armani Dubai
dubai.armanihotels.com
04 888 3888
Oozing style and extravagance, the Armani Hotel occupies six floors of the Burj Khalifa and has 160 exquisite rooms and suites. There are four restaurants, an opulent bar and a chic spa.
Map 2 B2 **Metro** Burj Khalifa/Dubai Mall

Essentials — Places To Stay

Atlantis The Palm
atlantisthepalm.com
04 426 0000
Situated on the crescent of the Palm Jumeirah, the sugary pink Atlantis offers 1,539 rooms including The Lost Chambers Suites which feature floor-to-ceiling windows looking into the aquarium. **Map** 1 C1 **Metro** Nakheel

Burj Al Arab
jumeirah.com
04 301 7777
Architecturally unique, one of the world's tallest hotels stands 321m high on a man-made island. It is dramatic, lavish and exclusive. Guests are looked after by a host of butlers. **Map** 3 E1
Metro Mall of the Emirates

Grosvenor House Dubai
grosvenorhouse-dubai.com
04 399 8888
Located at the mouth of Marsa Dubai, this accommodation features guest rooms, serviced apartments and some iconic nightlife venues, including Buddha Bar and the crow's nest Bar 44.
Map 3 B1 **Metro** DAMAC

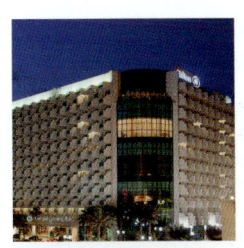

Hilton Dubai Jumeirah Resort
hilton.com
04 399 1111
Situated on a private beach a stone's throw from The Walk, this resort boasts good watersports facilities and popular eateries such as BiCE and The Wavebreaker beach bar. **Map** 3 A1 **Metro** Jumeirah Lakes Towers

Jumeirah Beach Hotel
jumeirah.com
04 348 0000
One of Dubai's icons, this hotel is built in the shape of a wave with a colourful interior, and all rooms have a sea view. Bars and restaurants include Villa Beach, 360° and a new branch of Jamie's Italian. **Map** 3 E1 **Metro** Mall of the Emirates

Jumeirah Zabeel Saray
jumeirahzabeelsaray.com
04 453 0000
Zabeel Saray is something of a structural wonder, combining Arabian and Turkish influences to create a hotel that screams luxury. It is also home to Talise Ottoman Spa, the largest spa in the Middle East. **Map** 1 C1 **Metro** DAMAC

Essentials

Places To Stay

Essentials — Places To Stay

Madinat Jumeirah
jumeirah.com
04 366 8888
This resort has two hotels, Al Qasr and Mina A'Salam, and exclusive summer houses, all linked by man-made waterways. Between the hotels is Souk Madinat Jumeirah. **Map** 3 E1
Metro Mall of the Emirates

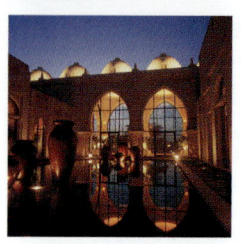

One&Only Royal Mirage
oneandonlyroyalmirage.com
04 399 9999
Blessed with an intimate atmosphere, this hotel features unparalleled service and dining, while a luxury spa treatment here is pure indulgence. Try Moroccan cuisine at Tagine, or enjoy late nights at Kasbar. **Map** 3 C1 **Metro** Nakheel

The Palace Downtown Dubai
theaddress.com
04 428 7888
Situated close to Burj Khalifa, The Palace boasts 242 deluxe rooms. There's butler service for all rooms, and views of the world's tallest building. Its Asado steak restaurant is recommended.
Map 2 B3 **Metro** Burj Khalifa/Dubai Mall

Park Hyatt Dubai
dubai.park.hyatt.com
04 602 1234
Mediterranean and Moorish in style, the Park Hyatt has 225 rooms, each with a balcony or terrace with great views. It has a prime waterfront location next to Dubai Creek Golf & Yacht Club.
Map 4 D5 **Metro** GGICO

Raffles Dubai
raffles.com
04 324 8888
With 248 stunning suites, the renowned Raffles Spa and a unique Botanical Sky Garden, this is one of Dubai's most noteworthy city hotels. It also houses the popular nightclub, People by Crystal.
Map 1 J3 **Metro** Dubai Healthcare City

The Ritz-Carlton Dubai
ritzcarlton.com
04 399 4000
Set right on the JBR beach, The Ritz-Carlton may stand low in comparison to the marina's towers but it excels in terms of style and service. Afternoon tea in the lobby is a must. **Map** 3 A1 **Metro** DAMAC

Essentials

Places To Stay

Essentials

Places To Stay

Le Royal Meridien Beach Resort & Spa
leroyalmeridien-dubai.com
04 399 5555
Set in landscaped gardens, this resort has a lush pool area and private beach, as well as excellent leisure facilities and a decent selection of bars and restaurants.
Map 3 B1 **Metro** DAMAC

Sheraton Dubai Mall of the Emirates
sheratondubaimalloftheemirates.com
04 377 2000
This plush hotel is a dream spot for keen shoppers. Also worth a mention is the roof terrace, which offers some of the best views in town. **Map** 3 E2 **Metro** Mall of the Emirates

The Westin Dubai Mina Seyahi Beach Resort & Marina
westinminaseyahi.com
04 399 4141
The Westin offers all the luxury you'd expect of a five-star hotel – in addition to popular evening venues and 1,200m of private beach close to Marsa Dubai.
Map 3 B1 **Metro** Nakheel

Dubai **Visitors'** Guide

Other Hotels

Burj Khalifa & DIFC

With easy access to Dubai's financial centre and tourist attractions such as The Dubai Mall and Burj Khalifa, the Sheikh Zayed Road and Burj Khalifa hotels offer a balance of work and play. The chic Sofitel Downtown (04 503 6666, sofitel-dubai-downtown.com), off Sheikh Zayed Road, features a modern design and breathtaking views of the Burj Khalifa. The glamorous Fairmont Dubai (04 332 5555, fairmont.com) sits opposite the city's financial hub and is home to a range of popular restaurants and nightspots. Nearby, the Shangri-La (04 343 8888, shangri-la.com) has a lovely pool area, as well as concept club The Act Dubai, which stylishly combines theatre, dining and nightlife. Located in the heart of Dubai's business district, the Ritz-Carlton Dubai International Financial Centre (04 372 2222, ritzcarlton.com) is a good bet for business trips, as is the boutique-style Four Seasons DIFC (04 506 0000, fourseasons.com).

Also in the area is Jumeirah Emirates Towers (04 330 0000, jumeirah.com), one of Dubai's most established luxury hotels.

The JW Marriott Marquis, in nearby Business Bay, is the world's tallest hotel, and is home to lively restaurants, bars and clubs.

Ski Stays

For the ultimate Dubai experience, check into Kempinski Hotel Mall of The Emirates (kempinski.com). Located in one of the world's busiest malls, the hotel's exclusive chalet rooms boast views of the snowy slopes of Ski Dubai.

Marsa Dubai

With sea views, swimming pools and private beaches, sun worshippers are spoilt for choice in Marsa Dubai (formerly Dubai Marina) and JBR. The Habtoor Grand Beach Resort & Spa (04 399 5000, habtoorhotels.com) is another good option right on the beach. The Address Dubai Marina (04 436 7777, theaddress.com), meanwhile, boasts easy access to Dubai Marina Mall. The Dubai Marriott Harbour Hotel & Suites (04 319 4000, marriott.com) has spacious suites, each with its own kitchen and well-stocked bathroom. Nuran Marina Serviced Residences (04 367 4848, nuran.com) is also a good choice if apartment hotel convenience in the vicinity of the beach is what you're after; the well-equipped apartments boast stunning marina views and the complex is conveniently located between Dubai Marina Yacht Club (dubaimarinayachtclub.com) and Dubai Marina Mall.

The Palm
Other luxurious resorts on Nakhlat Jumeira include Jumeirah Zabeel Saray (04 453 0000, jumeirah.com), One&Only The Palm (04 440 1010, oneandonlyresorts.com), and Anantara Dubai (04 567 8888, dubai-palm.anantara.com).

On The Creek

The creekside hotels are ideally located for soaking up the atmosphere of old Dubai. Jumeirah Creekside Hotel's unique, luxury interior will wow art lovers, and its Akaru Spa boasts plenty of awards. The Sheraton Dubai Creek Hotel & Towers' (04 228 1111, sheratondubaicreek.com) recent renovations mean upgraded comfort and services, and some stunning views. The brand new, ultra-extravagant Palazzo Versace (04 556 8888, palazzoversace.ae), situated on the creek in Culture Village, lives up to the reputation of the legendary fashion house whose name it bears. The Hilton Dubai Creek (04 227 1111, hilton.com) has some great restaurants, including Table 9. The five-star Radisson Blu Hotel, Dubai Deira Creek (04 222 7171, radissonblu.com) has a scenic pool and a host of popular dining options. Fish Market is particularly recommended.

Near The Airport
Le Meridien Dubai (04 217 0000, lemeridien-dubai.com) offers easy access to the airport and the resort is home to some of the city's favourite restaurants, including the Meridien Village Terrace and Yalumba. The Al Bustan Rotana (04 282 0000, rotana.com) is another alternative in and around this residential neighbourhood.

Guesthouses & Hostels
Guesthouses in Dubai are few and far between, but the XVA Art Hotel (xvahotel.com) is a real hidden gem, nestled in a unique location in the heart of Al Fahidi Historical Neighbourhood, one of the oldest heritage sites in the region. XVA Art Hotel's seven guestrooms ooze rustic charm and the adjacent gallery hosts interesting art exhibitions.

Dubai Youth Hostel (04 298 8151, uaeyha.com) in Al Qusais offers single, double, triple and dorm rooms starting from Dhs.100.

Villas are another option for short or longer stays. Visit mydubaistay.com for accommodation in different areas, with online availability, booking and a cost comparison chart.

Out of the City

Al Maha Desert Resort & Spa
04 832 9900
Dubai-Al Ain Rd, Remah
al-maha.com

Set in 225 sq km of desert, Al Maha Desert Resort is accessible only by a 4WD vehicle driven by your own field guide. It is congruously set on the slopes of a rising dune and styled as a Bedouin camp. Wild Arabian oryx (maha) wander around the resort, and each guestroom is a stand-alone property, designed to resemble a traditional Bedouin tent. The suites feature a private terrace and infinity plunge pool. You can opt to dine in private on your patio or at the Al Diwaan restaurant; the choice is varied and there is a great wine list. The Saray Spa offers the full range of pampering and there are several activities you can take part in. One of the most popular is a sunset camel ride and champagne toast on the dunes. **Map** 1 G7

Bab Al Shams Desert Resort & Spa
04 809 6100
Jabal Ali-Lehbab Rd, Mugatrah
meydanhotels.com

Like a desert mirage come to life, Bab Al Shams is a Bedouin fantasy escape. On approach, bamboo torches guide you to the building that blends into the imposing dunes that surround it, and the rooms have been designed to evoke a feeling of Bedouin living. Camel rides on the sand dunes are offered to guests, or you can chill out in one of the outdoor swimming pools. Take the pampering up a notch by heading to the Satori Spa and, as the evening sets in, Al Sarab Rooftop Lounge offers shisha and drinks. The Al Hadheerah restaurant offers a full-on Arabian experience, including a huge buffet, belly dancing and traditional music. **Map** 1 D7

JA Jebel Ali Golf Resort
Mena Jabal Ali

04 814 5555
jaresortshotels.com

Just far enough out of Dubai to escape the hustle and bustle, the JA Jebel Ali Golf Resort offers luxurious stays in resplendent surroundings, with a peaceful atmosphere. The resort is made up of two beach hotels, JA Palm Tree Court and the original JA Jebel Ali Beach Hotel, set within 128 acres of lush, landscaped gardens. The resort boasts an 800m private beach, a marina and a nine-hole, par 36 golf course, as well as three swimming pools. Guests can also enjoy horse riding, shooting, tennis, mini-golf and a variety of watersports. The resort houses a number of food and beverage outlets, and a few shops. **Map** 1 A2

Essentials

Exploring

Explore Dubai	76
At A Glance	78
Old Dubai: Around	
The Creek & Beyond	82
Al Qouz	92
Downtown & Sheikh Zayed Road	98
New Dubai: JBR & Marsa Dubai	106
Festival City & Garhoud	110
Jumeira: Beachside Life	114
Nakhlat Jumeira & Al Sufouh	120
Outside The City & Dubailand	126
Further Out	130
Tours & Sightseeing	138

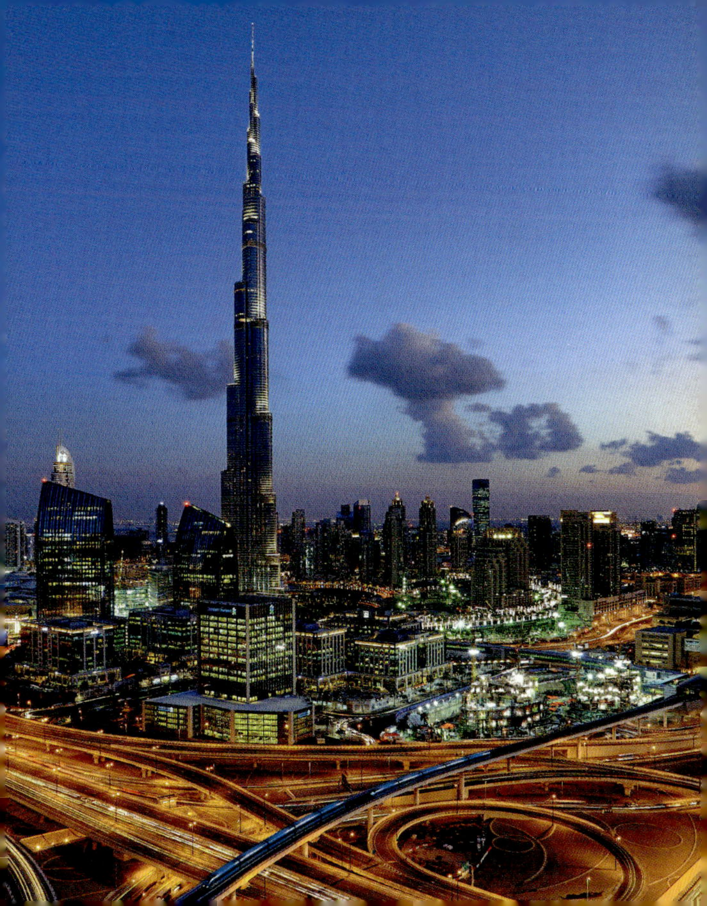

EXPLORE DUBAI

From slick city attractions to expansive deserts, Dubai is an emirate of superlatives that will impress even the most seasoned traveller.

Dubai provides a wealth of contrasting images: Ferraris parked outside falafel shops, massive skyscrapers shading pristine mosques, billionaires, cranes, camels, palaces and windtowers. The city is filled with luxurious five-star hotels and huge shopping malls. It has some of the top nightspots in the Middle East, and is home to a range of museums, heritage sites and places of cultural interest. There is quite a mix of experiences to be had.

Don't let the traffic and ever-expanding footprint disorientate you – Dubai itself is fairly easy to navigate and explore, especially with the introduction of the metro. The city runs along the Arabian Gulf coast, and the older and more bustling sections of the city, such as Deira and Bur Dubai, are situated in the northern end and around Dubai Creek. From there, the city stretches south along Sheikh Zayed Road towards developments such as Nakhlat Jumeira and Marsa Dubai.

Most of the city's historical attractions are located around the creek which, until recently, was the residential and commercial hub of the city. Al Fahidi Historical Neighbourhood and the souks of Deira have managed to retain much of the old Dubai character and multiculturalism, with narrow streets selling everything from wholesale grain to traditional Emirati dress. These are also the best areas to find a traditional Indian or Arabic meal.

The bright lights of Deira

If large and luxurious better describes the Dubai of your dreams, newer areas like Downtown Dubai, home to the world's tallest building, and Marsa Dubai should be your target destinations. The towering skyscrapers and enormous malls that fill these impressive developments contain some of the best shopping and nightlife in the Middle East. The Dubai Mall houses some 1,200 shops. Or head outdoors to soak up the sunshine on one of its sandy open beaches or luxurious beach clubs.

In the run up to Dubai's hosting of Expo 2020, new attractions and developments are being completed all the time, so look out for new theme parks, a safari park, giant Ferris wheel, opera house, new museums and much more.

Exploring

AT A GLANCE

Heritage, Arts & Culture

Al Ahmadiya School & Heritage House	p.83
Alserkal Avenue	p.94
Art Sawa	p.94
The Courtyard	p.95
Dubai International Art Centre	p.115
Dubai International Writers' Centre	p.85
Dubai Museum	p.86
Heritage & Diving Villages	p.86
Iranian Mosque	p.115
Jumeirah Mosque	p.116
The Majlis Gallery	p.88
Majlis Ghorfat Um Al Sheif	p.116
Sheikh Mohammed Centre For Cultural Understanding	p.88
Sheikh Saeed Al Maktoum House	p.89
Union House	p.117
XVA Gallery	p.89

Beaches & Parks

Creek Park	p.84
Dubai Miracle Garden	p.127
Jumeirah Beach Park	p.115
JBR Beach	p.106
Kite Beach	p.116
Mamzar Beach Park	p.88
Safa Park	p.117

Al Sufouh Beach	p.122
Zabeel Park	p.89

Amusement & Water Parks

Adventure Zone by Adventure HQ	p.92
Bounce	p.94
Children's City	p.83
KidZania	p.102
SEGA Republic	p.102
Ski Dubai	p.121
Wild Wadi Water Park	p.122
Xline by XDubai	p.103
Zoo Skatepark	p.95

Other Sights & Attractions

Atlantis The Palm	p.121
The Beach and the Walk at JBR	p.107
Burj Al Arab	p.121
City Walk	p.115
Creekside Souks	p.84
Dubai Aquarium & Underwater Zoo	p.100
Dubai Dolphinarium	p.84
The Dubai Fountain	p.100
Dubai Garden Centre	p.92
Global Village	p.127
Jumeirah Emirates Towers	p.102
Marina Walk	p.107
Plant Street	p.117
Souk Madinat Jumeirah	p.122

Exploring

At A Glance

Exploring — At A Glance

Dubai's Museums & Heritage Sites

Name / Location	Contact
Beit Al Rekkab	
Al Shindagha, Bur Dubai	dm.gov.ae
Al Boom Tourist Village	**04 324 3000**
Umm Hurair 2, Bur Dubai	alboom.ae
Burj Nahar	
Nr DEWA, Al Muteena, Deira	
Camel Museum	**04 392 0368**
Al Shindagha, Bur Dubai	dm.gov.ae
Coffee Museum	04 380 6777
Al Fahidi Historical Neighbourhood	coffeemuseum.ae
Coins Museum	**04 353 9265**
Nr The Ruler's Court, Al Souk Al Kabeer	dm.gov.ae
Crossroads of Civilisations Museum	04 393 4440
Al Shindagha, Bur Dubai	themuseum.ae
Dar Al Nadwa	
Nr Coin Museum, Al Souk Al Kabeer	
Dubai Maritime Museum	**04 221 5555**
Port Rashid, Bur Dubai	
Dubai Modern Art Museum	
Downtown Dubai, Burj Khalifa	emaar.com
Dubai Moving Image Museum	04 421 6679
MCN Hive, Tecom	dubaimovingimagemuseum.com
Dubai Municipality Museum	**04 225 3312**
Al Buteen, Deira	dm.gov.ae
Dubai Museum	**04 353 1862**
Al Fahidi Fort, Al Souk Al Kabeer	dubaiculture.ae

Dubai Transport Museum Roads & Transport Authority, Al Garhoud	04 290 3617
Falcon & Heritage Sports Centre Nr Nad Al Sheba Market	04 327 2854 dm.gov.ae
Heritage Island Nakhlat Jabal Ali, Al Wajeha Al Bahriah	emeg.ae
Horse Museum Al Shindagha, Bur Dubai	dubaiculture.gov.ae
Jean-Paul Najar Foundation Alserkal Avenue, Al Qouz Ind. 1	050 451 1948 jpnajarfoundation.com
Jumaa & Obaid Bin Thani House Al Shindagha, Bur Dubai	04 393 3240 dubaiculture.ae
Jumeirah Archaeological Site Nr Emirates Hospital, Jumeira 2	04 349 6874 dubaiculture.ae
Museum of the Poet Al Oqaili Nr Spice Souk, Deira	04 515 5000 dubaiculture.gov.ae

In The Pipeline

Dubai's many museums continue to multiply, with the Museum of the Future (motf.ae) set to showcase cutting-edge design, innovations and inventions when it opens near Jumeirah Emirates Towers in 2018.

Plans to establish Al Maktoum Hospital Museum are underway in Deira, with authorities crowd-sourcing experiences and memories from former patients and staff. Dubai Police Museum is also planned for Dubai Police General HQ in Deira. The building has been designed to resemble a giant policeman's cap.

OLD DUBAI: AROUND THE CREEK & BEYOND

Dubai Creek pumped life and trade into the city from its early days. The area surrounding this vital gateway is central to Dubai's heritage.

Dubai's trading tradition can still be witnessed today in the bustling streets around the creek. On one side, Deira is a maze of narrow convoluted streets bustling with activity, while gold, spices, perfumes and general goods are touted in its numerous souks. On the opposite bank, Bur Dubai is home to some of the oldest heritage sites in Dubai. Both sides of the creek are lined by corniches that come alive in the evenings as residents head out for a stroll and traders take stock.

This area is so central to Dubai's past that the emirate is bidding to have an almost 2 sq km site from Shindagha to Al Fahidi recognised as a UNESCO World Heritage site. Called Khor Dubai (Dubai Creek): The Traders' Harbour, the site evokes the city's centuries-old maritime traditions. It is still used by small traders from across the Gulf, and is home to almost 700 historic structures.

Al Fahidi Historical Neighbourhood on the Bur Dubai side of the creek is one of the oldest sites in the city, with a neighbourhood that dates back to the early 1900s. A wander around offers a beguiling glimpse into the Dubai of a bygone era, with its courtyards, a maze of winding and beautiful alleyways, and the distinctive four-sided windtowers (barjeel), seen on top of the traditional flat-roofed buildings – an early form of air conditioning. This atmospheric part of the city comes alive every year with the SIKKA (meaning *alleyways*) Art Fair as part of Dubai Art Season each spring.

Take the time to meander along the Deira side of the creek to witness the wooden dhows that are docked by the water's edge being loaded with everything from fruit and vegetables to televisions and cars. No visitor should leave without experiencing a trip across the water on a commuter abra for only Dhs.1, or a tourist abra (Dhs.100 for an hour's private trip).

Al Ahmadiya School & Heritage House   04 226 0286
Al Ahmadiya St, Al Ras   dubaiculture.ae

Established in 1912 for Dubai's elite, Al Ahmadiya School was the earliest regular school in the city. A visit here is an excellent opportunity to see the history of education in the UAE. Situated in what is becoming a small centre for heritage (Al Souk Al Kabeer), it is an interesting example of a traditional Emirati family home, and dates back to 1890. Open Saturday to Thursday 8.30am to 7.30pm and 2pm to 7.30pm on Friday. **Map** 4 C1 **Metro** Al Ras

Children's City   04 334 0808
Creek Park, Umm Hurair 2   childrencity.ae

Children's City offers kids hands-on educational amusement facilities. There's a planetarium, a nature centre and the Discovery Space, revealing the miracles of the human body. It is aimed at five to 12 year olds. **Map** 4 C5 **Metro** Dubai Healthcare City

Creek Park

Riyadh St, Umm Hurair 2

04 336 7633
dm.gov.ae

Creek Park is blessed with acres of gardens, fishing piers, barbecue sites, children's play areas and kiosks. Running along the park's 2.5km stretch of creek frontage is a cable car system, allowing visitors an unrestricted view from 30m in the air. **Map** 4 C6 **Metro** Oud Metha

Creekside Souks

Al Ras

Deira's three main souks – the spice souk, the fish souk and the gold souk – present some of the best examples of living heritage that Dubai has to offer. Smelly as it may be, an early morning trip through the fish souk makes for a great photo opportunity. The gold souk gets crowded on weekend afternoons, but spend an hour or two here during the week and enjoy a form of window shopping that's very different from a mall experience. For the best insight into the region's varied cuisines, take a walk through the spice souk where you'll be bombarded by the colours and smells of spices you've never heard of. Just across the creek on the Bur Dubai side sits the covered textile souk with its myriad of bright fabrics. An abra ride across the creek is a must while in this part of town.
Map 4 C2 **Metro** Al Ras

Dubai Dolphinarium > p, v, x

Creek Park, Umm Hurair 2

04 336 9773
dubaidolphinarium.ae

Located within Creek Park, the main attraction here is the seal and dolphin show, which runs twice a day during the week and three times daily at the weekends (closed on Sundays). Afterwards, you

can get your picture taken with the friendly mammals. Prices start at Dhs.100 for adults and Dhs.50 for children. Check the website for details of other options, including a chance to swim with the dolphins. Don't miss the mirror maze and the daily exotic bird show, which features performing parrots, cockatoos and macaws – the only show of its kind in the UAE. **Map 4 C5**
Metro Dubai Healthcare City

Dubai International Writers' Centre   04 355 9844
House No 290, Al Shindagha   diwc.ae

The Dubai International Writers' Centre hosts events regarding writing and literature, and also provides peaceful majlises for a spot of quiet reading when you wish to escape the hustle and bustle of the streets. **Map** 4 C1 **Metro** Al Ghubaiba

Exploring

Dubai Museum

04 353 1862
Al Fahidi St, Al Souk Al Kabeer
dubaiculture.ae

Located in and under Al Fahidi Fort, which dates back to 1787, this family-friendly museum was once the home of the ruler of Dubai and also functioned as a sea defence. Creative and well thought out, the museum represents all parts of life from Dubai's past in an attractive and interesting way. Walk through a souk from the 1950s, stroll along an oasis, see into a traditional house, get up close to local wildlife, learn about the archaeological finds and go 'underwater' to discover the pearl diving and fishing industries. There are some entertaining mannequins to pose with too. Entry costs Dhs.3 for adults and Dhs.1 for children under six years old. Open daily 8.30am to 8.30pm (2pm to 5pm on Fridays).
Map 4 C2 **Metro** Al Fahidi

Heritage & Diving Villages

04 393 7151
Al Khaleej St, Al Shindagha
dubaiculture.ae

Located near the mouth of Dubai Creek, the Heritage & Diving Villages focus on Dubai's maritime past, pearl-diving traditions and architecture. Visitors can observe traditional potters and weavers practising their craft the way it has been done for centuries. Camel rides are also available most afternoons and evenings. Local women serve traditionally cooked snacks – one of the many opportunities you'll have to sample genuine Emirati cuisine. The location is also home to the Kan Zaman creekside restaurant, which serves Arabic mezze and grills. The villages can be lively during the Dubai Shopping Festival and Eid celebrations, with performances including traditional sword dancing. Open daily 8.30am to 10pm (Fridays 3.30pm to 10pm). **Map** 4 C1 **Metro** Al Ghubaiba

Exploring

Old Dubai: Around The Creek & Beyond

askexplorer.com

The Majlis Gallery

04 353 6233

Al Fahidi Historical Neighbourhood,
Al Souk Al Kabeer

themajlisgallery.com

The Majlis Gallery is a converted Arabian house, complete with windtowers and courtyard. Small, whitewashed rooms lead off the central garden and host exhibitions by contemporary artists. In addition to the fine art collection, there's an extensive range of handmade glass, pottery, fabrics, frames and unusual furniture. The gallery is open Saturday to Thursday, 10am to 6pm. **Map** 4 C2 **Metro** Al Fahidi

Mamzar Beach Park

04 296 6201

Al Khaleej St, Al Mamzar

dm.gov.ae

With its four clean beaches, open spaces and plenty of greenery, Al Mamzar is a popular spot. The well-maintained beaches have sheltered areas for swimming and changing rooms with showers. Air-conditioned chalets, with barbecues, can be rented on a daily basis, costing from Dhs.160 to Dhs.210. There are two swimming pools with lifeguards on duty. Adults can hire bikes, jet skis and other equipment and kids have the run of play areas and climbing obstacles. **Map** 1 K2 **Metro** Al Qiyadah.

Sheikh Mohammed Centre For Cultural Understanding

04 353 6666

Al Fahidi Historical Neighbourhood,
Al Souk Al Kabeer

cultures.ae

This facility helps visitors and residents understand the customs and traditions of the UAE. It organises a walking tour of the Al Souk Al Kabeer area, guided tours in Jumeirah Mosque, as well as cultural breakfasts and lunches. There are majlis-style rooms around the courtyard and great views. The centre is open Sunday to Thursday 8am to 6pm and Saturday 9am to 1pm. **Map** 4 C2 **Metro** Al Fahidi

Sheikh Saeed Al Maktoum House
04 393 7139
Al Khaleej St, Al Shindagha
dubaiculture.ae

Dating from 1896, this carefully restored house-turned-museum is built in the traditional manner of the Gulf coast, using coral covered in lime and sand-coloured plaster. The interesting displays in many rooms show rare and wonderful photographs of life in Dubai before the discovery of oil. Entry is Dhs.2 for adults, Dhs.1 for children. **Map** 4 C1 **Metro** Al Ghubaiba

XVA Gallery
04 353 5383
Al Fahidi Historical Neighbourhood,
Al Souk Al Kabeer
xvagallery.com

This is one of Dubai's most interesting art gallery locations. Originally a windtower house, it's worth a visit for its architecture alone, which has an authentic look and feel. The gallery hosts exhibitions throughout the year and there's also a boutique hotel with guestrooms. Open daily. **Map** 4 C2 **Metro** Al Fahidi

Zabeel Park
04 398 6888
Shk Rashid Rd, Al Kifaf
dm.gov.ae

Providing an oasis of greenery in Dubai, Zabeel Park has several recreational areas, a jogging track, a mini cricket pitch, a football field, a boating lake and an amphitheatre, plus a number of kiosks serving snacks. On Friday mornings the park hosts the RIPE Market, which sells organic food. **Map** 4 A3 **Metro** Al Jafiliya

Exploring

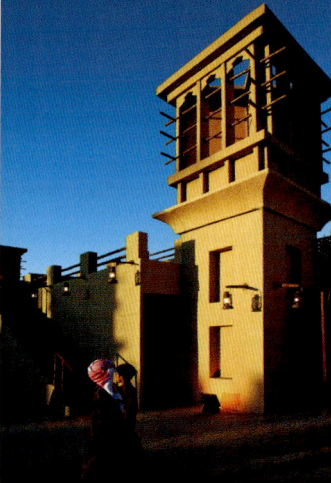

If you only do one thing in...
OLD DUBAI

Head to Dubai Museum to learn more about Dubai's rich past and the emirate's evolution into the spectacular superlative it is today.

Best for...

Eating & Drinking: For Arabian food in a traditional setting, try the Emirati machboos at Bastakiah Nights, or dine on a creekside terrace at Bait Al Wakeel.

Families: Give the kids an experience of a lifetime at the Dubai Dolphinarium inside Creek Park, where you can also admire the views over the water from a cable car.

Relaxation: Step into the calm courtyard of the Al Ahmadiya School & Heritage House, where you'll find some quiet in the Deira storm.

Shopping: The three souks in this area are a must-visit. Start at the textile souk in Bur Dubai then hop on an abra over the water to the spice souk and gold souk.

Sightseeing: The winding alleyways of Al Fahidi Historical Neighbourhood will linger in the memory long after you leave Dubai.

AL QOUZ

Tucked away in massive warehouses – often out of sight – are a collection of art galleries and impressive interior design shops.

The Al Qouz art scene, and Alserkal Avenue in particular, is at the heart of the Arab art world. It is here that lesser-known artists can find exhibition space, and the galleries are working to promote Arab art on an international scale. Add to that an endless selection of cheap south Asian cafeterias, trendy cafes, the Gold & Diamond Park, Times Square Center, the treasure trove of goods at Dubai Antique Museum and the gallery at The Courtyard, Al Qouz quickly becomes a destination worth exploring.

Adventure Zone by Adventure HQ
04 346 6824
Times Square Center, Shk Zayed Rd
adventurehq.ae
Adventure Zone consists of a 9m climbing wall with auto belays for beginner and experienced climbers, as well as a cable climb area, with swinging tyres and rope webs. **Map** 1 E3 **Metro** FGB

Alserkal Avenue
050 556 9797
8th St, Al Qouz Ind 1
alserkalavenue.ae
Alserkal Avenue is Dubai's foremost art hub, and it's a great place to spot new talent from the UAE and abroad. What began as 20 warehouses has since expanded to cover 500,000 sq ft of creative spaces, including galleries, concept stores, project spaces, black box theatre and outdoor event facilities, as well as Wild & the

Exploring

Al Qouz

askexplorer.com 93

Exploring

Al Qouz

Moon, a cold-pressed juice and smoothie bar. Many of the avenue's outlets are known for championing local artists, among them Salsali Private Museum, Mojo and Ayyam Gallery. Aside from just wandering around the avenue, the easiest way to explore is with the aid of ArtMap (artinthecity.com). **Map** 1 E3 **Metro** Noor Bank

Art Sawa

04 340 8660
Al Marabea St, Al Qouz Ind 1 · artsawa.com

Art Sawa focuses on the promotion of contemporary Arab art in a variety of mediums including collage, etching, installation, painting, photography, sculpture and video. It also hosts performing arts performances, music recitals and educational workshops aimed at engaging the local and international communities. **Map** 1 E3 **Metro** Noor Bank

Bounce

04 321 1400
Nr Ace Hardware, Al Qouz Ind 1 · bounce.ae

An unassuming warehouse on the outside, inside you'll find an urban playground with over 100 interconnected trampolines. Trampolining has become very popular and another venue Flip Out Dubai is also due to open in Al Qouz in the near future.
Map 1 E3 **Metro** Noor Bank

The Courtyard

04 347 5050
Nr Spinneys Warehouse, Al Qouz Ind 1 · courtyard-uae.com

A stone's throw from Alserkal Avenue is The Courtyard, home to the Total Arts Gallery, which has long showcased Middle Eastern art with an emphasis on Iranian artists, and the venue frequently exhibits traditional handicrafts and antique furniture. The gallery has featured the works of world-renowned artists such as Pierre-Auguste Renoir and Salvador Dali. There's also an innovative performing arts theatre here, The Courtyard Playhouse. **Map** 1 E3 **Metro** Noor Bank

Dubai Garden Centre
04 340 0006
Shk Zayed Rd, Al Qouz 3
dubaigardencentre.ae

A garden oasis within the city, this large store is filled with greenery and gifts. You will also find Roseleaf Cafe nestled inside, an adorable cafe serving up home cooked meals and great coffee. Stop for a light lunch and a little relaxation. **Map** 1 E3 **Metro** FGB

Zoo Skatepark
04 338 6126
Al Qouz Ind 1
ignite-wellness.com

If you love nothing more than pulling off tricks on a skateboard, Zoo Skatepark should be on your radar. Located near Al Qouz Bus Station, it is Dubai's largest indoor skate venue. Suitable for every skate fan, from total beginners right through to the advanced, there are ramps to suit every level of ability. Entry is available by the hour or in three-hour sessions. Day passes are also available. The skatepark can also arrange birthday parties, private hire and lessons if you are looking to improve your technique. **Map** 1 E3 **Metro** Noor Bank

> **Arty Alternative**
> **Based in Gate Village in Dubai's financial district, Opera Gallery (operagallery.com) has a permanent collection of art on display and for sale, mainly European and Chinese, with visiting exhibitions during the year.**

Exploring

If you only do one thing in...
AL QOUZ

Wander around Alserkal Avenue for a taste of the local art scene. The funky art district has a variety of exhibits and studios to admire from a diversity of local artists.

Best for...

Eating & Drinking: It's worth tracking down the Raw Coffee Company (rawcoffeecompany.com), hidden amid the warehouses to sample its various brewing techniques. It doesn't distract its baristas by serving food, however, so go to Tom & Serge or THE One to eat.

Families: Times Square Center on Sheikh Zayed Road has a high wires and climbing activity centre attached to outdoors store Adventure HQ.

Relaxation: Take a leisurely stroll around the galleries and creative spaces of Alserkal Avenue to soak up some art and culture.

Shopping: If the bustle and haggling of the gold souk in Old Dubai is a bit much, the Gold & Diamond Park offers similar wares in a more modern environment.

Sightseeing: This area's attractions are mostly hidden gems, but it will provide a fascinating insight into industrial Dubai.

Exploring

DOWNTOWN & SHEIKH ZAYED ROAD

The world's tallest building, Dubai's largest mall and the most photographed skyline in the city are all in Dubai's glitziest area.

Downtown Dubai is a spectacular mix of shops, restaurants, entertainment and architecture, while nearby is a stretch of Dubai's original stunning skyscraper strip, which lines either side of Sheikh Zayed Road and features some of the city's top hotels and building designs. At the heart of Downtown Dubai is the shimmering Burj Khalifa. The world's tallest tower points like a needle more than 800m skywards and counts an Armani hotel, viewing platforms At The Top and Burj Khalifa SKY, and the world's highest restaurant, At.mosphere, among its attractions. By its base are The Dubai Mall, Old Town and The Dubai Fountain, which plays in Burj Lake. Burj Park is an attractive green zone in the centre of this high-rise metropolis.

    The Dubai Mall is a huge shopping centre full of top-end retail brands, excellent eateries and some fantastic entertainment options, such as an Olympic-sized ice-skating rink, an aquarium, and entertainment centres KidZania and SEGA Republic. Old Town, which is home to the atmospheric Souk Al Bahar, takes

Exploring

Downtown & Sheikh Zayed Road

strong influences from traditional Arabia with its mosaics, passageways and fortress-like finishes, all of which are beautifully lit at night. Lights glitter across the length of Sheikh Mohammed bin Rashid Boulevard, which circles the Downtown area. Explore the boulevard from the top deck of Dubai Trolley, the world's first hydrogen-powered, emission-free tram, for some spectacular photo opportunities. The wide 3.5km stretch of skyscrapers is the subject of many a photo, as well as after-hours get-togethers. This area really comes alive at night.

Dubai Aquarium & Underwater Zoo > p.101

04 448 5200
The Dubai Mall, Downtown Dubai   thedubaiaquarium.com

More than 33,000 tropical fish are displayed to passing shoppers free of charge in a huge fish tank. For a closer view of the main tank's inhabitants, which include fearsome looking sand tiger sharks, you can pay to walk through the 270° viewing tunnel. The Underwater Zoo has residents such as penguins, piranhas and an octopus. One of its most popular residents is a giant crocodile called King Croc. He weighs 750kg and is more than 5m in length. If you're feeling adventurous, you can even go for a scuba dive in the tank (call ahead to book). **Map** 2 C3 **Metro** Burj Khalifa/Dubai Mall

The Dubai Fountain

800 382 246 255
Nr Burj Khalifa, Downtown Dubai   thedubaimall.com

This spectacular Downtown centrepiece draws crowds to witness the regular evening shows. Designed by the same team that created the famous Bellagio fountains in Las Vegas, the water, light and music combination is a captivating showstopper. Jets

"Nice extensions. I wonder how venomous they are!"
Did you know, the lionfish is armed with 18 poisonous needle-like dorsal fins? Get closer and make other interesting discoveries with over 160 species.
• Over 41,000 fish • 48-metre-long tunnel • Three different ecological zones: with numerous creatures of the not-so-deep: The Rainforest, The Rocky Shore & The Living Ocean • Spectrum of educational programmes • Aquatic experiences, including shark dive, glass boat ride, cage snorkelling & more
Up close & amazing
Located on LG & Level 2, The Dubai Mall
thedubaiaquarium.com
Follow us on
DUBAI AQUARIUM & UNDERWATER ZOO

of water shoot 150m into the air along the length of Burj Lake in synchronisation with classical and Arabic music, while the Burj Khalifa at night forms a memorable backdrop. The show takes place daily at 1pm and 1.30pm, and then every half hour from 6pm until 11pm (weekdays) or 11.30pm (weekends). **Map** 2 C3 **Metro** Burj Khalifa/Dubai Mall

Jumeirah Emirates Towers

04 330 0000
Shk Zayed Rd, Trade Center 2
jumeirah.com

These twin towers are a true Dubai landmark. At 350m, the office tower was the tallest building in the Middle East and Europe until the Burj Khalifa surpassed it. The smaller tower, at 305m, houses the Emirates Towers Hotel plus many eating and drinking spots. There is a mall that connects the two towers, full of restaurants and high-end shops. **Map** 2 D2 **Metro** Emirates Towers

KidZania > p.IBC

04 448 5222
The Dubai Mall, Downtown Dubai
kidzania.ae

A truly unique attraction that will keep the kids entertained for hours, this fantastic edutainment zone gives kids the chance to become adults for the day. Billed as a 'real-life city' for children, youngsters can dress up and act out more than 80 different roles, including everything from a policeman or fireman to being a pilot, doctor or a designer. **Map** 2 C3 **Metro** Burj Khalifa/Dubai Mall

SEGA Republic > p.IFC

04 448 8484
The Dubai Mall, Downtown Dubai
segarepublic.com

This indoor theme park located in The Dubai Mall offers a range of indoor thrills, courtesy of the nine main attractions and the 200 arcade games. A Power Pass gets you all-day access to the big attractions, which include stomach-flipping rides like the Sonic Hopper, the SpinGear and the Halfpipe Canyon. SEGA Republic is for all ages, and features some truly unique thrills. **Map** 2 C3 **Metro** Burj Khalifa/Dubai Mall

Xline by XDubai
Nr The Dubai Mall, Downtown Dubai   xdubai.com

For an exciting aerial perspective of the Dubai Fountain, try a zip-wire ride over the jets and Burj Lake. The wire reaches from a residential tower on Emaar Boulevard to The Dubai Mall. **Map** 2 C3 **Metro** Burj Khalifa/Dubai Mall

Exploring

Exploring

If you only do one thing in...
DOWNTOWN & SHEIKH ZAYED ROAD

Dine alfresco while watching the nightly Dubai Fountain shows.

Best for...

Eating & Drinking: Enjoy dinner at one of the several restaurants at Souk Al Bahar. Make sure to book early so you can have a seat on the terrace overlooking the Dubai Fountain show.

Families: Take your pick from any one of The Dubai Mall's attractions, such as SEGA Republic, KidZania or Dubai Aquarium.

Relaxation: Soothe shopped-out soles with a reflexology foot massage at The Spa at The Address Dubai Mall.

Shopping: With about 1,200 stores, The Dubai Mall is a shopaholic's paradise.

Sightseeing: Cocktails at Alta Badia at Emirates Towers are accompanied by fantastic skyline and Burj Khalifa views.

NEW DUBAI: JBR & MARSA DUBAI

Head to Marsa Dubai for high-rise heaven, a thriving cafe culture and bustling beach action.

Previously home to just a handful of waterfront hotels, Marsa Dubai (formerly Dubai Marina) is the epitome of the rise of 'New Dubai' to modern prominence. Apartment buildings (finished or still under construction) have sprouted up along every inch of the man-made waterway, while between the inland marina and the shore is the massive Jumeirah Beach Residence (JBR) development of residential towers. The walkways that run around the marina and parallel to the coast have evolved into lively strips of shops, cafes and restaurants, which are thronged with people in the evenings when the lit-up skyscrapers are at their most impressive. On the water, luxury boats fill the marina's berths, and thrill seekers take to the sea to parasail or waterski. Visitors can take a tour from the marina to the renowned luxury hotel, the Burj Al Arab, in a traditional wooden dhow or a yacht.

The Beach

Al Mamsha St, JBR, Marsa Dubai

04 431 0190
thebeach.ae

Shopping and dining destination The Beach is 30,000 sq ft of alfresco dining options located on the beach promenade, whilst shops and further dining options occupy the low-rise, open-air mall just behind it. Movie fans can get their fix at the 10 screen multiplex cinema or enjoy a movie alfresco at the outdoor cinema. The Beach also features an inflatable water park, outdoor gym equipment and markets. **Map** 3 A1 **Metro** DAMAC

JBR Beach
Nr Al Mamsha St, JBR, Marsa Dubai

At nearly 2km long, this bay of golden sand is very popular. The space in front of hotels is reserved for guests, but there are plenty of areas in between for others. The sea is calm and good for swimming, and hotels offer a variety of watersports such as parasailing that anyone can sign up for. The world's largest Ferris wheel is under construction off the shore. **Map** 3 A1 **Metro** DAMAC

Marina Walk
Marsa Dubai

Marina Walk boulevard starts at the base of Dubai Marina Towers and provides almost continuous pedestrian access around the 11km perimeter of the water. The area comes to life in the evenings and cooler months, when you can enjoy a meal in one of the waterfront restaurants and gaze out across the rows of yachts and the flashing lights of high-rise hotels and apartments. For speedier explorations, you'll find bicycle rental spots along the way.
Map 3 A1 **Metro** DAMAC

The Walk at JBR
Al Mamsha St, JBR, Marsa Dubai

04 390 0091
thewalk.ae

This cobbled strip embraces alfresco cafe culture, with streetside shops, cute stalls and plenty of outdoor restaurant seating, perfect for an evening amble towards The Beach. **Map** 3 A1 **Metro** DAMAC

Exploring

If you only do one thing in...
MARSA DUBAI & JBR

Head to the beach for a morning swim before treating yourself to an alfresco breakfast on The Walk.

Best for...

Eating & Drinking: Tuck into seafood alfresco at Dubai Marina Yacht Club's Aquara and watch marina life sail by as you dine.

Families: Challenge the family to find out who can stay on the longest on the slippery inflatables at The Beach Waterpark.

Relaxation: End your day with a movie on the beach, or pitch up to watch the game at one of The Beach's alfresco cinema screenings.

Shopping: Step off the beach and into the open-air mall, The Beach, where you can happily browse a choice of fashion, beauty, and kidswear.

Sightseeing: Board a wooden dhow for some spectacular views of the marina and JBR from the water. Try citysightseeing-dubai.com.

Waterside living in Marsa Dubai

Exploring

New Dubai: JBR & Marsa Dubai

FESTIVAL CITY & GARHOUD

Dubai Festival City can be both an oasis of calm and entertainment destination, with shopping, dining and waterways on the edge of the city.

Situated on the creek just down from Deira, Festival City has grown into a large eating, shopping and entertainment complex. With an open marina, a bowling centre and cinema, a world-class golf course and several restaurants, Festival City has enough attractions to warrant a day of exploring, strolling and window shopping.

Festival City is bounded at one end by Al Badia Golf Club and its gorgeous clubhouse, and at the other by the InterContinental and Crowne Plaza hotel towers which house the Belgian Beer Cafe. In between sits the Festival Waterfront Centre, one of Dubai's more spacious and relaxed shopping malls, as well as an outdoor concert venue that has hosted Paul Weller, Kylie Minogue, Maroon 5 and Queen. A canal-like waterway, complete with tiny passenger boats and alfresco dining options, meanders through the area and is perfect for post-meal, evening strolls. For a truly authentic dining experience, look no further than Al Fanar, an atmospheric restaurant that specialises in Emirati cuisine. Aside from shopping and dining, Festival City hosts several events throughout the year, including dragonboat races, children's events and fashion shows. Check out festivalcentre.com for a schedule of upcoming events.

Nearby in Garhoud, the Irish Village has long been an institution on the Dubai party scene with live music and several annual events such as Hopfest and St Patrick's Day celebrations. Next door, the Century Village is a collection of licensed alfresco restaurants including Sushi Sushi (04 282 9908) and St Tropez (04 286 9029). The Dubai Tennis Stadium is home of the Dubai Duty Free Tennis Championships, while The Aviation Club has good fitness and leisure facilities. Garhoud Park is so big it is split into three, offering children's play facilities, sports courts and jogging paths.

Dubai Transport Museum now gives details of future plans at the Roads & Transport Authority headquarters on Marrakech St.

Exploring

Exploring

If you only do one thing in...
FESTIVAL CITY & GARHOUD

Spend an evening over pints and live music at the Irish Village, one of the city's oldest and most popular pubs.

Best for...

Eating & Drinking: Kick back at one of the area's licensed restaurants along the waterfront for an evening cocktail and a bite to eat after the day's adventures.

Families: The bowling alley in Festival Waterfront Centre is a blast for all ages.

Relaxation: Take a stroll through Al Garhoud parks, and alongside the waterways at Festival City.

Shopping: Festival City Mall's large modern gold souk is great for perusing gold from all over the world in a quieter environment.

Sightseeing: If you're a nature-lover, visit Ras Al Khor Wildlife Sanctuary at 4pm to see a native flock of flamingos at feeding time.

JUMEIRA: BEACHSIDE LIFE

Jumeira's beaches, boutiques and art galleries offer a pleasant retreat from the high-rise side of the city, and its bustling core.

Jumeira's beaches, shopping centres and pleasant, wide roads make it one of the most desirable addresses for wealthy expats. In addition to enormous well-appointed villas, you'll find a distinctly upscale and independent vibe to the eateries and retail outlets here. Jumeira occupies a prime 9km strip of coastline and is popular for its beaches, some of which belong to hotels, but others are open to all free of charge. Construction of the Dubai Canal, from Jumeira to Business Bay, has disrupted some of the beaches, including Jumeirah Beach Park, but favourite the Jumeira Beach and Kite Beach still attract the crowds. The beachfront corniche offers a wide walkway, jogging track, retail kiosks, and public facilities. Just outside Jumeira, on the border with Satwa, lies 2nd December Street – the main destination for anyone needing to feed their post-club hunger, show off their expensive customised cars, or watch the city pass by as they enjoy some streetside Lebanese fare. Jumeira has a buzzing alfresco vibe with trendy developments popping up all around. Boxpark and City Walk are two recent developments that combine landscaped grounds with retail and dining establishments (see Shopping and Going Out).

City Walk
Al Safa St, Al Wasl

04 511 4670
citywalk.ae

Inspired by European-style, the tree-lined walkways of City Walk brings you a brand new retail space characterised by pleasant open spaces, water features, play areas, alfresco cafes and boutiques. You won't just shop here - you'll have a meal, grab a coffee and do some people watching, as well. **Map** 1 H2 **Metro** Emirates Towers

Dubai International Art Centre
Villa 27, 75B St, Jumeira 1

04 344 4398
artdubai.com

Since it was founded in 1976, Dubai International Art Centre has been a hub for all things artsy. In addition to nurturing local talent by organising training and workshops, the premises also house Gallery 76. This exhibition venue has been displaying paintings, sculpture and photography to outdoor installations by local and international artists alike since 2005. **Map** 1 G2 **Metro** Business Bay

Iranian Mosque
Al Wasl St, Jumeira 1

04 344 2886
3rdimam.com

Admire this mosque from the outside, but note that non-Muslims can't enter. The blue mosaic tiling, pillars, arches and elaborate minarets are very photogenic. **Map** 1 H2 **Metro** World Trade Centre

Jumeirah Beach Park
Jumeira St, Jumeira 2

04 349 2555
dm.gov.ae

The popular park is due to open by the end of 2016 after being closed for the Dubai Canal construction. As well as grassed picnic areas, a cafe and trees lining the beach, the park will have Dubai's new waterway running through it. **Map** 1 G2 **Metro** Business Bay

Exploring

Jumeira: Beachside Life

askexplorer.com

Jumeirah Mosque

04 353 6666
Jumeira St, Jumeira 1
cultures.ae

Non-Muslims are not usually permitted to enter a mosque, but the Sheikh Mohammed Centre for Cultural Understanding organises a highly recommended tour of Jumeirah Mosque, to improve awareness and understanding of Islam. Visitors are guided around the mosque and taught about the pillars and rituals of the religion, before being given the opportunity to ask any questions they have. Dress conservatively – no shorts or sleeveless tops. Women must also cover their hair with a head scarf, and all visitors should remove their shoes. Cameras are allowed and large groups can book private mosque tours. **Map** 1 H2 **Metro** World Trade Centre

Kite Beach

Nr Dubai Offshore Sailing Club
thekitebeach.com

Dubai's sportiest beach is by far its coolest, and a favourite with local kitesurfers. Other watersports taking place here include kayaking and stand up paddleboarding (SUP), or if you prefer to stay on dry land it's also a great spot for flying a kite. This area is developing all the time, adding new facilities such as children's climbing and high-wire activity zones, skatepark and an open-air gym. **Map** 1 F2 **Metro** Noor Bank

Majlis Ghorfat Umm Al Sheif

04 394 6343
Al Mehemal St, Jumeira 3
dubaiculture.ae

Constructed in 1955 from coral stone and gypsum, this simple building was used by the late Sheikh Rashid bin Saeed Al Maktoum as a summer residence. The ground floor is an open veranda, while upstairs the majlis (meeting place) is decorated with carpets, cushions, lanterns and rifles. Entry is Dhs.3 for adults and Dhs.1 for children under six years old. It is closed on weekends. **Map** 1 F2 **Metro** Business Bay

Plant Street
Al Hudaiba St, Al Satwa

Famous for pots and plants, pet shops, fabric shops and hardware outlets, Plant Street is another spot that hasn't changed much since the beginning of Dubai's boom. Head here on a Saturday evening to soak up the atmosphere, but women are advised to cover up (no miniskirts, shorts or strappy t-shirts) to avoid being stared at. **Map** 1 H2 **Metro** World Trade Centre

Safa Park
Al Wasl St, Al Wasl

04 349 2111
dm.gov.ae

A large and picturesque park with a boating lake, tennis and basketball courts, barbecue areas and plenty of kids' play areas. Entry costs Dhs.3 (free for children under three). There's a great running track around the park's perimeter. However, this park is also partially closed for the construction of Dubai Canal, which will eventually flow through it and out into the sea. **Map** 1 G2 **Metro** Business Bay

Union House
Jumeira St

04 345 3636
dubaiculture.ae

Union House is the birthplace of the nation. This is the location where the agreement forming the UAE was signed on 2 December 1971. The museum is expected to open next door in the near future. **Map** 1 H2 **Metro** World Trade Centre

Exploring

If you only do one thing in...
JUMEIRA

Learn more about Islam with a guided tour of the beautiful Jumeirah Mosque, one of few in the country open to non-Muslims.

Best for...

Eating & Drinking: Explore the trendy eateries based in the colourful containers that make up Boxpark.

Families: Spread out a towel on the sand of Kite Beach, paddle in the sea, and experience the Dubai you've seen in the brochures.

Relaxation: Feel like a 'Jumeira Jane' by slipping into SensAsia Urban Spa for a treatment.

Shopping: Enjoy a wander through the malls and independent fashion boutiques of Jumeira St.

Sightseeing: Stroll Jumeira Corniche late in the afternoon and glance back towards the city for a photo-worthy view as the sun sets.

NAKHLAT JUMEIRA & AL SUFOUH

With a modern man-made wonder, world-famous hotels, sandy shores and an indoor ski slope, this area is a must for any itinerary.

This stretch of coastline, between Marsa Dubai and Umm Suqeim, is home to some of the most prestigious and popular resorts in Dubai. From the exclusive, iconic Burj Al Arab and Jumeirah Beach Hotel at one end, along Al Sufouh Road past the One&Only Royal Mirage, The Westin and, finally, at the other end, Le Meridien Mina Seyahi (with everyone's favourite beach party bar, Barasti), this section of the Gulf contains more pricey hotels than a Monopoly set. In the middle of all this, stretching several kilometres out to sea, is Nakhlat Jumeira (Palm Jumeirah), Dubai's original mind-boggling man-made island, with its countless luxury villas and apartments, and the Disney-esque Atlantis hotel as its crowning showpiece. Within these resorts are dozens of excellent eating and drinking choices, open to all, while Souk Madinat Jumeirah and, nearby in Al Barsha, Mall of the Emirates are both great spots for shopping, dining and all-round entertainment.

Sun and water lovers are well catered for here too, with numerous beach clubs and two water parks. If the beautiful weather gets to be too much, there's always Ski Dubai where you can have a jaunt in the snow to cool you down.

Atlantis The Palm

Crescent St, Nakhlat Jumeira

04 426 0000
atlantisthepalm.com

As the name suggests, the water theme is an important part of the Atlantis set-up. Aquaventure is the resort's thrilling water park; get the adrenaline pumping by making the Leap of Faith, a 27.5m near-vertical drop, or take the various slides that shoot you through a series of tunnels surrounded by shark-infested waters. Alternatively, The Rapids will carry you around a 2.3km river, complete with waterfalls and wave surges. Another attraction here is Dolphin Bay, where you can get close up in the water with playful bottlenose dolphins, while inside the hotel is the Lost Chambers Aquarium, which contains 65,000 colourful inhabitants. The hotel is also home to several top restaurants. **Map** 1 C1 **Metro** Nakheel

Burj Al Arab

Jumeira St, Umm Suqeim 3

04 301 7777
jumeirah.com

The Burj Al Arab is one of the most photographed sights in Dubai. The billowing sail structure is a stunning piece of architecture – and inside it's no less spectacular. If your budget allows, you shouldn't miss the opportunity to sample extreme luxury at the spa, bars and restaurant. Keep in mind that you won't be allowed into the Burj Al Arab unless you have a reservation at one of the dining venues.
Map 3 E1 **Metro** Mall of the Emirates

Ski Dubai > *p.157*

Mall of the Emirates, Al Barsha 1

800 386
skidxb.com

The first indoor ski resort in the Middle East, it boasts more than 22,500 sq m of real snow over five runs and a freestyle area, as well as a snow park for the kids. With temperatures at around -4°C, this is a great place to cool off. It's also home to a colony of snow penguins that visitors can see through specially organised 'Peng Friend' encounters or during the March of the Penguins show. Remember to ask about special rates and promotions. **Map** 3 E6 **Metro** Mall of the Emirates

Souk Madinat Jumeirah   04 366 8888
Jumeira St, Al Sufouh 1   madinatjumeirah.com

Souk Madinat Jumeirah is located just a stone's throw from the Burj Al Arab and neighbouring Al Qasr hotel. Built to resemble a traditional Arabian market, it is a maze of alleyways with 95 shops and boutiques where you can find everything from swimwear to souvenirs. There are numerous coffee shops and bars, as well as Madinat Theatre. **Map** 3 E1 **Metro** Mall of the Emirates

Al Sufouh Beach
Al Sufouh St, Al Sufouh 1

This public beach, known unofficially as Black Palace Beach or 'secret beach', is on Al Sufouh Road, in a gap amid the grand palaces. There are no facilities, but the beach has a great view of the Palm and the Burj Al Arab. **Map** 3 D1 **Metro** Dubai Internet City

Wild Wadi Water Park > *p.vii*   04 348 4444
Jumeira St, Umm Suqeim 3   wildwadi.com

Beside Jumeirah Beach Hotel, Wild Wadi caters for all ages and bravery levels. The park features over 30 rides and attractions including sharp drops, a lazy river, a surfing simulator, and even skin-nibbling fish to finesse your feet. Thursday is ladies' night and there is also a 'sundowner' rate. **Map** 3 E1 **Metro** Mall of the Emirates

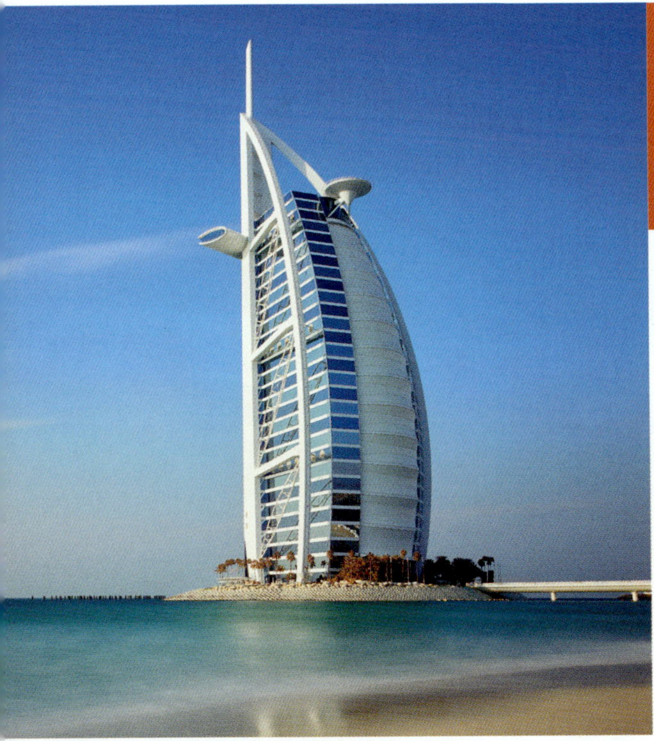

Exploring

If you only do one thing in...
NAKHLAT JUMEIRA & AL SUFOUH

Take in the (recreated) old Arabia by wandering around Souk Madinat Jumeirah's alleyways before heading to the beach for a view of the Burj Al Arab.

Best for...

Eating & Drinking: Sip with a view at Apres in Mall of the Emirates to watch people hurtle down Ski Dubai's slopes.

Families: Head to Atlantis' water attractions to kick back on the lazy river, watch the dolphins or stretch out on the hotel's private beach.

Relaxation: Be pampered in the incredible luxury of the Talise Spas at Burj Al Arab, Madinat Jumeirah or Jumeirah Zabeel Saray.

Shopping: Mall of the Emirates is a major 'New Dubai' dining and entertainment hub, not to mention the home of some of the region's best shopping.

Sightseeing: Take a ride on the Palm's monorail, which provides great views of the coastline.

OUTSIDE THE CITY & DUBAILAND

Vast development is taking place outside the city, meaning there is much to look forward to in the near future.

Dubai has a lot going on in the coming months so keep your eyes open for new developments, particularly outside the city. With three theme parks slated to open in 2016 and plans for several others floating around, everyone from adrenaline-fuelled thrill seekers to families with small children will have much more to choose from when it comes to planning the weekend.

Dubai Parks and Resorts will be the region's largest year-round theme park resort destination when it opens shortly along the E11 near Jabal Ali. The compound covers 2.3 million sq m, and includes Legoland Dubai, Legoland Waterpark, Bollywood Parks Dubai and Motiongate Dubai, between them count more than 100 rides and attractions.

IMG Worlds of Adventure in Dubailand will consist of four adventure zones featuring brands such as: MARVEL, Cartoon Network, Lost Valley – Dinosaur Adventure and IMG Boulevard, making it the world's largest indoor theme park.

Dubai Safari Park in Al Warqa is a much-anticipated replacement for the old zoo in Jumeira and will house almost 1,000 animals (including 350 rare and endangered species) across 1.2 million sq m.

The entire project – including an artificial wadi – will be eco-friendly and powered by solar energy.

Additional future projects include a 20th Century Fox park and The Pearl of Dubai with an underwater theme park at the Falconcity of Wonders development. Universal Studios Dubai remains on hold since the project stalled in 2009.

Dubai Miracle Garden
Shk Mohd Bin Zayed Rd, Arjan   04 422 8902
dubaimiraclegarden.com

This explosion of colour has been developed with the vision of becoming the world's biggest flower garden – no mean feat in the arid climate of Dubai. The sheer volume of blooms is astonishing, and you can walk under beautifully designed flower-covered arches and blooms fashioned into the shapes of pyramids, hearts and stars. Be sure to check out the world's longest wall of flowers. It is only open during the cooler winter months, but there is also a year-round butterfly park. **Map** 1 D4

Global Village
Shk Mohd Bin Zayed Rd, Wadi Al Safa 4   04 362 4114
globalvillage.ae

Between October and March a huge plot of paved desert outside of Dubai blossoms into a celebration of multiculturalism and fairground fun. There are big rides and action-orientated shows to entertain the family, but the main attraction is the shopping. Vendors come from over 45 countries across Africa, Asia and the Middle East to showcase their cultural wares. Each area has shops full of knick-knacks. You'll find some good quality as well as mass-produced clothing, furniture, decorations, technology, cosmetics, perfumes and food. **Map** 1 E6

Exploring

If you only do one thing in...
OUTSIDE THE CITY

Take a desert safari (arabian-adventures.com) out into the dunes to watch the sunset and experience some serious dunebashing.

Best for...

Eating & Drinking: A sundowner with spectacular views over the dunes is possible from the stunning Bab Al Shams Desert Resort & Spa (meydanhotels.com).

Families: Dubai Butterfly Garden next door to the Miracle Garden is a place where children can interact with moths and butterflies – in fact, they'll land all over you.

Relaxation: A stroll around the colourful Miracle Garden makes a soothing change from the hype of the city.

Shopping: Global Village is a coming together of traders from all over the world, selling everything from foodstuff to warm coats, ornaments to cosmetics and much more.

Sightseeing: Take a ride on City Sightseeing Dubai's Orange route, where you can hop on-hop off at both Dubai Miracle Garden and Global Village.

Top: An artist's impression of Motiongate Dubai; Global Village

FURTHER OUT

The UAE offers visitors some spectacular sights, from modern cities to ancient forts, and mountain pools to seemingly infinite deserts.

Dubai has a very distinct flavour and the other emirates which make up the UAE each also have a very different character. There's a lot to see, and many sights are just a short drive away so if you have time, hire a car or book a tour and hit the road. You'll quickly be surrounded by rolling sand dunes, wandering camels and imposing mountains. Heading out of Dubai to the other cities and emirates can be hugely rewarding and will add a worthy cultural perspective to your time in the UAE.

Abu Dhabi

Dubai is sometimes mistaken as the capital of the UAE, but that honour actually belongs to Abu Dhabi, which is also the largest emirate. Oil was discovered there before Dubai (1958 compared to 1966) and today it accounts for 6% of the world's known crude oil reserves, making it one of the richest cities on Earth. It is home to a growing number of renowned hotels, a selection of shiny shopping malls and a sprinkling of culture in the form of heritage sites, souks and the upcoming Abu Dhabi Guggenheim and Louvre galleries. Don't miss the 22,000 sq m Sheikh Zayed Grand Mosque (szgmc.ae).

Emirates Palace (kempinski.com) is another must-visit destination. The stunning hotel houses several excellent restaurants and is well worth the visit for the architecture alone.

UAE DAY TRIPPER

OVER 100 IDEAS TO INSPIRE A GREAT DAY OUT

Make the most of your free time!

askexplorer.com/shop

f ♥ ▶ 8+ ◉ in P /ask**explorer**

20 YEARS exploring the UAE

Off the coast, Yas Island is a thrill-seeker's delight. In addition to the annual Formula 1 Grand Prix, other events and driving experiences take place year-round at Yas Marina Circuit, while Ferrari World Abu Dhabi theme park (ferrariworldabudhabi.com) features petrol-fuelled attractions of every kind and Yas Waterworld (yaswaterworld.com), a huge water park, offers aquatic thrills. Yas Mall (yasmall.ae) is Abu Dhabi's largest mall and, at an impressive 2.5 million sq ft, it's the second largest in the UAE.

Nearby Saadiyat Island is a holiday paradise with a handful of classy hotels and resorts and the luxurious Saadiyat Beach Club (saadiyatbeachclub.ae). Visit askexplorer.com/shop to buy Explorer's *Abu Dhabi Visitors' Guide* and *Abu Dhabi Top Ten* guide for more advice on places to see in Abu Dhabi.

Al Ain

Al Ain is Abu Dhabi emirate's second city and a fertile oasis that sits on ancient trading routes between Oman and the Gulf. The birthplace of the late, revered Sheikh Zayed bin Sultan Al Nahyan, Al Ain is known as the Garden City because it is full of date plantations and pockets of greenery. These oases are lovely places to explore. Drive around the networks of walled, cobbled roads, park up, and wander through the lush green plantations. You might even get to taste some fresh fruit if you stumble across some harvested bounty (be sure to ask permission from the picker before you pop one in your mouth). Next to the main Al Ain oasis is the interesting Al Ain Palace Museum (03 751 7755, abudhabi.ae), which illustrates aspects of life in the UAE. Al Ain Zoo (03 799 2000, alainzoo.ae) is a nature lover's dream and easily one of the city's best attractions. Conservation is the keyword here, with natural habitats recreated to be as near to the real thing as possible. You can get the whole family up close to animals including giraffes, zebras and rhinos at the newly launched safari park.

For a great view over the city and desert landscape, take a scenic drive up Jebel Hafeet. A winding road rises to the summit, where you'll find the Mercure Grand Jebel Hafeet Hotel – a great place for a drink with a terrific view (03 783 8888, mercure.com). Below the mountain are a selection of beehive tombs dating back to about 3000BC, known as the Hafit tombs. You'll need a 4WD drive to visit them. At the foothill of the mountain is Wadi Adventure (wadiadventure.ae), which offers a range of adrenaline-pumping activities such as white-water rafting and kayaking.

Al Gharbia

Abu Dhabi's Western Region, Al Gharbia, is a vast 60,000 sq km or 60% of the total area of Abu Dhabi emirate and 51% of the UAE. The region boasts the highest sand dunes in the world and 350km of coastline with beaches, rare wildlife, and beautiful desert islands such as Delma and Sir Bani Yas fast becoming popular tourist destinations. For most visitors to Al Gharbia, however, all roads lead to Liwa.

Wildlife Watch
The International Fund for Houbara Conservation (IFHC) is a government organisation dedicated to the restoration and preservation of the local Houbara bustard. Since its first breeding centre in the UAE became operational in 1993, IFHC (houbarafund.org) has released 137,831 birds into the wild.

Liwa lies at the edge of the Rub Al Khali (Empty Quarter), one of the largest sand deserts in the world. Liwa Oasis is one of the largest oases on the Arabian Peninsula. This fertile crescent stretches for more than 150km and is home to the Bani Yas tribe, ancestors of the ruling family of Abu Dhabi. It's a quiet area, dotted with date plantations and small towns. Visitors go to see its ancient forts, traditional falconry, camel racing and trading, and because Liwa is the northern gate to the great desert. It's at Liwa that you'll find the legendary sand dune known as 'Tel Moreeb', or the Hill of Terror, a 300m high slope which attracts only the most confident off-roaders. Prepare for the most adventurous desert driving and incredible scenery the UAE has to offer.

East Coast

Even if you're only in the UAE for a short time, a trip to the east coast is a must. You can get there in less than two hours.

Divers consider it to be better than off Dubai's coast, mainly because of increased visibility. Snoopy Island off Dibba's coast is a favourite spot for snorkelling. The east coast is home to a few interesting areas, many of which are free to explore. The site of the oldest mosque in the UAE, Badiyah, is roughly halfway down the coast, north of Khorfakkan. The building is believed to date back to the middle of the 15th century and was restored in 2003. The village is considered one of the oldest settlements on the east coast, which is thought to have been inhabited since 3000BC. Located at the northernmost point of the coast, Dibba is made up of three fishing villages, each coming under a different jurisdiction: Sharjah, Fujairah and Oman. The villages share an attractive bay and excellent diving locations. The Hajar Mountains provide a wonderful backdrop to the public beaches. To reach Khasab, the capital of the Omani territory of Musandam, you now need to cross the border on the west coast (from Ras Al Khaimah), rather than via Dibba. You can stay at the Atana Khasab (+968 2 673 0777, atanahotels.com), which can organise dhow cruises and dolphin watching, or at the luxurious Six Senses Zighy Bay (+968 2 673 5555, sixsenses.com).

Further south on the coast lies Fujairah, the youngest of the seven emirates. Overlooking the atmospheric old town is a 300 year-old fort. The surrounding hillsides are dotted with more ancient forts and watchtowers, which add an air of mystery and charm. Hotels include Le Meridien Al Aqah Beach Resort (09 244 9000, lemeridien-alaqah.com), and Radisson Blu Resort, Fujairah (09 244 9700, radissonblu.com). Khor Kalba sits just south of Fujairah. It's the most northerly mangrove forest in the world, and home to a variety of plant, marine and birdlife not found anywhere else in the UAE.

Hatta

The road leading to Hatta from Dubai (E44) is a trip in itself. Watch as the sand gradually changes from beige to dark orange and then disappears, only to be replaced by jagged mountains. The famous Big Red sand dune lies on this road, and is a popular spot for dune driving in 4WDs or quad bikes.

Hatta is a small town, nestled at the foot of the Hajar Mountains, about 100km from Dubai city and 10km from the Dubai-Oman border. It is home to the oldest fort in Dubai emirate, which was built in 1790. You'll also see several watchtowers on the surrounding hills. On the drive you'll pass a row of carpet shops, ideal for putting your bargaining skills into practice. The town itself has a sleepy, relaxed feel, and includes the Heritage Village (04 852 1374), which charts the area's 3,000 year history and includes a 200 year-old mosque and the fortress built by Sheikh Maktoum bin Hasher Al Maktoum in 1896, which is now used as a weaponry museum.

Northern Emirates

North of Dubai and Sharjah are Ajman, Umm Al Quwain and Ras Al Khaimah. These three emirates are much smaller in size than Dubai and Abu Dhabi and are also less developed. Ajman is the smallest, but its proximity to Dubai and Sharjah has enabled it to grow considerably. It was once known as one of the largest dhow building centres in the region, and while it is mainly modern boats that emerge from the yards these days, you can still catch a glimpse of a traditionally built dhow sailing out to sea. Ajman also has some great beaches and a corniche with numerous five-star hotels.

Umm Al Quwain has the smallest population and little has changed over the years, though it is home to Dreamland Aqua Park (dreamlanduae.com) and Barracuda Beach Resort (barracuda.ae) which has an off-licence and gourmet food shop. The Flamingo Beach Resort (06 765 0000) offers crab hunting and mangrove tours.

Ras Al Khaimah is just over an hour's journey north of Dubai. With the jagged Hajar Mountains

Off-Road Antics
If hiring a 4WD and exploring is your style, grab a copy of Explorer's *UAE Off-Road* guide from petrol stations and supermarkets which details 33 routes across all emirates including Hafit Tombs, Liwa Oasis and Ras Al Khaimah's stunning mountains.

rising behind the city, and the Arabian Gulf stretching out from the shore, Ras Al Khaimah has some of the best scenery in the UAE. A creek divides the city into the old town and the newer Al Nakheel district. For a day trip, you should go to the souk in the old town and the National Museum of Ras Al Khaimah (07 233 3411, rakheritage.rak.ae). This is a good starting point for exploring the surrounding countryside and visiting the ancient sites of Ghalilah and Shimal. Check out RAK Sailing Academy for watersports.

Sharjah

Before Dubai's rise to prominence as a trading and tourism hotspot, neighbouring Sharjah was one of the wealthiest towns in the region, with settlers earning their livelihood from fishing, pearling and trade. Sharjah's commitment to art, culture and preserving its traditional heritage is recognised throughout the Arab world and the city is home to several museums. See sharjahmuseums.ae for details.

For some fun, Sharjah Golf & Shooting Club has a range where you can try out indoor pistols, rifles and revolvers. It also gives you a chance to try your hand at archery and paintball.

Sharjah city is built around Khalid Lagoon (known as the creek), and the surrounding Buhairah Corniche is a popular spot for an evening stroll. You can also hire a small dhow from various points on the lagoon. The heritage area is a fascinating old walled city, home to numerous museums and the traditional Souk Al Arsah. Shoppers should also make time for the beautiful Central Souk, and the arts area is a treat. A must is Al Qasba (06 556 0777, alqasba.ae), which has performance spaces and waterside restaurants. Another worthy stop-off is Sharjah Desert Park, home to Arabia's Wildlife Centre (06 531 1999, breedingcentresharjah.com).

TOURS & SIGHTSEEING

Whether it be by bus, plane, boat or 4WD, taking a tour is a fun and efficient way to see a different side of the UAE.

Tours are a great way to see the city and beyond, as well as to learn more about the landmarks and culture of Dubai. Hop-on, hop-off bus tours, such as those from City Sightseeing Dubai (citysightseeing-dubai.com), provide a useful overview of the main areas of interest and give the flexibility to spend longer at desired destinations, with inclusive transport. City Sightseeing Dubai offers four major routes, with audio commentary, and covers more than 45 stops. Check your ticket, as the package includes free boat tours, discounts and entry into attractions.

Helicopter and plane tours give an extensive aerial insight to the growing city. No visitor should leave without experiencing a desert safari of some sort. Expert drivers blast 4WDs up, down and around massive dunes while passing old Bedouin villages and pointing out incredible natural attractions. Mountain safaris lead passengers through the narrow wadis of the Hajar Mountains.

While most of the companies listed on the next page offer a wide range of experiences, some are more specialised. Both Aerogulf Services and Seawings concentrate on plane tours and Balloon Adventures is the city's main balloon ride operator.

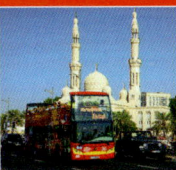

City Sightseeing Dubai

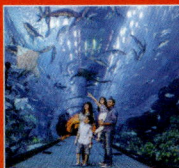

WE SHOW YOU DUBAI!

City Sightseeing Dubai's hop-on hop-off bus tours allow you to experience a scenic glimpse of Dubai's diversity. You will visit historical areas, Dubai Marina, the Palm Jumeirah, the tallest building in the world and experience a magical paradise along the coast.

24HR TICKET – OVER 15 INCLUSIONS

- 4 Routes, Over 45 Stops
- Dhow Cruise
- Water Taxi
- Dubai Museum
- Complimentary Water
- 3 Guided Walking Tours
- VIP Global Village Entry (Seasonal)
- Shopping & Dining Discounts
- Sheikh Saeed Al Maktoum's House
- 5 Other Museums

48HR TICKET IN ADDITION INCLUDES

- Dubai Aquarium & Underwater Zoo
- Sharjah hop-on hop-off Sightseeing tour (Shuttle Service to Sharjah available)

www.citysightseeing-dubai.com | City Sightseeing Dubai | @cssdubai | cssdubai

Contact: +971 4 316 7506, Email: info@cs-dubai.com

Tours & Sightseeing

Absolute Adventure	04 345 9900	adventure.ae
Aerogulf Services	04 877 6120	aerogulfservices.com
Alpha Tours	04 701 9111	alphatoursdubai.com
Arabian Adventures	04 343 9966	arabian-adventures.com
Balloon Adventures Emirates	04 285 4949	ballooning.ae
Bristol Middle East Yacht Solution	04 368 2480	bristol-middleeast.com
City Sightseeing Dubai > p.139	04 316 7506	info@cs-dubai.com
Delta Travel & Holidays	04 398 0909	delta.ae
Desert Adventures	04 450 4450	desertadventures.com
Desert Rangers	04 456 9944	desertrangers.com
Dubai Tourism & Travel Services	04 336 7727	dubai-travel.ae
Gulf Ventures	04 404 5880	gulfventures.ae
Knight Tours	04 343 7725	knighttours.ae
Oasis Palm Tourism	04 262 8889	opdubai.com
Omeir Travel Agency	04 337 7727	omeir.com
Orient Tours	04 282 8238	orient-tours-uae.com
Seawings	04 807 0708	seawings.ae
Sun City Tours & Safaris	04 357 1122	suncitydubai.com
Sunflower Tours	04 334 5554	sunflowerdubai.com
Tour Dubai	04 336 8407	tour-dubai.com
Travco	04 336 6643	travcotravel.ae

See *askexplorer.com* for a full directory of tour operators

Exploring

Tours & Sightseeing

askexplorer.com 141

Sports & Spas

Active Dubai	144
Sports & Activities	146
Spas	164

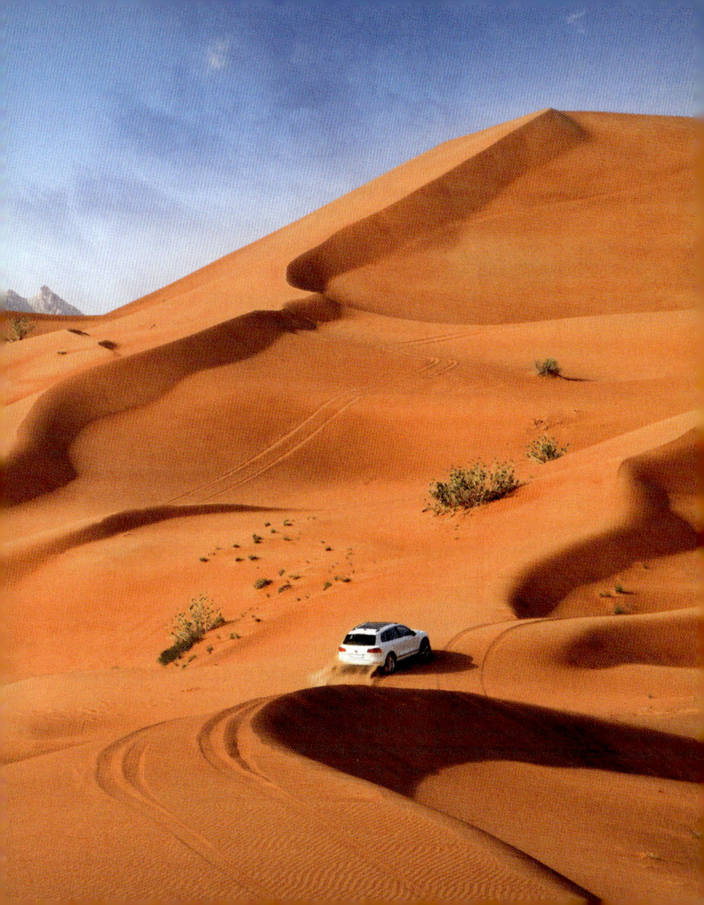

ACTIVE DUBAI

Dubai has a wealth of spas, sports and resorts dedicated to the art of relaxation.

It is not just shops and beaches that attract visitors to Dubai. Numerous world-class sporting events take place in the city throughout the year, drawing crowds of residents and tourists alike. The Dubai World Cup is the richest horse race in the world, the Dubai Rugby Sevens regularly pulls in crowds in excess of 70,000 and the Dubai Duty Free Tennis Championships see the world's leading players compete for multi million-dollar prizes.

Dubai is also home to several excellent golf courses, many designed by leading figures such as Robert Trent Jones II, Colin Montgomerie and Nick Faldo. Among them is the Emirates Golf Club, which hosts the annual Omega Dubai Desert Classic, a longtime fixture on the PGA European Tour.

Traditional sports, such as camel racing and falconry, offer an interesting perspective on local heritage, and should definitely not be missed.

A combination of Arabian Gulf shoreline and the vast expanses of desert just outside the city make Dubai a great adventure sports destination. From kitesurfing and diving to dune driving and sand skiing, there are many opportunities for exciting sports activities.

All this activity aside, those who are seeking blissful holidays spent relaxing and rejuvenating will find a collection of world-class spas offering a range of unique treatments in luxurious surroundings, usually at surprisingly reasonable prices.

Sports & Spas

SPORTS & ACTIVITIES

With its miles of sand dunes, clear seas, classic Arabian heritage and superb sports facilities, holidays in Dubai are action packed.

Beaches

Dubai has several beautiful beaches. There are public beaches, beach parks with good facilities and a nominal entrance fee, and private beaches which belong to hotels and beach clubs. Also check out Dubai Municipality's Dubai Parks and Beaches app.

The Beach
Jumeirah Beach Residence, Marsa Dubai   thebeach.ae

The waters are fairly calm at this busy beach, and the hotels offer a variety of watersports. It is one of the most fun, family friendly beaches in Dubai, and the skyscrapers of Marsa Dubai provide a spectacular backdrop. There are wide walkways, shower and toilet facilities, play areas for children, and a large choice of restaurants, cafes and boutiques. **Map** 3 A1 **Metro** DAMAC

Kite Beach
Nr Dubai Offshore Sailing Club, Umm Suqeim 1   thekitebeach.com

Dubai's sportiest beach, and by far its coolest, Kite Beach is a favourite with local kitesurfers. Other watersports taking place here include stand up paddleboarding (SUP). The long sweeping stretch of uninterrupted sand makes it the perfect playground. There are kayaks for hire, a kids' play area, skatepark, football and volleyball facilities, high-wire activity zones and an open-air gym. There are also numerous food outlets. **Map** 1 E2 **Metro** Noor Bank

Mamzar Beach Park
Al Khaleej St, Al Mamzar   04 296 6201

Mamzar Park has four clean beaches, green spaces, chalets for hire and play areas, and can be pleasantly empty during the week. The well-maintained beaches have sheltered, safe areas for swimming and there are also two swimming pools with changing rooms and showers, plus parasols and lifeguards. There are barbecue areas, a restaurant and several snack bars. **Map** 1 K2 **Metro** Al Qiyadah

Umm Suqeim Beach
Nr Jumeirah Beach Hotel, Umm Suqeim 3

This stretch of sand is also known as Sunset Beach because its spot next to the Burj Al Arab allows for some stunning photos. It is one of the busiest public beaches at weekends. **Map** 1 E2 **Metro** FGB

Boating

A stroll beside the creek, Dubai Marina or Jumeira's harbour will put you in the path of many companies that run tours (see also the Exploring chapter), or that charter boats for fishing, cruising or partying. Luxury yachts, catamarans and fishing boats and traditional wooden dhows are available, and many firms will consider letting out their tour boats for the right price. See askexplorer.com for a full directory of operators.

Al Boom Tourist Village

04 324 3000
alboom.ae

Shk Rashid Rd, Umm Hurair 2

Al Boom Tourist Village operates nine dhow boats on the creek, ranging from single-deckers with room for 20 people to the huge triple-decker Mumtaz, which can take 300 passengers. It offers a variety of packages, with prices varying accordingly. Late night trips can also be arranged. **Map** 4 C6 **Metro** Dubai Healthcare City

Khasab Travel & Tours

04 266 9950
khasabtours.com

Warba Centre, Al Muraqqabat

This operator organises day cruises in Khasab, Oman (including car transfers from Dubai). The route follows the rugged Musandam coastline, which has been dubbed the 'Norway of Arabia'. You'll pass small fishing villages in remote locations and may see dolphins and turtles. **Map** 4 E4 **Metro** Abu Baker Al Siddique

Diving & Snorkelling

The clear waters off the coast of Dubai are home to a variety of marine species, coral life and even shipwrecks. You'll see some exotic fish and possibly moray eels, small sharks, barracudas, sea snakes and stingrays. Most of the wrecks are located on the west coast of the UAE, while the best flora and fauna can be seen in Fujairah or Musandam, which is part of Oman (see the Exploring chapter). There are many tour companies and diving centres which provide instruction and PADI certification, and rent equipment.

More details on specific dives and sites can be found in Explorer's *UAE Diving* guide. For guaranteed interactions with marine life, the city's aquariums and water parks also offer diving experiences for all ages and abilities.

Al Boom Diving

Al Wasl St, Jumeira 1

04 342 2993
alboomdiving.com

Al Boom Diving is a purpose-built school with a fully outfitted diving shop, and it holds a variety of courses in Dubai and Fujairah (09 244 9000). For aquatic thrills right in the heart of the city, Al Boom Diving also offers the chance to dive with the sharks in The Dubai Mall's gigantic aquarium. **Map** 1 H2 **Metro** Emirates Towers

Pavilion Dive Centre

Jumeirah Beach Hotel, Umm Suqeim 3

04 406 8828
jumeirah.com

Offering courses for beginners through to instructors, Pavilion Dive Centre runs daily dive charters for certified divers in Dubai, and trips to Musandam on request. Pavilion also has professional Disabled Divers International (DDI) instructors and dive masters. **Map** 3 E1 **Metro** Mall of the Emirates

Golf

With an ideal climate for most of the year, golf is a popular sport in Dubai. Facilities include a number of international-standard courses designed by such names as South Africa's 'Big Easy' Ernie Els. As such, the emirate is host to a number of high-profile tournaments. Jumeirah Golf Estates is home to the DP World Tour Championship (europeantour.com), the grand finale of The Race to Dubai, the European Tour's season-long competition which features 50 tournaments in 27 destinations. Every year it attracts the cream of the golf world with a prize fund of $8 million. The Omega Dubai Desert Classic (dubaidesertclassic.com) at Emirates Golf Club, is a PGA European Tour competition which has previously involved Tiger Woods, Ernie Els and Henrik Stenson.

askexplorer.com

Al Badia Golf Club By InterContinental Dubai Festival City

04 601 0101

Dubai Festival City, Al Kheeran   albadiagolfclub.ae

World-renowned golf course designer Robert Trent Jones II is behind the InterContinental's offering. At the heart of Dubai Festival City, beside the creek, it enjoys great views across the city. The 7,303 yard, par 72 championship course has a plush clubhouse, extensive water features and salt-tolerant grass, meaning it can be irrigated with sea water. **Map** 1 J4 **Metro** Emirates

Arabian Ranches Golf Club

04 366 3000

Shk Mohd Bin Zayed Rd, Arabian Ranches,
Wadi Al Safa 6   arabianranchesgolfdubai.com

Designed by Ian Baker-Finch in association with Nicklaus Design, this par 72 grass course uses the natural desert terrain and features indigenous shrubs and bushes. You must have an official handicap to play, but can reserve a tee-off time six days in advance. Facilities include a golf academy with floodlit driving range, an extensive short game practice area and GPS on all golf carts. **Map** 1 D5

Dubai Creek Golf & Yacht Club

04 295 6000

Shk Rashid Rd, Port Saeed   dubaigolf.com

The par 71 course was designed by Thomas Björn and is open to all players with a valid handicap certificate. Those who are new to the game are encouraged to train with PGA qualified instructors at the academy. There is also a nine-hole, par three course, a floodlit range and extensive short game practice areas. The iconic clubhouse features several dining favourites and two pro shops. **Map** 4 C6 **Metro** Deira City Centre

The Els Club Dubai

04 425 1010
Dubai Sports City, Al Hebiah 4 elsclubdubai.com
Designed by Ernie Els, this 18 hole, par 72 course stretches 7,538 yards. There is also a Butch Harmon School of Golf for players of all ages and skills. Follow the game with dining options at the Mediterranean clubhouse. **Map** 1 C4 **Metro** Dubai Internet City

Emirates Golf Club

04 417 9999
Shk Zayed Rd, Al Thanyah 3 dubaigolf.com
Golfers can choose from two 18 hole courses: the 7,301 yard, par 72 Majlis Course, or the Faldo Course designed by Nick Faldo and IMG Design, which also offers night-time golfing. The club also has a Peter Cowen Golf Academy, along with two driving ranges, practice areas and clubhouse. **Map** 3 B2 **Metro** Nakheel

JA Jebel Ali Golf Resort

04 814 5555
Nr Palm Jebel Ali, Jabal Ali jaresortshotels.com
Situated in the landscaped gardens of the JA Jebel Ali Golf Resort & Spa, this nine-hole, par 36 course offers views of the Arabian Gulf. Renowned for its good condition all year, the course is also home to the Jebel Ali Golf Resort & Spa Challenge, the opener for the Omega Dubai Desert Classic.

Montgomerie Golf Club

04 390 5600
Emirates Living, Al Thanyah 4 themontgomerie.com
Designed by Colin Montgomerie and Desmond Muirhead, the 18 hole, par 72 course has some unique characteristics, including the 656 yard 18th hole. The facilities include a driving range and a swing analysis studio. **Map** 3 B3 **Metro** Nakheel

Motorsports

The UAE deserts provide ideal locations for rallying, and many events are organised throughout the year by the Emirates Motor Sports Federation and Automobile & Touring Club of the UAE. These cover all kinds of vehicles, from 4WDS and saloons to motocross, buggies and karts, The high-profile Abu Dhabi Desert Challenge (abudhabidesertchallenge.com) is one of the top events in World Cup Cross Country Rallying. Others include the Emirates Desert Championship (emiratesdesertchampionship.ae), the Dubai International Rally (dubaiinternationalrally.com) and the Gulf 12Hours (gulf12hours.com).

Yas Island (yasisland.ae), located a short drive away in Abu Dhabi, is home to the annual Formula 1 Etihad Airways Abu Dhabi Grand Prix. The circuit (yasmarinacircuit.com) hosts several other motorsports events throughout the year, and the theme park Ferrari World Abu Dhabi (ferrariworldabudhabi.com) features all manner of high-octane attractions for petrolheads.

Dubai Autodrome 04 367 8700
Dubai Motor City, Al Hebiah 1 dubaiautodrome.com

The Dubai Autodrome (part of Dubailand) is the home of motorsport in Dubai. It has six different track configurations, including a 5.39km FIA-sanctioned GP circuit, premium pit facilities and a 7,000 seat grandstand. The venue hosts events throughout the year, including the NGK Racing Series and UAE Sportbike Championship. You can experience the thrill of driving on a racetrack with the guidance of qualified instructors. A range of packages and experiences are offered, including McLarens, single-seaters, Audi R8s or TTs with prices starting at Dhs.875. **Map** 1 D5

Sports & Spas

Kartdrome

04 367 8744
dubaiautodrome.com

Dubai Motor City, Al Hebiah 1

Wannabe Vettels of any age can burn rubber at the Kartdrome, Dubai's primary go-karting track. After a safety briefing, you'll take to your powerful 390cc kart (there are smaller 120cc karts for the kids) and hit the tarmac on the exciting 1.2km circuit. **Map** 1 D5

Off-Roading

Most car rental agencies offer visitors 4WDs capable of desert driving. If renting a 4WD, make sure you get the details of the insurance plan, as many rental insurers won't cover damage caused by off-roading. Dune bashing, or desert driving, is one of the toughest challenges for both car and driver, but once you have mastered it, it's a lot of fun. The famous Big Red sand dune along the Dubai-Hatta road is a popular spot for dune driving in 4WDs, and there are places here that rent out quad bikes and all-terrain vehicles.

If you do venture out into the desert, it is a good idea to have at least one experienced driver and one other car to help if you get stuck. Most major tour companies offer a range of desert and mountain safaris if you'd rather leave the driving to the professionals.

Driving in wadis is usually a bit more straightforward. Wadis are (usually) dry gullies, carved through the rock by rushing floodwaters, following the course of seasonal rivers. The main safety precaution to take when wadi bashing is to keep your eyes open for rare, but not impossible, thunder storms developing. The wadis can fill up quickly and you will need to make your way to higher ground pretty fast to avoid flash floods. For further information and tips on off-road driving in the UAE, buy Explorer's *UAE Off-Road* at askexplorer.com/shop.

Rugby

Sports & Spas

Emirates Airline Dubai Rugby Sevens   04 321 0008
The Sevens Stadium, Al Marmoom   dubairugby7s.com

One of the biggest events in the UAE, the Dubai Rugby Sevens attracts a huge crowd each year. The three-day event is the first stop in the IRB Sevens World Series and plays host to the top 16 Sevens teams in the world. The first day of the event sees regional teams go head to head, with the international teams joining the fray for the last two days. As well as the international matches, you can also watch social, youth and women's games at the event. Tickets can sell out weeks in advance, so plan to get yours early. The whole weekend has a party atmosphere, with live bands, fancy dress and family entertainment making the Dubai Rugby Sevens an unmissable fixture for any sports fan. Plan this into your schedule if you're passing through the Emirates in December.

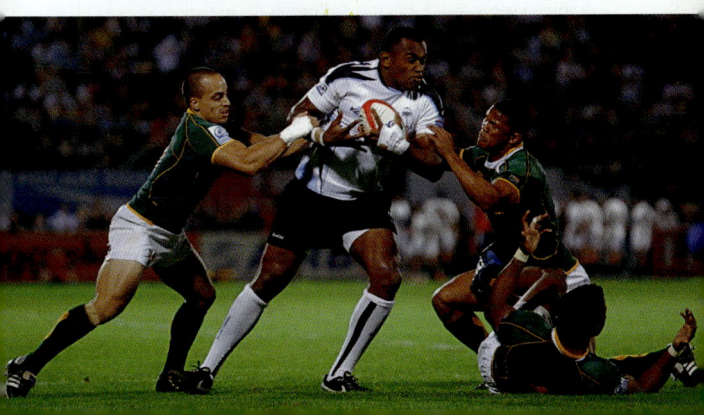

Skating & Skiing

Dubai's climate can get pretty hot, but the emirate has developed ingenious ways of keeping you cool when it all gets a bit much. If you need a break from the sun and sand, there are some refreshing options involving ice and snow.

Dubai Ice Rink

04 448 5111
The Dubai Mall, Downtown Dubai — dubaiicerink.com

This Olympic-sized arena on the ground floor of The Dubai Mall provides equipment and skating aids for little ones. For bigger kids, the rink is transformed into an ice disco in the evenings. **Map** 2 C3 **Metro** Burj Khalifa/Dubai Mall

Ski Dubai > *p.157*

800 386
Mall of the Emirates, Al Barsha 1 — skidxb.com

The first indoor ski resort in the Middle East, complete with 22,500 sq m of real snow, Ski Dubai has temperatures hovering around -4°C. Competent skiers and boarders can choose between five runs of different difficulty (there's even a black run) and a freestyle area, but lessons are available for beginners. There's a Snow Park, where you can take little ones tobogganing, and the attractions also include the opportunity to meet the cute resident penguins, and even go for a swim with them. If you don't ski, you can roll down the slope inside a giant inflatable ball or zip line on the Snow Bullet. Slope pass and lesson prices include the hire of jackets, trousers, boots, socks, helmets and equipment, but it's worth packing gloves, as you'll be charged extra for the hire of these. Don't forget to ask about special rates and promotions.
Map 3 E3 **Metro** Mall of the Emirates

HUG A PENGUIN.
RIDE A CHAIRLIFT.
BOBSLED.
RACE.
SCREAM.
REGAIN BREATH.
START ALL
OVER AGAIN.
Far from the heat. Far from lectures.
Far from your everyday routine, there's a
place that makes every day extraordinary.
- 4º FROM ORDINARY
SKI DUBAI
سكي دبي
SKI DUBAI APP NOW AVAILABLE ON
GET IT ON Google play
Download on the App Store
For more information visit www.skidxb.com
/SKIDXB /SKIDXB /SKIDUBAI /SKIDXB

Skydiving & Zip-lining

With its tall towers, there are many ways to get a bird's-eye view of Dubai. See also the Exploring chapter for aeroplane tours and hot-air balloons, but if you want to get higher still and adrenaline is what you're after, try these exciting ways to get some air.

iFLY Dubai

04 231 6292
City Centre Mirdif, Mirdif   theplaymania.com

If you like the idea of a skydive, but don't have the budget or head for heights, or would just prefer a practice run, iFLY simulates the sensation of jumping from a plane. You hover over powerful fans that blast you up to 10m in the air with winds of up to 200kph in its giant vertical wind tunnels. You can even take kids as young as three. **Map** 1 K5 **Metro** Rashidiya

SkyDive Dubai

04 377 8888
Nr Habtoor Grand Beach Resort, Marsa Dubai   skydivedubai.ae

This is the real thing, with options for beginners – a first-time tandem jump costs Dhs.1,999 with photos and DVD – and experienced divers. The company has two locations; opt for stunning views over Nakhlat Jumeira and Marsa Dubai, or there's a desert drop zone along the Dubai-Al Ain Road. **Map** 3 B1 **Metro** DAMAC

XLine by XDubai

Nr The Dubai Mall, Burj Khalifa   xdubai.com

This 558m long zip-line starts from the W1 Tower in Downtown Dubai and shuttles you at a height of 90m to The Dubai Mall. You'll pass over the Dubai Fountain and take in views of Burj Khalifa. Get tickets from the mall. **Map** 2 C3 **Metro** Burj Khalifa/Dubai Mall

Traditional Sports

If you're looking for a true taste of local culture, the traditional sports of the Emirates are your chance. Camel racing takes place in the winter months, usually early on a Friday morning, and additional meets are often held on public holidays. Equestrian activities are also popular in Dubai, especially endurance racing (dubaiequestrianclub.ae). The Arabian Saluki, the breed of dog most commonly associated with the region, can achieve speeds of more than 68kph and is also raced. Other traditional sports to look out for include falconry. You can often come across these activities at heritage festivals.

Al Marmoom Camel Racetrack
Al Marmoom dcrc.ae

This popular local sport is serious business, and racing camels are very valuable. Races are held during winter from 7am to 8.30am. There are many racetracks across the country, but this one holds the Marmoom Heritage Festival at the end of the season in March. The free event also features many traditional and cultural curiosities as well as camel-based escapades.

Meydan Racecourse
Nadd Al Shiba 1 04 327 0077
meydan.ae

This impressively large, state-of-the-art racecourse, with a 60,000 seat grandstand, a five-star hotel and several restaurants, is where the world's richest horse race, the Dubai World Cup, takes place. You can also see horse racing at Jebel Ali Racecourse (04 347 4914), near The Greens. Visit emiratesracing.com for the racing calendar and other courses. **Map** 1 G4

Water Parks

There is no better way to have fun in the sun than by splashing around at one of Dubai's exciting and expansive water parks. You'll find splash parks for children as well as the big ones for adults, and more are in the pipeline with Legoland Waterpark due to open in the near future. You'll find water parks all over the Emirates, with Dreamland Aqua Park (dreamlanduae.com) in Umm Al Quwain, Ice Land Water Park (icelandwaterpark.com) in Ras Al Khaimah, Al Montazah (almontazah.ae) in Sharjah, and Yas Waterworld (yaswaterworld.com) in Abu Dhabi. In Al Ain, Wadi Adventure (wadiadventure.ae) is an adventure park with surf pool, white-water rafting, kayaking, wakeboarding and more.

Aquaventure
04 426 0000
Atlantis Nakhlat Jumeira
aquaventurewaterpark.com

This is the ultimate destination for thrill-seekers. To get the adrenaline pumping, there's the Leap Of Faith, a near-vertical drop that shoots you through a series of tunnels surrounded by 'shark-infested' waters. There are rapids and a lazy river for those who want something calmer. You can also make use of the sun loungers on the park's private beach. Splashers is a giant water playground with slides specifically for little ones. **Map** 1 N1 **Metro** Nakheel

The Beach Waterpark
04 551 6180
Nr Al Mamsha St, Marsa Dubai
arabianwaterparks.com

An inflatable playground in the sea off the coast of JBR beach, The Beach Waterpark is fun for all ages. There are hills to clamber over, trampolines, climbing walls and, if you manage to pull yourself up to the top using the ropes and footholds (by no means an easy feat!), you get to whizz down on the slides or jump from some surprisingly scary heights. **Map** 3 A1 **Metro** DAMAC

Wild Wadi > *p.vii* 04 348 4444
Jumeira St Umm Suqeim 3 wildwadi.com

There's fun for all ages at this perennially popular water park beside Jumeirah Beach Hotel. The highlight is the Jumeirah Sceirah, where a trapdoor floor opens to shoot you down a 120m long slide at speeds of up to 80kph. For something more sedate, float round the lazy river or simply bob about in the wave pool. There's also a great water play area for younger kids. **Map** 1 S4 **Metro** FGB

Watersports

The emirate's stunning stretch of beaches offers plenty of opportunities for water-based fun and the different ocean breaks allow for a wide range of activities to take place within close proximity. Most beachside hotels offer watersports, including sea kayaking, sailing and windsurfing. Non-guests may have to pay beach fees to access the facilities, though sometimes you can enter the beach area for free if you make a prior reservation.

Kitesurfing is an extreme sport that fuses elements of windsurfing, wakeboarding and kite flying. Kite Beach (see Beaches) is the place to go, where Watercooled offers instruction and equipment hire. Stand up paddleboarding makes for a great workout and is a good way to get out on the water when the wind and waves are calm. As the board is a generous size, balancing on top of one is far easier than a surfboard.

Other popular watersports include wakeboarding, cableboarding, which allows you to wakeboard while being pulled along by a zip line, and jet-skiing. Flyboarding is a relatively recent craze in which you'll be strapped onto a miniature wakeboard that's connected to a giant hose, that in turn is connected to a jet ski. As soon as your jet-skier flips the throttle, water is sent through the hose at a very high pressure into the board on your feet giving you powerful propulsion.

Watersports Operators

Fun Beach Water Sports Nr Umm Suqeim Park, Umm Suqeim 2	050 705 0433 seaworlddsf.com
Nautica1992 Habtoor Grand Beach Resort & Spa, Marsa Dubai	04 399 5000
Sea Breeze The Beach, JBR, Marsa Dubai	800 637 227 thebeach.ae
Sea Riders UAE Dubai Marina Mall Water Taxi Station	055 510 3739 searidersuae.com
SeaWake Dubai International Marine Club, Marsa Dubai	055 166 3344 seawake.ae
Sky & Sea Adventures Hilton Dubai Jumeirah Resort, Marsa Dubai	04 399 9005 watersportsdubai.com
Wake Evolution Riva Beach Club, Nakhlat Jumeira	056 765 4312 wake-evolution.com
Water Adventure Dubai Rixos The Palm Dubai, Nakhlat Jumeira	04 453 7544 wateradventure.ae
Watercooled JA Jebel Ali Golf Resort, Mena Jabal Ali	04 887 6771 watercooleddubai.com
Waves Water Sports & Luxury Yacht Charters Nr Umm Suqeim Park, Jumeira 3	04 256 2479 wwsdubai.com

A range of watersports is available off Dubai's shores

Sports & Spas

SPAS

Take some time out from the city's frenetic pace to enjoy a massage, facial or hammam. You won't have to go far to find one.

A comprehensive range of treatments is on offer in the city and you can find spas offering anything from Balinese massage, hammams and Moroccan baths, to ayurvedic treatments and hot-stone therapy in Dubai's five-star hotels.

The price of treatments varies between spas, and while basic treatments like manicures and pedicures can be cheaper in the smaller spas and salons, you will often pay a high price for more exotic treatments in the upmarket hotels. Lesser known options are just as good and often cheaper. Jumeira has several smaller spas, treatment centres and nail salons that cater for those on a more modest budget and you'll find them inside fancy villas along the beach road and Al Wasl Road. It's also a good idea to check sites like Groupon and Cobone for discounted spa offers and treatments.

Spas will often offer set packages that combine a few treatments to make your visit more cost-effective. Compare packages between spas to get the best deal – and ask about their facilities as you will often be allowed to use the sauna, pool or Jacuzzi before or after your treatment.

Some spas only serve women, but others offer treatments for couples in private rooms, or have separate areas for men. Grooming lounges like 1847, which cater exclusively to men, are also increasingly popular.

1847

04 399 8989
1847uae.com

Grosvenor House, Marsa Dubai

A grooming lounge dedicated to men, 1847 offers manicures, professional shaves and massages in a decidedly masculine setting. Several of the treatments take place in private studies, with personal LCD TVs. There is also an inhouse retail boutique that stocks skincare and grooming products, as well as travel packs and accessories. There is another lounge in The Boulevard at Emirates Towers (04 330 1847) and The Walk at Jumeirah Beach Residence (04 437 0252). **Map** 3 B1 **Metro** DAMAC

Ahasees Spa & Club

04 317 2335
dubai.grand.hyatt.com

Grand Hyatt Dubai, Umm Hurair 2

Although this is a relatively large spa, its atmosphere and attention to detail are spot on. The relaxation area is lit by rows of candles and the wet area (which has a Jacuzzi, plunge pool, steam room and spacious showers) is peppered with rose petals. A broad range of treatments is available, from facials designed to preserve youthfulness, to relaxing massages using aromatic essential oils. **Map** 4 B6 **Metro** Dubai Healthcare City

Akaru Spa

04 230 8565
jumeirah.com

Jumeirah Creekside Hotel, Al Garhoud

The autumnal colours, natural decor, wooden fittings and glass features create a truly tranquil retreat at this luxurious Garhoud favourite. The menu of exotic treatments on offer range from various specialised facials and wraps to microdermabrasion and CACI micro-current treatments to tone, lift and firm the face, eyes and body. **Map** 4 D6 **Metro** GGICO

Spas

Amara Spa Dubai
04 602 1661
Park Hyatt Dubai, Port Saeed   dubai.park.hyatt.com
Nestled in stunning surroundings on the banks of the Dubai Creek, Amara Spa is a luxurious treat. The treatment rooms act as your personal spa and, after being treated to one of the fantastic facials or massages, you'll get to enjoy your own private outdoor shower and relaxation area. **Map** 4 D5 **Metro** GGICO

Armani/Spa
04 888 3888
Armani Hotel Dubai, Burj Khalifa   dubai.armanihotels.com
Armani/Spa is modern, elegant and sleek. There are three categories of treatment classified as stillness (relaxing), freedom (rejuvenating) and fluidity (detoxifying). The menu encompasses massages, facials and body wraps. Pod-like treatment rooms create a feeling of being truly cocooned from the stress of the outside world. **Map** 2 B2 **Metro** Burj Khalifa/Dubai Mall

B/Attitude Spa
04 402 2200
Grosvenor House, Marsa Dubai   battitudespa-dubai.com
Sister venue to Buddha Bar, this stylish spa oozes oriental chic. Dark colours and soothing DJ tunes set the scene and the treatments range from eastern-style massages to Ayurvedic therapies. Swiss Bellefontaine facials are also available. **Map** 3 B1 **Metro** DAMAC

Cleopatra's Spa & Wellness
04 324 7700
Wafi, Umm Hurair 2   cleopatrasspaandwellness.com
Cleopatra's Spa may not have the grand entrance that some hotel spas share, but what it lacks in ostentation it makes up for in other ways. The relaxation area is modelled on ancient Egypt, with

Sports & Spas

Spas

askexplorer.com 167

drapes, silk cushions and majlis-style seats. The spa menu features massages and facials, body wraps and anti-ageing treatments.
Map 4 B5　**Metro** Dubai Healthcare City

De La Mer Day Spa
04 328 2775
Jumeira St, Umm Suqeim 2　　delamerspa.com
This retreat is perfect for a girly get together, with massages, manicures and pedicures on offer. Soak up some sun in the secluded garden, which has a swimming pool and an outdoor Jacuzzi. You can book the VIP suite for special occasions and bring your own food, drink and decorations.　**Map** 1 E2　**Metro** FGB

Dreamworks Spa
04 447 5511
Shoreline Apartments, Nakhlat Jumeira　　dreamworks.ae
If it's a massage you're looking for, then you can't go wrong with a trip to this mid-range chain of spas, which specialise in kneading out your knots. Let go of your daily stresses by treating yourself to some foot reflexology, a Balinese head massage or even an exquisite four hands massage. There are many locations other than Shoreline so check the website. The branches at Marsa Dubai and Business Bay offer couples' massages.　**Map** 3 C1　**Metro** Nakheel

Heavenly Spa By Westin Dubai Mina Seyahi Beach Resort
04 511 7901
Marsa Dubai　　westinminaseyahi.com
Similar to other luxury spas in the immediate area, the service here leaves nothing to be desired. The contemporary decor still manages to feel warm and inviting, helping to clear your mind for the gorgeous treatments that await.　**Map** 3 B1　**Metro** Nakheel

Mandara Spa

04 501 8270

The H Hotel Dubai, Trade Center 1   mandaraspa.com

The epicentre of this elegant spa is a circular, cocoon-like chamber containing a grand Jacuzzi pool, and from here you'll find your way to the communal changing room, sauna, steam room and atmospheric treatment rooms. Many of the body therapies on offer start with a foot washing ritual, and the quality of service is evident.
Map 2 E1   **Metro** World Trade Centre

One&Only Private Spa

04 440 1040

One&Only The Palm   thepalm.oneandonlyresorts.com

The emphasis in this serene spa is on understated decor, with plenty of neutral colours and natural light. The relaxation room is an ideal spot to savour the sensations after your treatment. Its speciality is the 'canyon love stone therapy', an energy-balancing massage using warm and cool stones.   **Map** 3 B1   **Metro** Nakheel

Sports & Spas

Spas

Oriental Hammam

04 315 2130

One&Only Royal Mirage, Al Sufouh 2   oneandonlyresorts.com

This is the ultimate in Arabian luxury. The surroundings are elegant with a warm traditional feel. The hammam and spa is an impressive area with mosaic-covered arches and intricate carvings. The wonderfully invigorating treatment involves being bathed, steamed, and washed with traditional black soap. **Map** 3 B1 **Metro** Nakheel

Raffles Spa

04 314 9870

Raffles, Umm Hurair 2   raffles.com

Prepare to be tempted by every treatment on the menu at Raffles Spa, located in the famous Raffles Hotel. Get a taste of it all by starting with the Dubai Decadence, a full six hours of head-to-toe pampering treatment, including a steam bath, body scrub, hot stone massage, facial, manicure and pedicure. There is also a gym, pool, sauna and steam room. **Map** 4 B5 **Metro** Dubai Healthcare City

The Ritz-Carlton Spa

04 318 6521

The Ritz-Carlton, Marsa Dubai   ritzcarlton.com

The opulence of the Ritz-Carlton quietly asserts itself amidst the brash, trendy spots that dominate Dubai's beachfront and the hotel's spa is in keeping with the resort's general character. With treatments like Ritz's 24 carat gold massage, don't expect bargains here, but sheer delight, yes. **Map** 3 A1 **Metro** DAMAC

Saray Spa

04 319 4630

Dubai Marriott Harbour Hotel & Suites, Marsa Dubai   marriott.com

Taking its name from the caravanserais of the ancient Silk Route, the Saray Spa offers an Arabian-inspired experience. The spa's signature product range features natural and traditionally used elements from around the region including lemon, coffee, mint, frankincense, honey, rose, pomegranate and dates, as well as Dead Sea salts and mud. **Map** 3 B1 **Metro** DAMAC

Satori Spa
Bab Al Shams Desert Resort, Mugatrah

04 809 6232
meydanhotels.com

This spa makes the most of its desert location. The treatment rooms feature a window with a blind – unusual for spas in Dubai, which are usually cosseted away in the heart of a hotel. The sense of being close to the desert wilderness seeps into the gently lit room, and the quiet music empties your mind of everything but the rhythmic strokes of the therapist. Aromatherapy Associates is the oil of choice here.

Spas

SensAsia Urban Spa
04 349 8850
The Village Mall, Jumeira 1
sensasiaspas.com

SensAsia is one of the most popular spas among Dubai expats and it's not hard to see why. The quality of service is excellent, the therapists well-trained and whichever branch you choose to visit, the treatments delivered in a gorgeous Asian-inspired setting. The emphasis is on Balinese and Thai-style treatments, although Elemis and Eve Lom facials are also available. In addition to the Jumeira venue, branches are located in Palm Jumeirah (04 422 7115), Emirates Golf Club (04 417 9820) and Dukkan Al Manzil Souk (04 456 0866). **Map** 1 H2 **Metro** Al Jafiliya

The Spa at The Address
04 438 8025
The Address Dubai Mall, Downtown Dubai
theaddress.com

This luxurious spa features signature rituals and exceptional expertise to create an unforgettable experience. Therapists use a carefully curated range of wellness products from the Arabian inspired brand Shiffa, and global names like Natura Bissé and Aromatherapy Associates. **Map** 2 C3 **Metro** Burj Khalifa/Dubai Mall

The Spa at The Palace
04 428 7805
The Palace Downtown, Downtown Dubai
theaddress.com

This spa truly makes the most of its enviable location with its lakeside spa cabanas. These luxurious treatment beds directly overlook Burj Khalifa lake, providing gorgeous views of the world's tallest building and the Dubai Fountain, while ensuring the utmost privacy despite the glamorous outdoor setting. Attentive therapists ensure that your treatment is personalised to meet your needs.
Map 2 B3 **Metro** Burj Khalifa/Dubai Mall

The Spa at Shangri-La

04 405 2441

Shangri-La, Trade Center 1

shangri-la.com

This spa offers a holistic approach to healing, featuring a tempting menu of traditional Asian treatments. The relaxation facilities are extensive, with a salon, barber, juice bar and boutique. Every treatment begins with a welcome drink and foot bath, with therapists pairing holistic spa rituals with the finest European skin care products. Spa treatments are customised to realise personal health and wellness goals. The minimalist surroundings and the communal areas lean more towards fitness club than spa. **Map** 2 C1 **Metro** Financial Centre

Spa Cordon   04 421 3424

Sky Gardens, Zaa'beel 2

spacordon.com

Located on the concourse level of DIFC's Sky Gardens, Spa Cordon is an oasis of tranquillity in the middle of the bustling financial district. Designed to make guests feel like they are outdoors, this bright and airy spa is decorated with water features. It offers the usual

Nail Bars

Dubai's nail bars are pampering havens where you can enjoy basic treatments and massages in style. You will find at least one in each of the malls, and popular salons like NStyle Nail Lounge (nstyleintl.com) and N.Bar (nbaruae.com) have several locations. Also try The Organic Glow Beauty Lounge (04 380 4666), Sisters Beauty Lounge (sistersbeautylounge.com) or Tips & Toes (tipsandtoes.com).

treatments, plus an oriental bath. If you opt for a massage, you have the option of concocting your own custom massage oil. **Map** 2 D2 **Metro** World Trade Centre

Talise Ottoman Spa
04 453 0456
Jumeirah Zabeel Saray, Nakhlat Jumeira jumeirah.com

With 50 treatment rooms, mineral pools, saunas, ice chambers, couples' suites, gyms and stunning hammams, Talise Ottoman Spa lays claim to being the biggest in the Middle East and one of the largest in the world. Relax with an indulgent massage, or splash out in the authentic Turkish hammam. **Map** 1 C1 **Metro** Nakheel

Talise Spa
04 366 6818
Madinat Jumeirah, Al Sufouh 1 madinatjumeirah.com

This regal spa is made up of luxurious lounges and treatment rooms, connected by garden walkways. The spa boasts 26 treatment rooms, inclusive of two couples' suites. The focus of the treatments is on natural therapies, with each designed to transform the mind, body and soul. The spa also runs Full Moon Yoga sessions on the beach. **Map** 3 E1 **Metro** Mall of the Emirates

Waldorf Astoria Spa
04 818 2244
Waldorf Astoria, Nakhlat Jumeira waldorfastoria3.hilton.com

Impressive, opulent and elegant, this spa includes six treatment rooms, a nail care studio, a Spa boutique, thermal and water flotation lounges, an ice fountain, a herbal steam room and Himalayan salt stone saunas. Treatments are tailored for ladies and gents in separate zones. For couples who really want a special treat, there are also two private VIP Spa suites. **Map** 1 D1 **Metro** Nakheel

Sports & Spas

Spas

ask**explorer**.com

Shopping

Do Buy	178
Where To Go For...	182
Souks & Markets	188
Shopping Malls	196
Department Stores	210

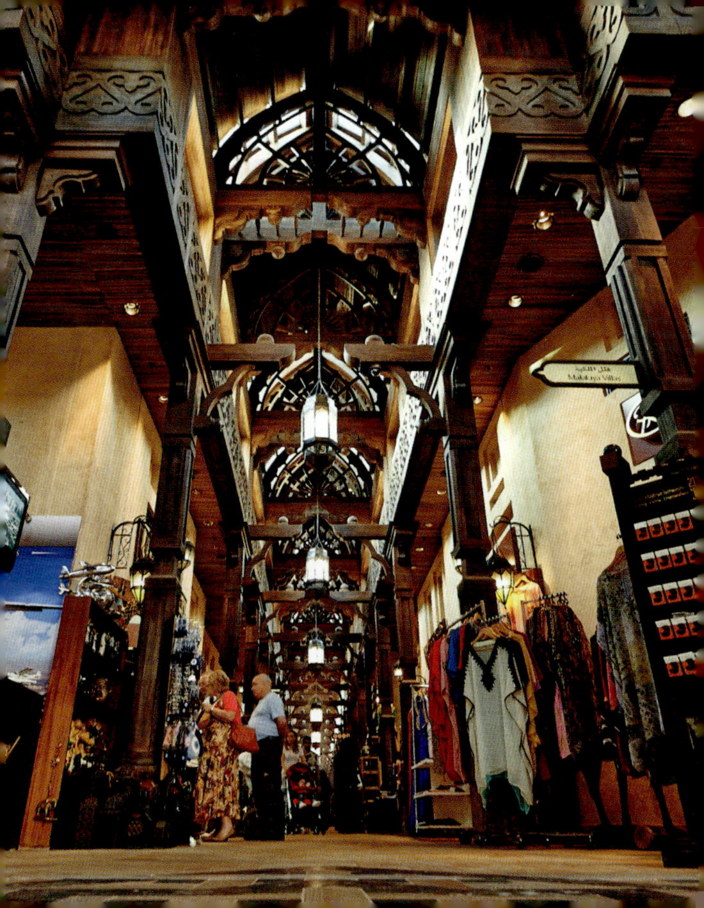

DO BUY

With souks, boutiques and mammoth malls at every turn, you won't have any problems spending your holiday money in Dubai.

Dubai provides many opportunities to indulge in a shopping spree. It is either a shopaholic's dream or nightmare, depending on who's paying the bill. Dubai's malls are gleaming hubs of trade filled with a mix of international high-street brands and designer names. While prices for most items are comparable to elsewhere in the world, there are not many places that can beat Dubai's range and frequency of sales. Most people head to the malls as their first stop, but it is also worth checking out some of Dubai's independent shops for some unique finds and good deals.

In the summer, malls are a good place to escape the soaring heat, and with most shops open until at least 10pm every night, and some until midnight at the weekends, there's plenty of time to browse. It takes a dedicated shopper to tackle the malls when they are at their busiest on a Friday evening.

Not content with the large number of existing malls, developers are building even more. City Walk in Jumeira is a new development with retail and dining options, extending along Al Safa from the funky Boxpark development. The Pointe, located just across the bay from Atlantis on Nakhlat Jumeira, is due to open in 2016 and will house over 100 shops and restaurants. Nakheel Mall, which promises to rival the world's most iconic fashion destinations, is scheduled to open in the second half of 2016.

Alternatively, souks provide a more authentic way to shop. They hold a broad range of items, including souvenirs and traditional gifts, and you are able to bargain with traders to get a good price.

There are several places to buy carpets and gold jewellery, but you'll need to bargain hard to get a good price. Electronics can be cheaper than they are in the UK or the US, and Dubai is the world's leading re-exporter of gold. For most items, there is enough choice to find something to fit any budget, from the streets of Karama with its fake designer goods, to the shops in the malls that sell the real thing. Read on to see the Where To Go For... section for the lowdown on where to find your essential Dubai buys.

Shopping

Sizing

Figuring out your size is fairly straightforward. International sizes are often printed on garment labels or the store will usually have a conversion chart on display. Otherwise, a UK size is always four higher than a US size (so a UK 10 is a US 6). To convert European sizes into US sizes, subtract 32 (so a European 38 is a US 6). To convert European sizes into UK sizes, a 38 is roughly a 10. As for shoes, a woman's UK 6 is a European 39 or US 8.5 and a men's UK 10 is a European 44 or a US 10.5.

Bargaining

Bargaining is still a common practice in the souks and shopping areas of the UAE. You'll need to give it a go to gain the best prices. Before you take the plunge, try to get an idea of prices from a few shops, as there can often be a significant difference. Once you've decided how much you are willing to spend, offer an initial bid that is roughly half that price. Stay laid back and vaguely disinterested. When your initial offer is rejected (and it will be), keep going until you reach an agreement or until you have reached your limit. If the price isn't right, say so and walk out – the vendor will often follow and suggest a compromise price. The more you buy, the better the discount. When the price is agreed, it is considered bad form to back out of the sale.

While common in souks, bargaining isn't usually accepted in malls and independent shops. However, use your discretion, as some shops such as jewellery stores, smaller electronics stores and eyewear optical centres do operate a set discount system and the price shown may be 'before discount'. Ask whether there is a discount on the marked price and you may end up with a bargain.

Shipping

The large number of international and local shipping and courier agencies in Dubai means your shopping needn't be limited by the size of your suitcase. Transporting anything from a coffee pot to a car is feasible, as air and sea freight are both available. Air freight is faster but quite a bit more expensive and not really suitable for large or heavy objects. Sea freight, on the other hand, may take several weeks to arrive but it is cheaper and, as it is possible to rent containers, size and weight are not as much of an issue.

With so many shipping companies to choose from, it is worth getting a few quotes and finding out what will happen when the goods arrive. Some companies offer no services at the destination while others, usually the bigger ones, will clear customs and deliver your goods right to your door. For smaller items, or those that have to be delivered quickly, air freight is typically better, and the items can be tracked. Empost (empostuae.com) offers both local and international courier and air freight services at competitive prices. Aramex (aramex.com), DHL (dhl.ae), FedEx (fedex.com), TNT (tnt.com) and UPS (ups.com) also offer international shipping services from Dubai.

Forget The Food Court
Dubai also has fantastic cafes and restaurants in its malls. At Mall of the Emirates try Almaz by Momo inside Harvey Nichols, or Tribes, a delicious South African joint on the ground floor. Parker's is an exclusive new concept at The Dubai Mall – you must find a key first via social media to enter.

WHERE TO GO FOR...

Art

The art scene in Dubai is enjoying rapid growth and the city is now home to a number of arty hubs suitable for browsing and shopping. There are galleries and exhibitions displaying traditional and contemporary art by Arabic and international artists working in a range of media. Al Qouz is Dubai's burgeoning art district, located in an industrial area of the city. See the Exploring chapter for galleries in this part of the city, and visit artinthecity.com for more.

There is also a concentration of galleries and independent artists at Dubai International Financial Centre (DIFC), in particular at Gate Village, where you'll find international names like Christie's alongside galleries such as The Empty Quarter, founded locally.

D3 (Dubai Design District) is a free zone and community of artists and designers in Zabeel, which hosts events and exhibitions. Al Fahidi Historical Neighbourhood provides the perfect peaceful setting for artists, especially during its SIKKA Art Fair in March, and Souk Madinat Jumeirah also has a few art shops.

Outside these hotspots, places to look up include Art Source (artsource-llc.com) or MacKenzie Art (dubaimurals.com) for a range of original artwork. For fine art photography of the Middle East region, check out Explorer Art (explorerart.com). You can order high-quality portraits, cityscapes and landscapes from Explorer's award-winning photographers in a variety of finishes.

An Arabian Shopping Experience

There are a few places in Dubai where you can sidestep the glitzy mall experience and enjoy more authentic Arabian-style shopping.

The souks around Deira and Bur Dubai have atmosphere, but mainly sell mass produced goods. Al Fahidi Historical Neighbourhood, has narrow walkways, traditional windtowers and courtyards, which provide the perfect setting for artisans to sell their wares.

Souk Madinat Jumeirah's winding walkways are a great place to shop for jewellery, photography and art, while Souk Al Bahar has some quirky boutiques and furniture stores selling traditional items.

Wafi's underground marketplace, Khan Murjan, houses 150 stalls underneath its spectacular stained glass ceiling, selling souvenirs and gifts including jewellery, antiques, Arabic perfume and souvenirs.

Fake Goods

The consumer protection department of the Dubai Department of Economic Development (dubaided.gov.ae) has been cracking down on the sale of counterfeit goods; however, the sale of such items is still very common in Dubai. If it has a logo, then you'll be able to find a 'genuine copy' version of it in Karama. The quality of goods varies, with some items being almost indistinguishable from the originals, and others being hilariously bad imitations. You'll want to inspect items properly to ensure you are buying the genuine article and not a very good fake.

Carpets

Carpets are one of the region's signature items, although they tend to be imported from Iran, Turkey and Pakistan. The price of a piece depends on a number of factors: its origin, the material used, the number of knots and whether or not it is handmade. The most expensive carpets are usually those that have been handmade with silk in Iran. The higher the quality, the neater the back, so turn the carpets over – if the pattern is clearly depicted and the knots are all neat, the carpet is of higher quality than those that are indistinct.

Try to do some research so that you have a basic idea of what you are looking for before you go, just in case you happen to meet an unscrupulous carpet dealer. Fortunately, most vendors are eager to share their knowledge with you, and will happily spread the carpets out to explain the differences between the rugs. If you ask the dealer, you can often also garner some interesting information about the carpets and where they were made – for example, some carpets have family names sewn into the designs.

Don't be shy. Ask to see a selection of various carpets and get a feel for the differences between handmade or machine-made silk, as well as wool or blend carpets. Expect prices to range from a few hundred dirhams to tens of thousands of dirhams, depending on the material and the craftsmanship. It is always worth bargaining to get a better price. The best place in the UAE to buy carpets is the Central Souk in Sharjah, but if you're not planning a trip out of the city, try Fabindia (04 398 9633) on Mankhool St, Bur Dubai, or browse around Pride of Kashmir (04 368 6110) or National Iranian Carpets (04 368 6001) at Souk Madinat Jumeirah. The Red Carpet (04 379 4740) based in the Mall of the Emirates also carries a wide selection, and there's a good collection of places in Deira as well.

Gold

Gold is notably cheaper in the UAE than in Europe, making it a popular souvenir and a main attraction for many visitors. Dubai is the world's leading re-exporter of gold and you'll find a jeweller in even the smallest of malls. It is available in 18, 21, 22 and 24 carats and is sold according to the international gold rate. This means that, for an identical piece, whether you buy it in Mall of the Emirates or in the gold souk, there should be very little difference in price. You should do your research before buying anything though, especially if you decide to get a piece custom made to a design, such as a necklace with your name in Arabic. Of course, don't forget to bargain.

Many of the world's finest jewellery stores have outlets in Dubai. Both Cartier and Tiffany & Co. have numerous branches throughout the city. Simply asking for a discount, even in these upmarket retailers, can sometimes get good results. You'll find a large selection of outlets, most of which are open to some bargaining, in the Gold & Diamond Park (goldanddiamondpark.com) near FGB metro station on Sheikh Zayed Road. This venue offers a slightly cooler, less frenetic shopping experience than the gold souk.

Souvenirs

There is the usual selection of tacky souvenirs available in Dubai, but an equally impressive range of tasteful items may be much more worthy of your money. Hand-carved wooden trinket boxes, sometimes filled with traditional oudh (a kind of incense) are popular, as are beaded wall hangings from the textile souk, khanjars (traditional Arabic daggers), pashminas and keffiyeh headscarves, embroidered slippers, hand-woven carpets and shisha pipes. For the ultimate in Arabian kitsch, you can pick up a gaudy mosque alarm clock that wakes you up with the sound of the call to prayer – it won't win you any style awards though. You can also stock up on plush camels at stores like The Camel Company. Good places to hunt for souvenirs include the lower ground floor of Dubai Mall and At The Top Burj Khalifa where you'll find Explorer's photography books and Rihla brand of Arabian scented candles.

Tailoring

If you happen to be staying in town for longer than a few days, it is a great opportunity to get some garments made. Tailors can be found in most areas, but the area around Dubai Museum in Al Souk Al Kabeer, or Plant Street in Satwa, are good places to start. A proficient tailor will be able to make a garment from scratch (rather than just make alterations), either from a photo or diagram, or by copying an existing item. If they don't get the garment spot on, they will happily make the necessary alterations. Allow one week or more to make sure you don't run out of time for any alterations you may require after the first fitting.

Dream Girl Tailors (04 349 5445) in Satwa has a huge following. It is great for everything from taking up trousers to making custom ballgowns. Skirts here cost about Dhs.60 and dresses from around Dhs.150, depending on the complexity of the pattern. Lobo Tailors (04 352 3760), in Meena Bazaar, is good for shirts and suits, as is Whistle and Flute (04 342 9229) in Satwa. Shirts usually start from Dhs.85 and suits from around Dhs.1,000. One of Dubai's most highly regarded tailors is Kachins (04 352 1386), where you may pay a little extra for a suit or shirt, but the fabric and cut will definitely be worth it.

Shopping

SOUKS & MARKETS

If you want to add a slice of cultural indulgence to your shopping list, head to the souks where you'll find bargains amid the bustle.

There are a number of souks and markets in Dubai. The souks are the traditional trading areas, some more formally demarcated than others. In keeping with tradition, bargaining is expected and cash gives the best leverage. The gold, spice and textile souks line either side of the creek, but parking is limited, so if possible it is better to go to these areas by metro or taxi. To visit all three, head for one side of the creek and take an abra to the other side.

Western-style markets are becoming more popular. They are usually based around food and crafts and are often seasonal. Marina Market is set up along Marina Walk during the cooler months, Market at The Beach (thebeach.ae) at JBR also sells food and crafts. The Farmers' Market On The Terrace at Bay Avenue in Business Bay, and the RIPE Market sell local and organic produce. The RIPE Market (ripeme.com) is held in Zabeel Park on Friday mornings and Al Barsha Pond Park on Saturday evenings during winter, with indoor locations found during the summer. All are great launch pads for local talents.

Global Village (globalvillage.ae) is a huge collection of stalls, food and entertainment from all over the world held on the outskirts of the city. It runs from October to March every day of the week, and is a good spot to pick up everything from Chinese lanterns to honey from Yemen. Organised by country, you can spend hours exploring the wares before enjoying a unique range of dishes in the international food court. Just don't overdo dinner before getting on the fairground rides. See the Exploring chapter for more on Global Village.

Artisans of the Emirates (ARTE)

Artisans of the Emirates was established in 2005 and takes place on select dates only at the Times Square Center, Oasis Centre, the InterContinental in Festival City, and occasionally outside of Dubai. Check arte.ae for dates. It was established to provide a platform for talented locally based artisans to sell and showcase their work. In the time since, ARTE's network has grown to include more than 2,000 artisans from over 60 different countries. You'll find hand-printed cards, personalised artwork, bags, cushions and jewellery created by talented local designers. **Map** 1 E3 **Metro** FGB

Shopping

Electronics Souk

At the heart of Bur Dubai's traditional shopping area, and bordering the textile souk, Al Fahidi Street is home to Dubai's electronics souk. A great place to wander round in the cooler evenings, it's perfect for a bit of local colour and some great shopping. This area is always busy but it really comes to life at night – if you're unsure whether you're in the right place, just head for the neon lights. Take the time to look around at the range and prices available. Although goods are often cheaper here, if you are making a big purchase, it may be worth paying that bit extra at a major retailer, so that you have more security if something goes wrong. **Map** 4 C2 **Metro** Al Ghubaiba

The Farmer's Market On The Terrace

The Farmers' Market On The Terrace sells local produce grown on UAE farms, as well as fresh bread and cakes baked by Baker & Spice and Sweet Connections Gluten Free Baking. Produce is harvested just hours before it is sold and the farmers are on hand to answer any questions. More stalls packed with goodies make up the market which takes place every Friday from 9am to 1pm during winter at Bay Avenue, Business Bay. **Map** 2 B2 **Metro** Business Bay

Friday Market

At the Friday Market near Hamriya Shopping Centre in Hor Al Anz East, Deira, you'll see Emiratis and expats selling a range of local commodities. Along with fresh fruit and vegetables, you'll be able to buy tasty local and Indian delicacies. The prices are cheaper than in the shops. There's also a selection of local souvenirs and handicrafts. **Map** 1 K2 **Metro** Abu Hail

Gold Souk

In addition to being an exotic experience to remember, the souk is a good place to buy customised jewellery for unique souvenirs and gifts at a reasonable price. On the Deira side of the creek, the meandering lanes are lined with shops selling gold, silver, pearls and precious stones. These can be bought as they are, or in a variety of settings so this is definitely a place to try your bargaining skills – let the vendor offer you the best discount to get the ball rolling. Gold is sold by weight according to the daily international price and so will be much the same as in the shops in malls – the price of the workmanship is where you will have more bargaining power. Try not to visit between 1pm and 4pm as many shops will be closed. **Map** 4 C2 **Metro** Al Ras

Karama Complex

Karama is one of the older residential districts in Dubai, and it has a big shopping area that is one of the best places to find a bargain. The best spot is the Karama Complex (also known as Karama Market), a long street running through the middle of the district that is lined by shops on both sides. The area is best known for bargain clothing, sports goods, gifts and souvenirs, and it is notorious for being the hotbed of counterfeit items in Dubai.

As you wander round, you will be offered copy watches and copy bags, and if you show any interest you will be whisked into a back room to view the goods. Two of the most popular shops are Blue Marine and Green Eye, while the imaginatively named Asda is around the corner, and offers high-quality handbags and accessories crammed into two floors. It's pretty claustrophobic but the range is excellent. **Map** 4 B3 **Metro** ADCB

Shopping — Souks & Markets

Khan Murjan

For something a little different, head to Wafi's underground souk. Khan Murjan's magnificent stained glass ceiling (which stretches for 64m) and long curved arches help make this an atmospheric place to shop. The souk features more than 150 stalls selling jewellery, antiques, Arabic perfumes and souvenirs. It is particularly good if you wish to spice up your home with traditional decorative pieces, as there are workshops where artisans can create various bits of arts and crafts on site. In the centre of the souk, you'll find an open air marble courtyard and the Khan Murjan Restaurant (04 327 9795), which serves tasty pan-Arabic culinary treats. **Map** 4 B5 **Metro** Dubai Healthcare City

Marina Market

The promenade behind Dubai Marina Mall is the home for this cute little market, which is packed full of funky clothes, accessories, souvenirs, home decor items and children's products. Having moved along Marina Walk from the far end, the new location means that the mall cafes provide a pit stop, and views across the marina make for a pleasant backdrop. The market runs every Wednesday from 10am to 10pm, and every Thursday to Saturday from 10am until 11pm. There's parking at Dubai Marina Mall.
Map 3 A1 **Metro** Jumeirah Lakes Towers

RIPE Food & Craft Market

Taking place on Fridays in Zabeel Park, RIPE Food & Craft Market is the place to go in Dubai for fresh, organic, locally grown fruit and veg, as well as pantry essentials such as coconut oil, honey and gluten-free products. But you'll find more than groceries at RIPE.

The market hosts over 100 of Dubai's local businesses, fashion designers and artists selling everything from freshly made treats to jewellery and other handicrafts. There is also live music and kids' activities. A second RIPE Market is held at Al Barsha Pond Park on Saturday evenings. **Map** 1 H2 **Metro** Al Jafiliya

Souk Al Bahar

While this isn't a souk in the conventional sense, Souk Al Bahar, in Downtown Dubai, is a modern take on the concept. Similar to the souk at Madinat Jumeirah, the Arabian-style mall features dimly lit corridors, carved wood and a small range of shops. Compared to the retail extravaganza of the adjacent Dubai Mall, Souk Al Bahar is unlikely to set a serious shopper's pulse racing but the wafting scent of toasted nuts creates an intriguing atmosphere, and falcon handlers in the entrance ensure excellent photo opportunities.

It's also a good spot to stock up on souvenirs. Stop by Fortix Art Gallery (04 420 3680) for small gifts to bring home, or try Pride of Kashmir (04 420 3606) to bag an exotic rug. The main reason for turning up at Souk Al Bahar is the centre's vibrant bar and dining scene. Claw (04 432 2300) offers ribs, lobsters, crabs and steaks, while Fuego (04 449 0977) serves up a range of creative Mexican dishes, including guacamole that's made right at your table. Once darkness falls, there are several bars for a post-shop cool down and refuelling opportunity. **Map** 2 B3 **Metro** Burj Khalifa/Dubai Mall

Souk Madinat Jumeirah

Souk Madinat Jumeirah is a recreation of a traditional souk, complete with narrow alleyways, authentic architecture and motorised abras. The blend of outlets is unlike anywhere else in

Shopping

Dubai, with boutique shops, galleries, cafes, restaurants and bars. The layout can be a little confusing, but there are maps throughout and the main features are signposted. If you're really lost, staff will happily direct you. The stalls in the outside areas sell souvenirs, some tasteful and some tacky. For holiday clobber, eye-catching but expensive swimming gear can be found at Vilebrequin (04 368 6531) and Kiwi St Tropez (04 454 1507).

There are more than 20 waterfront cafes, bars and restaurants to choose from, including some of Dubai's hottest night spots like Trader Vic's and Left Bank. There's also the impressive Madinat Theatre (madinattheatre.com) which sees international and regional artists perform everything from ballet to comedy.
Map 3 E1 **Metro** Mall of the Emirates

Spice Souk

Souks & Markets

With its narrow streets and exotic aromas, a wander through the spice souk, next to the gold souk, is a great way to get a feel for the way the city used to be. Most of the stalls sell the same ranges and the vendors are usually happy to advise on the types of spices and their uses. This is a good spot to pick up an exotic souvenir or two – you may even be able to pick up some saffron at a bargain price. The shops operate split shifts, but there is more bustle in the evenings. Friday is not the best day to visit as many of the shops are closed until the evening. **Map** 4 C2 **Metro** Al Ras

Textile Souk

The textile souk in Al Souk Al Kabeer is stocked with every fabric and colour imaginable. Textiles are imported from all over the world, with many of the more elaborate ones coming from South

Spice souk

Dubai **Visitors'** Guide

and East Asia. There are silks and satins in an amazing array of colours and patterns, velvets and intricately embroidered fabrics. Basic cottons can sometimes be harder to find but you can always try Satwa. Prices are negotiable and there are often sales, particularly around the major holidays of Eid and Diwali, and the shopping festivals. It is worth having a look in a few shops before parting with your cash as stock and prices vary considerably. The mornings tend to be a more relaxed time to browse.

Nearby, Meena Bazaar is the area that most taxi drivers head for if you ask for the textile souk. It has an impressive number of fabric stores. Rivoli Textiles (04 335 0075) has a good selection. Be sure to haggle to get the best price. **Map** 4 C2 **Metro** Al Ghubaiba

Shopping

SHOPPING MALLS

More than merely shopping destinations, Dubai's malls are epicentres of activity, with eating, drinking and even skiing on offer.

The Beach
04 317 3999
The Walk at Jumeirah Beach Residence, Marsa Dubai thebeach.ae

The Beach isn't what you typically think of when you hear the world 'mall'. Set along the beachfront opposite JBR, this open air shopping centre is the only place in Dubai where you can go straight from playing in the surf to browsing the boutiques. Perfectly situated for those staying in JBR or Dubai Marina, The Beach consists of over 70 retail, food, drink and entertainment venues, including a 10 screen cinema. Shop around stores such as Victoria's Secret, Adventure HQ and Sephora before taking a break for lunch at one of the many cafes and restaurants. Be sure to save room for dessert though, as the popular Magnolia Bakery has a branch here (try the banana pudding). It's also a great place for a night-time stroll. The restaurants and cafes are open until midnight every day, while the retail outlets are open until 10pm during the week and midnight at the weekends. **Map** 3 A1 **Metro** DAMAC

Boxpark
800 637 227
Al Wasl St, Al Wasl boxpark.ae

This trendy collection of colourful shipping container-style units houses cafes and restaurants, as well as a number of sports fashion and speciality stores. **Map** 1 E2 **Metro** Business Bay

Shopping

Shopping Malls

Shopping Malls | **Shopping**

BurJuman
Shk Khalifa Bin Zayed St, Mankhool

04 352 0222
burjuman.com

One of Dubai's original shopping havens, BurJuman is renowned for its blend of designer and high-street labels attracting many a well-heeled shopper. The mall houses many famous brands including Dior, Escada, Prada and Versace, as well as some interesting smaller shops and legendary New York department store Saks Fifth Avenue. In addition to clothing and fashion, you can stock up on electronics, home decor and sports goods. There are also a few independent music shops that sell a good range of CDs and DVDs, and a branch of Virgin Megastore. The two food courts and numerous cafes are well arranged for people-watching, including the popular Dome Cafe and Paul on the ground floor, where you can dine outside during the cooler months. The mall can be accessed directly from Dubai Metro and there is plenty of underground parking and a taxi rank just outside (this gets pretty congested after 6pm and at weekends). There is also a branch of Carrefour supermarket. **Map** 4 B3 **Metro** BurJuman

City Centre Deira
Ittihad St, Port Saeed

04 295 1010
citycentredeira.com

A stalwart of Dubai's mall scene, this centre attracts the most cosmopolitan crowd. The three floors offer a diverse range of shops where you can find anything from a postcard to an Arabian carpet. There's a 12 screen cinema, a children's entertainment centre, a jewellery court, a bowling alley, a textiles court and an area dedicated to local furniture, gifts and souvenirs. It's all anchored by a huge Carrefour hypermarket, Paris Gallery and Debenhams. In addition, many high-street brands are represented and the mall has two food courts: one on the first floor, next to Magic Planet, serving mainly fast food, and one on the second floor, featuring several good sit-down restaurants. Thanks to the Deira City Centre metro station, it is now easier to get to and from than before – which is great because the taxi queues can get very long, especially during weekends and in the evenings. **Map** 4 D5 **Metro** Deira City Centre

City Centre Mirdif
Shk Mohd Bin Zayed Rd, Mirdif

04 602 3000
citycentremirdif.com

What makes this mall stand out from the rest? Its bright, modern interior, its mix of high-street and designer brands, and a good few stores that don't have a presence elsewhere in Dubai. The mall's highlights include branches of Debenhams, Carrefour and Pottery Barn, as well as Hamleys, CH Carolina Herrera, Sacoor Brothers, Gap and Karen Millen. If you have kids in tow, Playmania is an emporium of fun times with highlights that include an indoor skydiving centre, a climbing wall, a water-themed play centre, 10 pin bowling, an edutainment centre and an arcade. Top it off with a large car park and well-stocked food courts, and this is definitely worth a visit if you're near Mirdif or are staying with friends or relatives based in this part of town. **Map** 1 K5 **Metro** Rashidiya

City Centre Al Shindagha
Al Khaleej St, Shindagha

800 2744
citycentreshindagha.com

Having just opened in January 2016, City Centre Al Shindagha is one of Dubai's newest malls. You won't find the luxury shopping Dubai is known for at this mall, but it does have 75 retail outlets, including brands such as Adidas, Giordano, Jockey and Splash.

There is also a Magic Planet, full of games and rides for the kids, and a VOX Cinema for when you need to take a rest from all the shopping. **Map** 4 C1 **Metro** Al Ghubaiba

City Walk
04 511 4670
Al Safa St, Al Wasl citywalk.ae

This development is airy and al-fresco. Located at the junction of Al Wasl Road and Safa Road, it aims to create a European town centre feel with chic fashion, Georgian-style replica architecture and tree-lined walkways. It is characterised by open spaces, water features, play areas, alfresco cafes and boutiques. Phase 2 has launched with high-end shops and eateries, and once complete will provide more than a kilometre of tree-lined walkways, shopping, hospitality and entertainment. **Map** 1 F2 **Metro** Burj Khalifa/Dubai Mall

Dragon Mart
04 453 4282
Al Awir Rd, Warsan 1 dragonmart.ae

This huge concentration of Chinese traders (shaped like a dragon and over 1km long) is vaguely divided into zones by commodity; from building materials to toys, household items to quad bikes. Everything is available, and cheaper than elsewhere in the city. Dragon Mart 2 has now opened next door, with a hypermarket, cinema, entertainment offerings, restaurants and more. **Map** 1 J6

Dubai Festival City
800 332
Crescent Dr, Al Kheeran festivalcentre.com

Dubai Festival City incorporates the Festival Mall and The Festival Waterfront Centre, all of which is evolving as part of a Dhs.1.5 expansion. More than 100 retail outlets have been added to

Shopping

the existing mall in the last year, with highlights including US favourite Old Navy. John Lewis will also open in the near future. The waterfront strip of restaurants has also expanded. Facilities include a cinema and bowling alley. **Map** 1 J4 **Metro** Emirates

The Dubai Mall > p.203   04 362 7500
Financial Centre St,
Downtown Dubai, Burj Khalifa   thedubaimall.com

The Dubai Mall is one of the world's largest malls with more than 1,200 stores, including 160 eateries. The huge shopping and entertainment complex houses an extensive range of stores, an Olympic size ice skating rink, a catwalk for fashion shows, an enormous aquarium, a 22 screen cinema, an indoor theme park called SEGA Republic, a luxury hotel and a children's edutainment centre called KidZania.

The shopping highlights are manifold, but unique to The Dubai Mall are the regional flagship stores for New York department store Bloomingdale's, French department store Galeries Lafayette and the world-renowned toy shop Hamleys. It also houses UK upmarket food retailer Waitrose on the lower ground floor. You'll find all of the haute couture designer brands along Fashion Avenue and there is a sprawling souk with 66 jewellery outlets. Given its gigantic dimensions, it could be easy to get lost inside this mall. Fortunately, touch-screen maps and knowledgeable staff make it easy to find your way around the shops and other draws.

For a complete contrast, cross the wooden bridge over Burj Lake and you'll find yourself in Souk Al Bahar. The tranquillity of its dimly lit passageways offers a more relaxing shopping experience after the big, bright mall. **Map** 2 C3 **Metro** Burj Khalifa/Dubai Mall

THE DUBAI MALL

THEDUBAIMALL.COM

Dubai Marina Mall

04 436 1020
dubaimarinamall.com

Al Marsa St, Marsa Dubai

Located in Marsa Dubai's thriving community, and within walking distance of the popular beachfront promenade in Jumeirah Beach Residence, this mall's 160 outlets offer a mix of plush designer goods and high-street regulars. Shops like New Look, Reiss, Karen Millen, Ted Baker and Accessorize anchor the mall's offering of reasonably priced fashion. You can also pick up children's items at Mamas and Papas or the Early Learning Centre. The Njoi play area provides plenty of entertainment for kids, and there is a branch of Reel Cinemas. If you get hungry while browsing, there are several restaurants and cafes. The large top-floor food court features many of the usual fast-food suspects. On the ground floor and mezzanine levels, you'll find more varied options, with restaurants such as Carluccio's, Gourmet Burger Kitchen and Yo! Sushi among the popular draws. Many of these restaurants also boast attractive alfresco areas along the water's edge. There's also the seven-storey, licensed Pier 7, which is home to numerous lively restaurants serving up a variety of cuisine types, with waterfront views.

Map 3 A1 **Metro** Jumeirah Lakes Towers

Dubai Outlet Mall

04 423 4666
dubaioutletmall.com

Dubai-Al Ain Rd, Umm Nahad 1

In a city where the emphasis is on excess, it is refreshing to find a mall dedicated to saving money. Dubai's first 'outlet' mall may be quite a way out of town, but bargain hunters will find it's worth the drive. A wide range of luxury brands and designer labels are on offer at discounted prices, in addition to a good selection of bargain sports goods and children's wear. **Map** 1 G7

Shopping

Al Ghurair Centre

Al Riga'a St, Al Muraqqabat

800 24227
alghuraircentre.com

Al Ghurair Centre is a long established mall with international brands, including Bhs, Le Chateau, Mango and Marks & Spencer, as well as smaller boutiques, a Carrefour, cinema and family entertainment centre. **Map** 4 D3 **Metro** Union

Ibn Battuta Mall

Shk Zayed Rd, Jabal Ali

04 362 1900
ibnbattutamall.com

This mall is divided into six zones, each based on a region that explorer Ibn Battuta visited in the 14th century. There are several anchor stores, including Debenhams and a Geant hypermarket. Shops are loosely grouped: China Court is dedicated to entertainment, with several restaurants and a 21 screen cinema, including an IMAX screen. For electronics, there is Sharaf DG, and iStyle for fans of Apple products. iStyle also does repairs in case you dropped your iPad into the hotel pool.

The fashion conscious should head to India Court for the likes of Sacoor Brothers, Topshop, Oasis, and popular independent boutique Ginger & Lace, while Egypt Court hosts Le Chateau, Gap, Giordano and New Yorker. The food courts are at either end of the mall. To reward the kids for trailing around after you, there's a Fun City in Andalusia Court. **Map** 1 B2 **Metro** Ibn Battuta

Mall of the Emirates

Shk Zayed Rd, Al Barsha 1

04 409 9000
malloftheemirates.com

Mall of the Emirates is more than a mall, it's a lifestyle destination. It houses an indoor ski slope (Ski Dubai), the Kempinski hotel, the Sheraton hotel and the Dubai Community Theatre & Arts Centre.

There are more than 500 outlets selling everything from forks to high fashion. The Fashion Dome features a selection of restaurants and fashion outlets including a MORE Cafe, a Boutique 1 store and Sephora. Label devotees will find no shortage of luxury brands, with labels such as Burberry, Dolce & Gabanna, Salvatore Ferragamo, Tod's and Versace all present.

Mall of the Emirates is anchored by a Carrefour, Dubai's largest branch of Debenhams, Harvey Nichols and Centrepoint, which includes Babyshop, Lifestyle, Shoe Mart and Splash.

A new third level also opened in 2015, home to an expanded VOX Cinemas where you can enjoy a film in Gold Class, which means enormous leather armchairs and waiter service throughout, or even enjoy fine dining by Gary Rhodes with your cinema experience at ThEATre by Rhodes. The extension adds more shops and funky eateries to the mall.

The sizeable Magic Planet includes a bowling alley, and a myriad of games and rides. You'll need to keep your energy up to explore this large mall so it's fortunate there is a wide range of dining options, from the Swiss chalet feel of Apres to a large selection of cafes, two food courts and the Sheraton and Kempinski hotels.
Map 3 E2 **Metro** Mall of the Emirates

Mercato Shopping Mall
04 344 4161
Jumeira St, Jumeira 1   mercatoshoppingmall.com

Mercato is the largest mall in Jumeira, with more than 90 shops, restaurants, cafes and a cinema. As you drive along Jumeira St, the renaissance-style architecture really makes Mercato stand out, and, once inside, the huge glass roof provides natural light and enhances the Mediterranean feel. The mall is anchored by a large Spinneys supermarket, a Virgin Megastore and Gap. There are designer boutiques and high-street brands, and shops range from the reasonably priced Pull and Bear to the more exclusive Reiss.

There is a food court and a number of cafes and restaurants, including French cafe Paul and the popular Shake Shack. The cinema and large Fun City play area should keep most of the family occupied. **Map** 1 G2 **Metro** Financial Centre

Wafi
04 324 4555
Shk Rashid Rd, Umm Hurair 2 wafi.com

Wafi's Egyptian theme, designer stores and layout make this one of the more interesting malls to wander around, and it rarely feels busy. The distinctive building has three pyramids, two of which are decorated with stained glass, depicting Egyptian scenes. Among the mall's more interesting boutiques is Ginger & Lace, which stocks a mix of funky fashion styles, as well as Salam department store and Marks & Spencer. There's a children's play area called Kids Connection, glow-in-the-dark crazy golf, and events include the Return of the Pharaohs light show and Movies Under the Stars screenings on the rooftop. Wafi is also home to the exclusive Raffles Dubai hotel. **Map** 4 B5 **Metro** Dubai Healthcare City

The Walk At Jumeirah Beach Residence
04 390 0091
Jumeirah Beach Residence, Marsa Dubai

While this isn't strictly a mall, and the selection is rather limited, The Walk is great for browsing and cafe culture. It is a fully pedestrianised shopping area that stretches 1.7km along the beachfront. Outlets are either on the ground level or on the plaza level of six clusters of

towers called Murjan, Sadaf, Bahar, Rimal, Amwaj and Shams. The plaza level of each cluster can be accessed by stairs or lifts at ground level and in the car park. The largest cluster of shops is concentrated at the Murjan end of the strip. Fashion favourite Boutique 1 is here. The Style Outlet carries discounted designer clothing – to the delight of fashion-conscious bargain hunters. During the cooler months, you will also find pop-up markets along The Walk selling all manner of goods. In the afternoons, people congregate in the many cafes in the area – particularly popular are Le Pain Quotidien and Paul, and there are also plenty of alfresco restaurants to dine in. Parking is available along the beach near Bahar, or in the designated visitors' area of the Murjan car park. Most of the shops are open from 10am to 10pm.
Map 3 A1 **Metro** DAMAC

Shopping

DEPARTMENT STORES

The scope of department stores covers the full shopping spectrum, from the epitome of chic at Saks Fifth Avenue to the affordable Centrepoint.

Bloomingdales
The Dubai Mall, Downtown Dubai

04 350 5333
bloomingdales.com

This famous upscale department store houses merchandise for the home as well as fashion items. There are two locations in The Dubai Mall – one over three levels selling clothing and accessories, and another single-level Bloomingdales home store. Staff can provide personalised assistance, and when the shopping is done you can treat yourself to a cupcake at the Magnolia Bakery. **Map** 2 C3 **Metro** Burj Khalifa/Dubai Mall

Centrepoint
Mall of the Emirates, Al Barsha 1

04 341 1988
centrepointstores.com

Centrepoint is the go-to shop for family and home essentials that won't break the bank. This vast and versatile shopping destination houses Babyshop, Splash, Lifestyle, Shoe Mart and Beautybay, all under one roof. Dress your family, stock up on baby products, or decorate your home, all on one easy shopping trip. All the brands are known for their affordability, making it popular and busy during peak hours at the mall. Additional branches are located around the city, including at Dubai Festival City Mall, City Centre Mirdif, and City Centre Meaisem. **Map** 3 E2 **Metro** Mall of the Emirates

Debenhams
Mall of the Emirates, Al Barsha 1

04 419 0472
debenhams.com

A stalwart of the British high street, Debenhams has five stores in Dubai: City Centre Deira, Ibn Battuta Mall, Mall of the Emirates, City Centre Mirdif and The Dubai Mall. The branches all stock perfumes and cosmetics, clothing and homewares. They carry the popular Designers at Debenhams range with lines from John Rocha, Betty Jackson and Jasper Conran. **Map** 3 E2 **Metro** Mall of the Emirates

Galeries Lafayette
The Dubai Mall, Downtown Dubai

04 339 9933
galerieslafayette-dubai.com

This French department store adds more designer brands to The Dubai Mall's extensive store list, with the vast stock including glamorous frocks and stylish shoes, cosmetics, children's wear, lingerie and a homeware section. Expect prices to match the exclusive surroundings and labels, but the quality is worth the investment. The Lafayette Gourmet food store stocks a range of original and innovative edible treats, and you can even dine in.
Map 2 C3 **Metro** Burj Khalifa/Dubai Mall

Harvey Nichols
Mall of the Emirates, Al Barsha 1

04 409 8888
harveynichols.com

Dubai simply couldn't call itself a luxury destination without its own Harvey Nichols. The largest branch outside the UK, the Harvey Nichols store at the Mall of the Emirates contains a large selection of high-rolling fashion, food, beauty and homeware brands, as well as an intimidating selection of sunglasses. There is even a food market that stocks a small range of gourmet products. Pick up fashion treats from Jimmy Choo, Diane Von Furstenberg, Juicy Couture, Hermes and Sergio Rossi, then head to the top floor for the popular Almaz by Momo (04 409 8877), a restaurant, juice bar and shisha cafe all in one. **Map** 3 E2 **Metro** Mall of the Emirates

Saks Fifth Avenue
BurJuman, Mankhool

04 501 2700
saksfifthavenue.com

Anchoring the extension to BurJuman is the second-largest Saks Fifth Avenue outside the US. The stylish store for the label conscious is spread over two floors of paradise. You'll find designers galore, including Alexander McQueen, Dolce & Gabbana, Dior, Moschino, Marc Jacobs and Roberto Cavalli, in addition to a personalised shopping service. **Map** 4 B3 **Metro** BurJuman

Supermarkets & Hypermarkets

The city's large supermarkets and hypermarkets stock a good range of international products and a comprehensive range of electronics, household goods, luggage and mobile phones. Carrefour (carrefouruae.com) has several locations in the city, and it is the best place to buy French products (particularly good are its crusty bread and selection of French cheeses). Its stores also stock camping gear, clothes, music, DVDs and stationery. Similarly, Geant stocks a massive selection of products, from fresh produce to reasonably priced electronics and media. There is a huge branch located at Ibn Battuta Mall (04 368 5858).

LuLu, the local hypermarket chain, stocks a similar range of products – often across many floors in stand-alone mall complexes.

You won't find quite as many Western imports, but you will discover more exotic fare, and its hot food counters and salad bar are particularly good value.

Upmarket UK store Waitrose has branches in Dubai Marina Mall and The Dubai Mall. It is well known for its premium range of British produce and gourmet goods, and its deli counter is great for picnic items and snacks. You can also buy Waitrose products at Spinneys supermarkets. Choithrams, with locations across the city, is known for stocking British, American and Asian products, including Tesco-branded items. Park n Shop also sells a great range of imported food items.

Shopping

Independent & Noteworthy Shops

Dubai's independent scene has improved greatly in recent years. You'll find the odd store in Souk Al Bahar or The Walk At Jumeirah Beach Residence, but Jumeira St in Jumeira is one of the most popular destinations. In addition to individual stores in converted villas, the local malls here are fruitful grounds to hunt for unique items and hard-to-find brands. City Walk Phase 2 and Boxpark also feature a number of independent shops, most of which you won't find elsewhere in the UAE.

The industrial area of Al Qouz is known as the city's art district, and is also home to cutting-edge designer fashion, with boutiques like The Cartel (thecartel.me) at Alserkal Avenue bringing together international designers.

The Village Mall in Jumeira is a good place to start for fashionable boutiques. It is home to the likes of Ayesha Depala (ayesha-depala.myshopify.com) who has made a name internationally for her fashion forward designs, operating out of her flagship Jumeira store.

West L.A. is an ultra-cool boutique selling women's and menswear by brands from across the world.

S*uce (shopatsauce.com) stocks a range of funky

Gold & Diamonds
The Gold & Diamond Park (goldanddiamondpark.com), near FGB metro station, has many of the same shops as the gold souk, but in a calmer, air-conditioned atmosphere. You can still barter, and there are cafes to wait in while the jeweller makes any alterations. Like at the outlets in the souk, you are able to commission pieces.

accessories, outfits and gifts at its locations at The Village Mall, City Walk and The Dubai Mall, while its S*uce On-Sea branch at The Beach at JBR adds some quirk to your swimming attire.

Fabindia (fabindia.com) now has two branches in Dubai, in Mankhool and City Centre Al Shindagha mall. A riot of bright colours and subtle hues, the clothing ranges for men and women combine Indian and western styles. The hand-crafted fabrics, including soft furnishings, tablecloths and cushion covers, will add decorative flair to your home. Fans of designer labels can head out to Boutique 1 (boutique1.com) on The Walk in JBR. A bigger branch is also located in Mall of the Emirates.

The Antique Museum (fakihcollections.com), in Al Qouz, is full to the brim with everything from souvenirs to furniture, pashminas and Omani silver. The prices are less than in tourist hotspots like Souk Madinat Jumeirah and wandering through its passageways and secret rooms is a treat in itself.

For home decoration that's easier to carry with you, look no further than Explorer Art (explorerart.com), which offers fine art photography of the Middle East region. Breathtaking portraits, cityscapes and landscapes are available in a variety of sizes and finishes to suit your space and luggage.

If you've forgotten your mobile charger at home, Sharaf DG (sharafdg.com) is one of the more popular spots to buy electronics. You'll find branches in several of the malls but its largest store is in Times Square Center.

For something for the kids – or grown-ups with a soft spot for sweet treats – head to Candylicious (candyliciousshop.com). This super-sized sweet shop in The Dubai Mall has enough goodies to keep those with a sweet tooth grinning from ear to ear.

Going Out

Dine, Drink, Dance	218
Entertainment	222
Area Directory	226
Cuisine Finder	238
Restaurants & Cafes	246
Bars, Pubs & Clubs	310

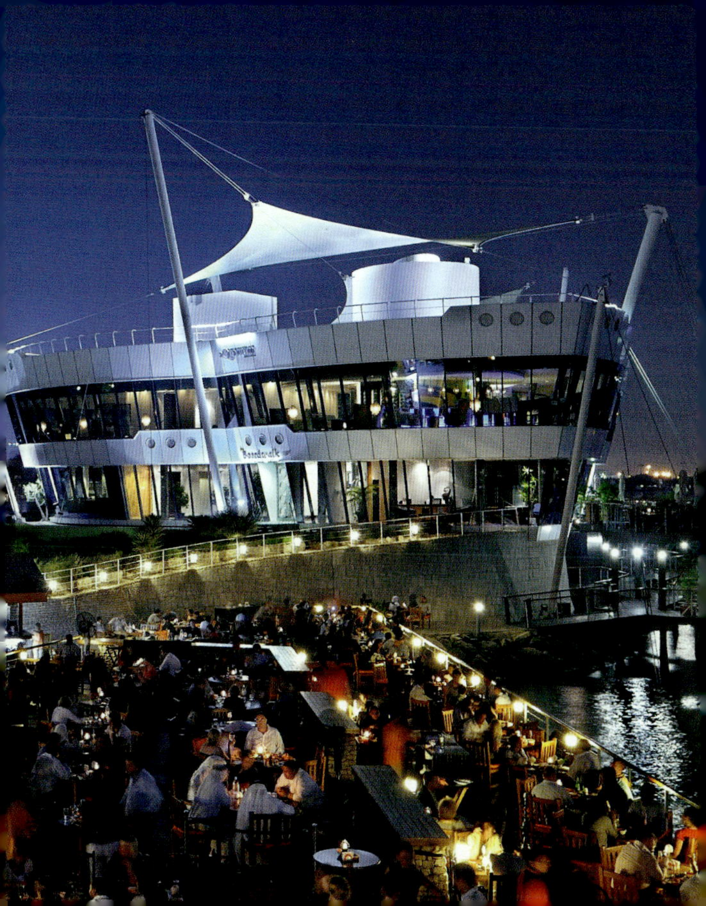
Boardwalk

DINE, DRINK, DANCE

Celebrity chefs, world-class nightlife and eclectic eateries; Dubai's dining and entertainment options are endless.

Dubai's gastronomic landscape is huge and constantly growing. Cosmopolitan culinary treats, picturesque bars and cosy shisha joints combine to form the region's most exciting nightlife. The city's varied population has produced a demand for exceptional food. Fine-dining aficionados will be impressed with the diversity, quality and abundance of first-rate restaurants, while culinary tourists can dine on authentic Arabic kebabs for lunch and fiery Pakistani dishes for dinner.

Thursday and Friday nights are the big ones, with reservations required in the restaurants and international DJs in the clubs. However, during the week you'll find drinks deals across the city and all manner of dining promotions. Dubai doesn't lend itself to pub crawls by foot or evening strolls around restaurant districts. You'll usually need to take a short taxi ride between locations, although there are some hubs, like Souk Madinat Jumeirah and Souk Al Bahar. For a venue to serve alcohol, it must usually be attached to a hotel or a sporting facility. The legal drinking age is 21, and it's best to avoid getting staggeringly drunk as it may land you behind bars. Most importantly, don't even think about getting behind the wheel of a car after drinking – Dubai maintains a strict zero tolerance stance on drink driving. Respect the laws and you'll have nothing to worry about.

Brunch & Other Deals

With so many venues to choose from, Dubai's restaurants and bars face stiff competition in attracting punters. As a result, there are some excellent deals on food and drink almost every day of the week. Buffet deals abound, and some of the city's best restaurants offer time-specific deals that let diners experience exquisite creations at extreme discounts. Tuesday has become the official ladies' night for several of Dubai's drinking institutions.

The king of all Dubai deals is the Friday brunch, a lazy, drawn out, all-you-can-eat-and-drink afternoon. Many of the finest five-star hotels, including Al Qasr, Burj Al Arab, Park Hyatt Dubai and Jumeirah Beach Hotel put on lavish spreads every Friday afternoon and they're almost always packed with revellers. These extravagant affairs often include unlimited champagne and food from all over the world. Of course, such luxury comes at a price – usually upwards of Dhs.350 for the premium options, while the cheap and cheerful versions start at about Dhs.199.

Vegetarian

There are plenty of delicious local delicacies that will thrill herbivores. Rahib salad, a hot combination of aubergine and tomato, is a great option when eating Lebanese food, or you could go with tasty tabouleh, fattoush and falafel, all served with fluffy fresh bread. Middle Eastern food traditions aside, the huge South Asian population means there are plenty of authentic vegetable dishes to be had. Head to Karama or Satwa to try a veg thali, which consists of up to 10 small pots of curries, pickles and sauces into which you can dip chapatti, or mix with rice. You'll find plenty of small restaurants in and around Karama; Saravanaa Bhavan is an exceptionally good choice, and the experience will rarely cost you more than Dhs.12.

Nightclubs

Massive sound systems, international DJs, incredibly diverse interiors and just enough musical variety to keep things interesting – Dubai's club scene has long been the best in the region, and it keeps getting better. House and popular R&B dominate Dubai's dancefloors, but some clubs regularly promote theme nights such as Arabic, Indian and cheesy music (for the worst kind of cheese, and least pretentious vibe, go to Rock Bottom in TECOM or Bur Dubai). Door policies differ from venue to venue. Some of the most exclusive spots, such as Cavalli Club and Cirque Le Soir Dubai (056 115 4507), won't let you in unless you're on the guest list, while others merely require a decent pair of shoes.

Street Food

The shawarma is to Dubai what the hot dog is to New York. The popular snack, consisting of rolled pita bread filled with lamb or chicken carved from a rotating spit, can be found throughout the city, and tiny cafeterias serving the delicacy are around every corner. At about Dhs.5 each, they're the perfect end to a big night out or a tasty pre-club snack. A huge shawarma spit is a good sign that the cafeteria has a high turnover. Streetside cafeterias also serve some of the best and least expensive fresh juices in the city.

Arabian Experience

Al Fanar and Bastakiah Nights are among the handful of restaurants specialising in local Emirati dishes like al machboos or al harees. In addition, there's plenty of opportunity to experience Arabic food from other parts of the region, especially Lebanon and Syria. Tabouleh (chopped parsley with bulgar, tomato and herbs), fattoush (salad seasoned with sumac and topped with toasted pita), arayes (grilled flat bread with spiced meat in the middle) and many kinds of grilled, skewered meat can be found in any Arabic restaurant.

Real foodies can discover the hidden gems and street-food superstars of Dubai's old town with Frying Pan Adventures (fryingpanadventures.com). These guided walks have different themes to educate you about Arabic and Indian street foods, with loads of sampling, so go with an empty stomach. Book well in advance of your trip because they're very popular. It's not cheap, but you'll eat very well and the individuals who run them are extremely informative.

If you're visiting in March, you're in luck, as Dubai Food Festival (visitdubai.com) and Taste of Dubai (tasteofdubaifestival.com) make Dubai's gourmet scene even more exciting with tastings and exclusive events.

Shisha

It's common to see people relaxing in the evening with a shisha pipe. Shisha is a popular method of smoking tobacco with a water-filled pipe. It comes in a variety of flavours, including grape and apple. Some of the best places to try shisha in Dubai are Reem Al Bawadi and QD's at Boardwalk.

ENTERTAINMENT

With a popular film festival, massive concerts and a growing theatre scene, Dubai is a regional entertainment hub.

Cinema

Most of the Hollywood and Bollywood blockbusters make it to Dubai screens. The big cinemas are located in the shopping malls, and tend to be run by one of three operators, Novo Cinemas, Reel Cinemas and VOX Cinemas. Most of the big theatres show 3D movies and there are IMAX theatres at Meydan in Nadd Al Shiba and Ibn Battuta Mall. The Dome Box at the Boxpark in Jumeira has a 360° screen to immerse the viewer, and shows interesting animations.

As with everything in Dubai, you can also find a luxury cinema experience. Gary Rhodes opened a fine-dining restaurant for cinema-goers at VOX in Mall of the Emirates and Reel Cinemas' Platinum suites offer butler service, pillows and blankets.

During the temperate winter evenings, you can watch a movie under the stars at Galleria Mall in Al Wasl, where VOX has opened its OUTDOOR concept on the rooftop. Wafi Mall also holds free rooftop viewings on Sundays from October to the end of May, and on Fridays The Address Montgomerie puts on Dive In Movies where you can relax on inflatable chairs, in the pool or on the deck. Movies & Munchies at Desert Palm and poolside movies at Dubai Polo & Equestrian Club are also worth checking out.

Movie buffs in town during December are in for a treat with Dubai International Film Festival (DIFF) taking place.

Comedy

Comedy nights in Dubai tend to be semi-regular, rather than weekly events. The Laughter Factory (thelaughterfactory.com) organises monthly performances, with comedians from the UK coming over to play various venues. Shows are usually held at Zinc at the Crowne Plaza, the Movenpick Hotel at JBR, and the Grand Millennium at TECOM. Also look out for shows staged by Punchline Comedy Club at Jumeirah Creekside Hotel. Dubai Comedy Festival (dubaicomedyfest.ae) started in 2015, and there are also several one-off events, some of which are organised by Dubomedy (dubomedy.com).

Live Music

Dubai hosts a number of concerts each year, and as the city grows it attracts bigger names. Past acts include Muse, J-Lo, Kylie, Kanye West, Sting, Mariah Carey and Robbie Williams. The bigger names usually play at outdoor venues such as the tennis stadium, Dubai Autodrome, Dubai Festival City, Dubai World Trade Centre, and the amphitheatre at Media City. Smaller gigs with the likes of The Proclaimers, UB40 and Billy Ocean, Bob Geldof, Texas and the Happy Mondays have been held at the Irish Village.

All That Jazz
The Emirates Airline Dubai Jazz Festival (dubaijazzfest.com) is a major highlight of the musical calendar. The event has attracted big names from all around the world – Courtney Pine, John Legend, James Blunt, Sting, James, TOTO and David Gray have all performed previously.

The Music Room in Bur Dubai has live bands and jam sessions, and Barasti at Le Meridien Mina Seyahi Beach Resort & Marina has live bands. As well as gigs and superstar DJs visiting beach clubs and lounge bars across the city, musical entertainment is the focus of the Dubai Music Week, an annual festival of rock, pop, urban, Latin and Arabic music. In addition, RedFestDXB has seen the likes of The Lumineers, Jessie J and Mark Ronson take to the main stage. Dance music extravaganza Sensation sees revellers dress in white and enjoy a huge outdoor party with phenomenal light shows.

Abu Dhabi also draws the crowds to du Arena with a regular line-up of headliners. Particularly around the Formula 1 weekend, it's the place to catch the biggest bands.

Theatre

The theatre scene in Dubai continues to grow and Dubai Opera (dubaiopera.com) is eagerly expected to open in September 2016, with a line-up including Placido Domingo, The Barber of Seville and the ballet Giselle. You can also catch stage shows at Madinat Theatre (madinattheatre.com), which hosts a variety of performances, from serious stage plays to comedies, children's performances and music. Dubai World Trade Centre's large venues have held Cirque du Soleil shows, Michael Jackson THE IMMORTAL World Tour and Swan Lake. Dubai Community Theatre and Arts Centre (ductac.org) is also behind a thriving local theatre scene, from its location at Mall of the Emirates.

On the 42nd floor of the Shangri-La hotel, The Act (theactdubai.com) also puts on a show as a cabaret/nightclub hybrid, complimented by an innovative Peruvian restaurant.

Most tickets can be purchased at ticketmaster.ae.

Going Out

Entertainment

askexplorer.com

AREA DIRECTORY

Al Barsha

Almaz By Momo	Mall of the Emirates	p.247
Brunswick Sports Club	Sheraton Mall of the Emirates	p.256
The Butcher Shop & Grill	Mall of the Emirates	p.257
Emporio Armani Caffe	Mall of the Emirates	p.264
Fauchon	Mall of the Emirates	p.265
MORE Cafe	Mall of the Emirates	p.280
Salero – Tapas & Bodega	Kempinski Mall of the Emirates	p.294
Salmontini Le Resto	Mall of the Emirates	p.295
St Moritz Cafe	Mall of the Emirates	p.302
Tribes	Mall of the Emirates	p.305

Al Corniche

Al Dawaar	Hyatt Regency Dubai	p.263

Al Garhoud

Biggles Pub	Millennium Airport Hotel	p.312
Blue Elephant	Al Bustan Rotana	p.253
The Irish Village	31A St	p.318

Al Hamriya

Antique Bazaar	Four Points by Sheraton Bur Dubai	p.247
Picante	Four Points by Sheraton Bur Dubai	p.289

Al Hudaiba

Magnum	Ramada Jumeirah Hotel	p.321
Al Mallah	2nd December St	p.278
Shabu Shabu	Al Hudaiba Bldg	p.298

Al Jadaf

Enigma	Palazzo Versace Dubai	p.264
La Vita	Palazzo Versace Dubai	p.328

Burj Khalifa

Armani/Amal	Armani Hotel Dubai	p.248
Armani/Hashi	Armani Hotel Dubai	p.249
Armani/Prive	Armani Hotel Dubai	p.310
Armani/Ristorante	Armani Hotel Dubai	p.249
Asado	The Palace Downtown	p.250
At.mosphere	Burj Khalifa	p.250
Baker & Spice	Souk Al Bahar	p.251
BiCE Mare	Souk Al Bahar	p.253
Cabana	The Address Dubai Mall	p.312
Cafe Bateel	The Dubai Mall	p.258
Cafe Habana	Souk Al Bahar	p.258
The Cheesecake Factory	The Dubai Mall	p.260
Claw BBQ	Souk Al Bahar	p.261
Eataly	The Dubai Mall	p.264
Ewaan Lounge	The Palace Downtown	p.265
FAI	The Palace Downtown	p.316
Fortnum & Mason	Nr The Dubai Mall	p.266
Fuego	Souk Al Bahar	p.267
Karat	The Address Dubai Mall	p.273
Karma Kafe	Souk Al Bahar	p.274
Katsuya by Starck	The Dubai Mall	p.274
Maison Bagatelle	Shk Mohd Bin Rashid Blvd	p.277
The Majlis Dubai	The Dubai Mall	p.277
The Meat Co	Souk Al Bahar	p.279
NA3NA3	The Address Dubai Mall	p.282
Nezesaussi Grill	Manzil Downtown Dubai	p.322

Going Out

Area Directory

La Postreria	Souk Al Bahar	p.290
Roseleaf Cafe	Souk Al Bahar	p.294
La Serre Bistro	Vida Downtown Dubai	p.297
Thiptara	The Palace Downtown	p.303

Business Bay

Ananta	The Oberoi Hotel	p.247
Garden	JW Marriott Marquis Hotel	p.268
Iris	The Oberoi Hotel	p.271
Izakaya	JW Marriott Marquis Hotel	p.272
Nine7One	The Oberoi Hotel	p.283
Tong Thai	JW Marriott Marquis Hotel	p.304
Umai	The Oberoi Hotel	p.306

Dubai International Airport

The Dubliner's	Le Meridien Dubai	p.316
Long Yin	Le Meridien Dubai	p.276
Mahec	Le Meridien Dubai	p.277
Warehouse	Le Meridien Dubai	p.307
Yalumba	Le Meridien Dubai	p.308

Emirates Towers

The Ivy	The Boulevard	p.271

Jabal Ali

Sicilia	Movenpick Hotel Ibn Battuta Gate	p.299

Jumeira

Coya	Four Seasons Resort Dubai	p.262
Al Khayma	Dubai Marine Beach Resort & Spa	p.274
The Lime Tree Cafe	Nr Jumeirah Mosque	p.276

Loca	Dubai Marine Beach Resort & Spa	p.320
Malecon	Dubai Marine Beach Resort & Spa	p,278
Reem Al Bawadi	Nr Sunset Mall	p.292
Sho Cho	Dubai Marine Beach Resort & Spa	p.326

Al Karama

Kris With A View	Park Regis Kris Kin Hotel	p.275
Rock Bottom	Regent Palace Hotel	p.324
Saravanaa Bhavan	Abdul Aziz Mirza Bldg	p.295

Al Kheeran

Belgian Beer Cafe	Crowne Plaza Festival City	p.312
Choix	InterContinental Festival City	p.261
Reflets Par Pierre Gagnaire	InterContinental Festival City	p.292
Vista Lounge	InterContinental Festival City	p.328

Madinat Dubai Al Melaheyah

Mannaland Korean	Al Mina St	p.279

Mankhool

The Music Room	Majestic Hotel Tower Dubai	p.321
Paul	BurJuman	p.288

Marsa Dubai

25°55° Cafe Bistro	Dubai Marina Yacht Club	p.246
Aprons & Hammers	Dubai International Marine Club	p.248
Aquara	Dubai Marina Yacht Club	p.248
Asia Asia	Pier 7	p.250
Atelier M	Pier 7	p.250
Barasti	Le Meridien Mina Seyahi	p.311
Benihana	Amwaj Rotana JBR	p.252

Going Out

Area Directory

Going Out

Area Directory

BiCE Ristorante	Hilton Dubai Jumeirah Resort	p.253
Blue Jade	The Ritz-Carlton Dubai Hotel	p.254
Buddha Bar	Grosvenor House Dubai	p.312
Bussola	The Westin Mina Seyahi	p.257
Cargo	Pier 7	p.313
Cavalli Cafe	The Beach	p.260
El Chico	Al Mamsha St	p.261
Embassy Dubai	Grosvenor House Dubai	p.316
Fogueira Restaurant	Ramada Plaza JBR	p.266
Frankie's	Al Fattan Marine Tower	p.266
Fratelli La Bufala	The Beach	p.267
Fume	Pier 7	p.267
Girders	JA Ocean View Hotel	p.317
The Grape Escape	Hilton Dubai The Walk	p.318
Indego by Vineet	Grosvenor House Dubai	p.271
Kosebasi	Rimal 5	p.275
Luciano's	Habtoor Grand Beach Resort & Spa	p.276
Maya Modern Mexican Kitchen & Lounge	Le Royal Meridien Beach Resort & Spa	p.279
The Observatory	Dubai Marriott Harbour	p.284
Operation: Falafel	The Beach	p.285
Ossigeno	Le Royal Meridien Beach Resort & Spa	p.286
Pachanga	Hilton Dubai Jumeirah Resort	p.286
Pots, Pans & Boards	The Beach	p.290
Rhodes In Residence	Grosvenor House Dubai	p.292
Rhodes Twenty10	Le Royal Meridien Beach Resort & Spa	p.293
Sama Lounge	Ramada Plaza JBR	p.325
Sapori di BICE	The Beach	p.295
The Scene	Pier 7	p.326

Going Out / Area Directory

Siddharta Lounge By Buddha Bar	Grosvenor House Dubai	p.326
Societe	Marina Byblos Hotel	p.327
Speakeasy	Ramada Plaza JBR	p.327
Spice Emporium	The Westin Mina Seyahi	p.301
Splendido Restaurant	The Ritz-Carlton Dubai Hotel	p.301
Stereo Arcade	DoubleTree by Hilton Jumeirah Beach	p.327
El Sur	The Westin Mina Seyahi	p.302
Toro Toro	Grosvenor House Dubai	p.304
The Underground Pub	Habtoor Grand Beach Resort & Spa	p.328
Wavebreaker	Hilton Dubai Jumeirah Resort	p.307
XL Beach Club	Habtoor Grand Beach Resort & Spa	p.329
Zero Gravity	Jumeirah Beach Residence	p.329

Mena Jabal Ali

White Orchid	JA Jebel Ali Golf Resort	p.307

Mugatrah

Le Dune Pizzeria	Bab Al Shams Desert Resort	p.263
Al Forsan	Bab Al Shams Desert Resort	p.266
Al Hadheerah Restaurant	Bab Al Shams Desert Resort	p.268
Al Sarab Rooftop Lounge	Bab Al Shams Desert Resort	p.325

Al Muraqqabat

JW's Steakhouse	JW Marriott Hotel Dubai	p.273

Nadd Al Shiba

Farriers	The Meydan Hotel	p.265
Prime Steakhouse	The Meydan Hotel	p.290

askexplorer.com

Going Out

Area Directory

Qube Sports Bar	The Meydan Hotel	p.324
Shiba Restaurant & Bar	The Meydan Hotel	p.299
White Dubai	The Meydan Hotel	p.329

Nakhlat Jumeira

101 Dining Lounge & Bar	One&Only The Palm Dubai	p.246
Beach House Cabana	Shoreline Apartments	p.252
La Brasserie	Atlantis The Palm	p.254
Bread Street Kitchen	Atlantis The Palm	p.254
Bushman's	Anantara The Palm Resort & Spa	p.257
Frevo	Fairmont The Palm Dubai	p.267
Hong Loong	Sofitel Palm Jumeirah	p.270
Imperium	Jumeirah Zabeel Saray	p.271
Kaleidoscope	Atlantis The Palm	p.273
Levantine	Atlantis The Palm	p.276
Mekong	Anantara The Palm Resort & Spa	p.279
Moana	Sofitel Palm Jumeirah	p.280
Nasimi Beach	Atlantis The Palm	p.322
Nobu	Atlantis The Palm	p.283
Ossiano	Atlantis The Palm	p.286
Porterhouse	Sofitel Palm Jumeirah	p.290
Ronda Locatelli	Atlantis The Palm	p.293
Saffron	Atlantis The Palm	p.294
Seafire Steakhouse & Bar	Atlantis The Palm	p.296
Seagrill on 25	Fairmont The Palm Dubai	p.296
Social by Heinz Beck	Waldorf Astoria Palm Jumeirah	p.300
STAY By Yannick Alleno	One&Only The Palm Dubai	p.302
Yuan	Atlantis The Palm	p.308

Oud Metha

| Singapore Deli Restaurant | Nr Lamcy Plaza | p.300 |

Port Saeed

Boardwalk	Dubai Creek Golf & Yacht Club	p.254
Casa de Tapas	Dubai Creek Golf & Yacht Club	p.258
QD's	Dubai Creek Golf & Yacht Club	p.323
The Thai Kitchen	Park Hyatt Dubai	p.303

Al Raffa

Signature By Sanjeev Kapoor	Melia Dubai	p.299
Troyka	Ascot Hotel	p.306
Xiao Wei Yang Hotpot	Rolla Residence	p.308

Al Rigga

Shabestan	Radisson Blu Hotel Deira Creek	p.298

Riggat Al Buteen

Bateaux Dubai	Nr Emirates NBD HQ	p.251
Creekside Restaurant	Sheraton Dubai Creek	p.262
Table 9	Hilton Dubai Creek	p.303
Vivaldi by Alfredo Russo	Sheraton Dubai Creek	p.306

Al Safa

Bundoo Khan Express	Al Rostamani Business Center	p.256
Smiling BKK	Wasl Square	p.300

Al Satwa

Ravi Restaurant	2nd December St	p.292

Al Shindagha

Al Bandar Restaurant	Nr Heritage Village	p.251

Going Out

Area Directory

askexplorer.com

Al Souk Al Kabeer

Arabian Tea House	Al Fahidi St	p.248
Bastakiah Nights	Al Fahidi Hist Neighbourhood	p.251
Puranmal	Meena Bazaar	p.291
XVA Cafe	XVA Art Hotel	p.308

Al Sufouh

Bahri Bar	Mina A'Salam	p.311
Beach Bar & Grill	One&Only Royal Mirage	p.252
Celebrities	One&Only Royal Mirage	p.260
Crab Tavern	Media One Hotel	p.262
THE DEK On 8	Media One Hotel	p.314
Eauzone	One&Only Royal Mirage	p.264
Al Hambra	Al Qasr	p.270
The Jetty Lounge	One&Only Royal Mirage	p.318
Koubba Bar	Al Qasr	p.320
Left Bank	Souk Madinat Jumeirah	p.320
Nina	One&Only Royal Mirage	p.283
Olives	One&Only Royal Mirage	p.284
Pacha Ibiza	Souk Madinat Jumeirah	p.323
Pai Thai	Al Qasr	p.286
Pierchic	Al Qasr	p.289
Q43	Media One Hotel	p.323
The Rooftop Terrace & Sports Lounge	One&Only Royal Mirage	p.324
Shimmers	Mina A'Salam	p.299
Story Rooftop Lounge	Holiday Inn Express Dubai Internet City	p.327
Tortuga	Mina A'Salam	p.305
Trader Vic's	Souk Madinat Jumeirah	p.328
Zheng He's	Mina A'Salam	p.309

Al Thanyah

Cocktail Kitchen	Armada BlueBay Hotel	p.313
Jazz@PizzaExpress	Nr Movenpick Hotel JLT	p.272
Lock Stock & Barrel	Grand Millennium Dubai	p.320
McGettigan's Irish Pub	Bonnington JLT	p.321
Nelson's	Media Rotana	p.322
Nola	Armada BlueBay Hotel	p.284
Urban Bar & Kitchen	Movenpick Hotel JLT	p.328

Trade Center

40 Kong	The H Hotel Dubai	p.310
Alta Badia	Jumeirah Emirates Towers	p.247
Benjarong	Dusit Thani	p.252
Bentoya Kitchen	Al Kawakeb Bldg D	p.253
Catch	Fairmont Dubai	p.260
Cavalli Club	Fairmont Dubai	p.313
Cirque Le Soir	Fairmont Dubai	p.313
Double Decker	Al Murooj Rotana	p.314
The Exchange Grill	Fairmont Dubai	p.265
Fibber Magee's	Saeed Tower 1	p.316
Hakkasan	Emirates Towers	p.270
Harry Ghatto's	The Boulevard at Emirates Towers	p.318
Hoi An	Shangri-La Hotel Dubai	p.270
Movida	Nassima Royal Hotel	p.321
Al Nafoorah	The Boulevard at Emirates Towers	p.282
Nando's	Saeed Tower 2	p.282
Noire	Fairmont Dubai	p.283
Okku	The H Hotel Dubai	p.284
Options by Sanjeev Kapoor	Dubai World Trade Centre	p.285
Oscar's Vine Society	Crowne Plaza Dubai	p.322
Pax	Dusit Thani	p.288

Going Out

Area Directory

askexplorer.com

Going Out

Area Directory

Purobeach Urban Oasis	Conrad Dubai	p.323
Rodeo Drive	The Stables Bar & Restaurant	p.324
Shakespeare and Co.	Al Saqr Business Tower	p.298
Shang Palace	Shangri-La Hotel Dubai	p.298
Tokyo@thetowers	The Boulevard at Emirates Towers	p.304
Zaroob	Jumeirah Tower	p.309
Zinc	Crowne Plaza Dubai	p.329

Umm Hurair 2

Crossroads Cocktail Bar	Raffles Dubai	p.314
Al Dahleez	Al Boom Tourist Village	p.262
iZ	Grand Hyatt Dubai	p.272
Khan Murjan Restaurant	Wafi	p.274
Manhattan Grill	Grand Hyatt Dubai	p.278
Peppercrab	Grand Hyatt Dubai	p.288
Qbara	Nr Raffles Dubai	p.291
Raffles Garden	Raffles Dubai	p.291
Sushi	Grand Hyatt Dubai	p.302
Tomo	Raffles Dubai	p.304
Wafi Gourmet	Wafi	p.306
Wox	Grand Hyatt Dubai	p.307

Umm Suqeim

360° Bar Lounge & Club	Jumeirah Beach Hotel	p.310
Bu Qtair	Nr Burj Al Arab	p.256
Dhow & Anchor	Jumeirah Beach Hotel	p.314
Gold on 27	Burj Al Arab	p.317
Jamie's Italian	Jumeirah Beach Hotel	p.272
Junsui	Burj Al Arab	p.273
Al Mahara	Burj Al Arab	p.277
Al Muntaha	Burj Al Arab	p.282

Sahn Eddar	Burj Al Arab	p.294
SALT	Kite Beach	p.295
Scoopi	Jumeira St	p.296
Skyview Bar	Burj Al Arab	p.326

Warsan
Rare Restaurant	Desert Palm	p.291

Al Wasl
Bubbleology	Boxpark	p.256
Mo's	City Walk	p.280
Slider Station	The Galleria	p.300
Taste of Italy by Heinz Beck	The Galleria	p.303

Zaa'beel
Burger & Lobster	Burj Daman	p.257
Cafe Belge	The Ritz-Carlton DIFC	p.258
Cipriani	Gate Village 10	p.261
Gaucho	Gate Village 5	p.268
The Gramercy	DIFC Gate 3	p.317
Al Grissino	Emirates Financial Tower 1	p.268
Mint Leaf of London	Emirates Financial Tower 1	p.280
La Petite Maison	Gate Village 8	p.288
Roberto's	Gate Village 1	p.293
Zuma	Gate Village 6	p.309

CUISINE FINDER

Restaurants & Cafes

African	Almaz By Momo	p.247
	Tribes	p.305
American	Catch	p.260
	The Cheesecake Factory	p.260
	Claw BBQ	p.261
	Mo's	p.280
	Nola	p.284
	SALT	p.295
	Slider Station	p.300
Australian	Bushman's Restaurant & Bar	p.257
Cafe	Arabian Tea House	p.248
	Baker & Spice	p.251
	Bubbleology	p.256
	Fortnum & Mason	p.266
	Karat	p.273
	The Lime Tree Cafe & Kitchen	p.276
	The Majlis Dubai	p.277
	MORE Cafe	p.280
	Roseleaf Cafe	p.293
	Sahn Eddar	p.294
	Shakespeare and Co.	p.298
	XVA Cafe	p.308
East Asian	Armani/Hashi	p.249
	Benihana	p.252

Going Out

Cuisine Finder

	Bentoya Kitchen	p.253
	Creekside Restaurant	p.262
	Hakkasan	p.270
	Hong Loong	p.270
	Izakaya	p.272
	Junsui	p.273
	Katsuya by Starck	p.274
	Long Yin	p.276
	Mannaland Korean Restaurant	p.279
	Nobu	p.283
	Okku	p.284
	Shabu Shabu	p.298
	Shang Palace	p.298
	Sushi	p.302
	Tokyo@thetowers	p.304
	Tomo	p.304
	Umai	p.306
	Xiao Wei Yang Hotpot	p.308
	Yuan	p.308
	Zheng He's	p.309
	Zuma	p.309
European	25°55° Cafe Bistro	p.246
	Alta Badia	p.247
	Armani/Ristorante	p.249
	Atelier M	p.250
	BiCE Mare	p.253
	BiCE Ristorante	p.253
	Boardwalk	p.254
	La Brasserie	p.254

askexplorer.com

Going Out

Cuisine Finder

European		
	Bread Street Kitchen	p.254
	Bussola	p.257
	Cafe Belge	p.258
	Casa de Tapas	p.258
	Cavalli Cafe	p.260
	Celebrities	p.260
	Choix	p.261
	Cipriani	p.261
	Le Dune Pizzeria	p.263
	Eataly	p.264
	El Sur	p.302
	Emporio Armani Caffe	p.264
	Fauchon	p.265
	Frankie's	p.266
	Fratelli La Bufala	p.267
	Fume	p.267
	Al Grissino Restaurant & Lounge	p.268
	Al Hambra	p.270
	Imperium	p.271
	Jamie's Italian	p.272
	Jazz@Pizza Express	p.272
	Luciano's	p.276
	Maison Bagatelle	p.277
	Al Muntaha	p.282
	Nando's	p.282
	Olives	p.284
	Ossigeno	p.286
	Paul	p.288
	Pax	p.288

	La Petite Maison	p.288
	Picante	p.289
	La Postreria	p.290
	Reflets Par Pierre Gagnaire	p.292
	Rhodes In Residence	p.292
	Roberto's	p.293
	Salero – Tapas & Bodega	p.294
	Sapori di BICE	p.295
	La Serre Bistro	p.297
	Sicilia	p.299
	Social by Heinz Beck	p.300
	Splendido Restaurant	p.301
	STAY By Yannick Alleno	p.302
	Table 9	p.303
	Taste of Italy by Heinz Beck	p.303
	Vivaldi by Alfredo Russo	p.306
	Warehouse	p.307
International	101 Dining Lounge & Bar	p.246
	Al Dawaar	p.263
	Al Forsan	p.266
	At.mosphere	p.250
	Bateaux Dubai	p.251
	Brunswick Sports Club	p.256
	Enigma	p.264
	Farriers	p.265
	Iris	p.271
	The Ivy	p.271
	Kaleidoscope	p.273

Going Out — Cuisine Finder

	Nine7One	p.283
	Noire	p.283
	The Observatory	p.284
	Pots, Pans & Boards	p.290
	St Moritz Cafe	p.302
	Wavebreaker	p.307
	Yalumba	p.308
Middle Eastern	Al Bandar Restaurant	p.251
	Bastakiah Nights	p.251
	Cafe Bateel	p.258
	Al Dahleez	p.262
	Ewaan Lounge	p.265
	Al Hadheerah Restaurant	p.268
	Khan Murjan Restaurant	p.274
	Al Khayma	p.274
	Kosebasi	p.275
	Levantine	p.276
	Al Mallah	p.278
	NA3NA3	p.282
	Al Nafoorah	p.282
	Operation: Falafel	p.285
	Qbara	p.291
	Raffles Garden	p.291
	Reem Al Bawadi	p.292
	Shabestan	p.298
	Wafi Gourmet	p.306
	Zaroob	p.309
Russian	Troyka	p.306
Seafood	Aprons & Hammers	p.248

	Aquara	p.248
	Beach Bar & Grill	p.252
	Bu Qtair	p.256
	Burger & Lobster	p.257
	Crab Tavern	p.262
	Al Mahara	p.277
	Moana	p.280
	Ossiano	p.286
	Pierchic	p.289
	Salmontini Le Resto	p.295
	Seagrill on 25 Restaurant & Lounge	p.296
	Shimmers	p.299
South American	Asado	p.250
	Beach House Cabana	p.252
	Cafe Habana	p.258
	El Chico	p.261
	Coya	p.262
	Fogueira Restaurant	p.266
	Frevo	p.267
	Fuego	p.267
	Garden	p.268
	Malecon	p.278
	Maya Modern Mexican Kitchen	p.279
	Pachanga	p.286
	Toro Toro	p.304
	Tortuga	p.305
South Asian	Ananta	p.247
	Antique Bazaar	p.247
	Armani/Amal	p.248

Going Out

Cuisine Finder

	Bundoo Khan Express	p.256
	Indego by Vineet	p.271
	iZ	p.272
	Karma Kafe Restaurant Lounge	p.274
	Mahec	p.277
	Mint Leaf of London	p.280
	Nina	p.283
	Options by Sanjeev Kapoor	p.285
	Ravi Restaurant	p.292
	Saravanaa Bhavan	p.295
	Signature By Sanjeev Kapoor	p.299
South-East Asian	Asia Asia	p.250
	Benjarong	p.252
	Blue Elephant	p.253
	Blue Jade	p.254
	Eauzone	p.264
	Hoi An	p.270
	Kris With A View	p.275
	Mekong	p.279
	Pai Thai	p.286
	Peppercrab	p.288
	Saffron	p.294
	Shiba Restaurant & Bar	p.299
	Singapore Deli Restaurant	p.300
	Smiling BKK	p.300
	Spice Emporium Flavours of Thailand	p.301
	The Thai Kitchen	p.303
	Thiptara	p.303
	Tong Thai	p.304

Thiptara

Steakhouse	White Orchid	p.307
	Wox	p.307
	The Butcher Shop & Grill	p.257
	The Exchange Grill	p.265
	Gaucho	p.268
	JW's	p.273
	Manhattan Grill	p.278
	The Meat Co	p.279
	Porterhouse	p.290
	Prime	p.290
	Rare Restaurant	p.291
	Rhodes Twenty10	p.293
	Seafire Steakhouse & Bar	p.296
Vegetarian	Puranmal	p.291

Going Out

RESTAURANTS & CAFES

Dubai's culinary landscape includes everything from mountainous buffet spreads to low-key streetside snacks.

There isn't much you can't find in Dubai when it comes to food. Whether it's a quick-fix burger, super fresh fish and chips or sizzling curries, the variety is extraordinary. Dining in one of Dubai's five-star hotel resorts is a must, if only to witness the tremendous variety and quality.

101 Dining Lounge & Bar   International
One&Only The Palm Dubai, Nakhlat Jumeira   04 440 1030

A chic bar and lounge located right by the resort's private marina, 101 Dining Lounge and Bar offers amazing views of Marsa Dubai. The alfresco seating and sophisticated atmosphere make it a great spot for a romantic dinner. **Map** 1 C2 **Metro** DAMAC

25°55° Cafe Bistro   European
Dubai Marina Yacht Club, Marsa Dubai   04 362 7955

Whether you come to enjoy a pie and pint while watching the big match or for a must-have full-English breakfast after a big night out, this bistro/pub/yacht club/restaurant will satisfy your hunger. **Map** 3 A1 **Metro** Jumeirah Lakes Towers

Almaz By Momo
African
Mall of the Emirates, Al Barsha 1 04 409 8877
This Moroccan restaurant tucked away in Harvey Nichols provides a contrast to the retail buzz outside. Take a break from shopping with refreshing mocktails, tasty stews, tender lamb and fluffy couscous, served in generous portions. **Map** 3 E2 **Metro** Mall of the Emirates

Alta Badia
European
Jumeirah Emirates Towers, Trade Center 2 04 319 8771
This Italian restaurant serves up simple Ladin cuisine from the Alta Badia region in the heart of the Dolomites. It is inspired by traditional recipes that emphasise seasonal products and fresh ingredients. Located high on level 50, you can enjoy sweeping views of the city with your meal. **Map** 2 D2 **Metro** Emirates Towers

Ananta
South Asian
The Oberoi Hotel, Business Bay 04 444 1407
Ananta is The Oberoi Hotel's signature Indian restaurant. The dining room features crisp white linens and bright red chairs, and is dominated by the large show kitchen. Watch the chefs create tasty Indian dishes right before your eyes using traditional coal-fired clay ovens. **Map** 2 A2 **Metro** Business Bay

Antique Bazaar
South Asian
Four Points by Sheraton Bur Dubai, Al Hamriya 04 397 7444
Antique Bazaar offers a full range of Indian culinary delights to an ever-present musical accompaniment. When in full swing, the live music show is a memorable cultural experience. Arrive early for conversation, late to party. **Map** 4 C2 **Metro** Al Fahidi

Restaurants & Cafes

Aprons & Hammers
Seafood
Dubai International Marine Club, Marsa Dubai — 04 454 7097
Soak up some incredible views of Marsa Dubai and The Palm on board this traditional dhow. A visit here is a must-do for seafood fans. Armed with a wooden hammer and a giant bib, diners are served huge buckets of delicious crab and other fresh catch, and invited to get cracking. **Map** 3 B1 **Metro** DAMAC

Aquara
Seafood
Dubai Marina Yacht Club, Marsa Dubai — 04 362 7900
Aquara is chic but understated, allowing the views of the marina's skyscrapers and million-dirham yachts to speak for themselves. It specialises in seafood and the Friday brunch is excellent – the centrepiece is the seafood bar with lobster, oysters, prawns, crab, clams, sushi and sashimi. **Map** 3 A1 **Metro** Jumeirah Lakes Towers

Arabian Tea House
Cafe
Al Fahidi St, Al Souk Al Kabeer — 04 353 5071
Previously known as Basta Art Cafe, this courtyard cafe and gallery offers quiet sanctuary amid busy and atmospheric Al Fahidi Historical Neighbourhood. Visitors can sit on majlis-style cushions or under a canopy. **Map** 4 C2 **Metro** Al Fahidi

Armani/Amal
South Asian
Armani Hotel Dubai, Burj Khalifa — 04 888 3888
With its open kitchen and vaulted framework, this award-winning Indian restaurant is a hip with high-end cuisine. Outside, the terrace is a magical spot to watch the Dubai Fountain light show. **Map** 2 B2 **Metro** Burj Khalifa/Dubai Mall

Armani/Hashi
Armani Hotel Dubai, Burj Khalifa
East Asian
04 888 3888

What better way to impress than to dine in the Armani Hotel, inside the world's tallest building, the Burj Khalifa? Inside, the restaurant is beautifully elegant, but the prime seats are outside with the Burj Khalifa's sky-piercing spire above you and the romantic Dubai Fountain in front. **Map** 2 B2 **Metro** Burj Khalifa/Dubai Mall

Armani/Ristorante
Armani Hotel Dubai, Burj Khalifa
European
04 888 3888

If you have a taste for Italian cuisine, Ristorante is your place to experience the glamorous surroundings of Armani Hotel. Select your table in the bright, contemporary interior and choose from a menu of classic Italian dishes. **Map** 2 B2 **Metro** Burj Khalifa/Dubai Mall

Going Out

Asado
South American
The Palace Downtown Dubai, Burj Khalifa   04 888 3444
Asado is a meat lover's dream. Excellent meat and an enormous wine selection, with terrace views of Burj Khalifa thrown in, make this Argentinean restaurant something special. **Map** 2 B3
Metro Burj Khalifa/Dubai Mall

Asia Asia
South-East Asian
Pier 7, Marsa Dubai   04 276 5900
Asia Asia impresses upon arrival with grand statues and low-lit ambience. The sushi and specials that include moromi miso black cod and miso and sake duck breast, are excellent. The cocktail menu is creative – though the squid ink and sesame seed fog is not for the weak stomached. **Map** 3 A1 **Metro** Jumeirah Lakes Towers

At.mosphere
International
Burj Khalifa, Downtown Dubai   04 888 3444
The wow factor at the world's highest restaurant goes beyond the stupendous views. The Grill serves lunch and dinner and is the equal of any of the UAE's top restaurants. The Lounge opens from midday to 2am for drinks and snacks. **Map** 2 B2
Metro Burj Khalifa/Dubai Mall

Atelier M
European
Pier 7, Marsa Dubai   04 450 7766
Atelier M offers fresh French cuisine with a contemporary twist. During the day the restaurant is bright and airy, and becomes an intimate venue in the evening. There is also a rooftop terrace and art-deco lounge. **Map** 3 A1 **Metro** Jumeirah Lakes Towers

Baker & Spice

Cafe — 04 425 2240

Souk Al Bahar, Burj Khalifa

The menu here is based on organic ingredients sourced from local farmers, and changes daily. What is constant, however, is the carefully prepared 'home-cooked' flavour of every dish. If you're lucky, Barista Henji (a visual artist) will 'paint' the Burj Khalifa on the top of your cappuccino. **Map** 2 B3 **Metro** Burj Khalifa/Dubai Mall

Al Bandar Restaurant

Middle Eastern — 04 393 9001

Nr Heritage Village, Al Shindagha

With an idyllic creekside location and good seafood, Al Bandar is the perfect venue to ease visitors into the Arabian dining experience. The restaurant is good value and caters for a dressed down clientele. **Map** 4 C1 **Metro** Al Ghubaiba

Bastakiah Nights

Middle Eastern

Al Fahidi Historical Neighbourhood, Al Souk Al Kabeer 04 353 7772

This is a magical place celebrating local cuisine and culture, and a good spot to soak up the atmosphere. The venue offers a perfect amalgamation of great location and delectable food. Choose from the fixed menus or a la carte offerings. **Map** 4 C2 **Metro** Al Fahidi

Bateaux Dubai

International — 04 814 5553

Nr Emirates NBD HQ, Riggat Al Buteen

Take your date on a boat cruise while you dine and watch Dubai's twinkling city lights glide past. This sleek, glass-topped vessel offers an intimate setting, four-course fine dining from a varied international menu, and five-star views of the city. A bubbly Friday brunch is also available. **Map** 4 D3 **Metro** Union

Beach Bar & Grill
Seafood
The Palace At One&Only Royal Mirage, Al Sufouh 2   04 399 9999

Seafood lovers must take a trip to this opulent, romantic beach bar. There are seafood platters to share, and surf and turf options for people who can't pick just one dish. The chef's recommendation is the cataplana of shellfish. **Map** 3 B1 **Metro** Nakheel

Beach House Cabana
South American
Shoreline Apartments, Nakhlat Jumeira   04 361 8856

Hot and cold tapas, hearty mains, reasonable prices and a good cocktail selection add to the convivial feel at this South American eatery. Once the sun goes down, salsa music entices diners onto the dancefloor. **Map** 1 C2 **Metro** Nakheel

Benihana
East Asian
Amwaj Rotana JBR, Marsa Dubai   04 428 2000

Dining at Benihana is a pleasure and an experience. The restaurant is part of an internationally renowned chain, and the quality is excellent. It's also great value for money. The terrace is lovely, or sit at the teppanyaki grills where the chefs cook your food in front of you. **Map** 3 A1 **Metro** Jumeirah Lakes Towers

Benjarong
South-East Asian
Dusit Thani, Trade Center 2   04 317 4515

If you're searching for Thai cuisine in a luxury setting, you'll think you've struck gold at Benjarong. Although this is a chain, the traditional closed-palm welcome and tempting menu soon make this restaurant stand out from the crowds. Book to avoid disappointment. **Map** 2 C2 **Metro** Financial Centre

Bentoya Kitchen
Al Kawakeb Bldg D, Trade Center 2

East Asian
04 343 0222

Bentoya's popularity with Dubai's Japanese expats vouches for the authenticity of its fresh, good-quality maki, sushi and bento boxes. The compact, double-storey restaurant is well priced and ideal for a casual bite to eat. **Map** 2 C2 **Metro** Financial Centre

BiCE Mare
Souk Al Bahar, Burj Khalifa

European
04 423 0982

Sister to BiCE Ristorante, the 'mare' signifies a seafood-dominated menu of delicious dishes that bring fish lovers back time and time again. Dine inside and be entertained by the sultry jazz hands of the resident pianist or take in the splendid Dubai Fountain show from the terrace. **Map** 2 B3 **Metro** Burj Khalifa/Dubai Mall

BiCE Ristorante
Hilton Dubai Jumeirah Resort, Marsa Dubai

European
04 318 2520

The old European feel of the place is a far cry from the trattoria-style bistro, but Italian is what this restaurant unashamedly is. Pizzas and pastas feature heavily, barely overshadowed by imaginative meat cuts and seafood. Prices are fairly high but it's full all week. **Map** 3 A1 **Metro** Jumeirah Lakes Towers

Blue Elephant
Al Bustan Rotana, Al Garhoud

South-East Asian
04 282 0000

This stalwart of Dubai's Thai restaurant scene has changed little in years. The food is excellent. Blue Elephant sticks to what it knows – pad thai, curries, and dim sum – plus adds more unusual options such as fresh lime sea bass. **Map** 4 D6 **Metro** GGICO

Going Out

Restaurants & Cafes

Blue Jade

South-East Asian
04 318 6150

The Ritz-Carlton Dubai Hotel, Marsa Dubai

Blue Jade transports diners across the Indian Ocean, taking them on a culinary tour of the Far East. The menu, crafted by the Vietnam-born chef Ta Van, is a melting pot of cooking techniques and Asian flavours. **Map** 3 A1 **Metro** DAMAC

Boardwalk

European
04 295 6000

Dubai Creek Golf & Yacht Club, Port Saeed

Boardwalk's water views are unmatched as it stands on wooden stilts overlooking the creek. The menu features an array of generous and well-presented starters and mains including seafood and vegetarian options. **Map** 4 D6 **Metro** GGICO

La Brasserie

European
04 426 2626

Atlantis The Palm, Nakhlat Jumeira

Chef de Cuisine Aaron Gillespie has created a menu featuring the highest quality prime and secondary cuts, along with innovative dishes including saltbush lamb, pumpkin pearl barley risotto, and the decadent D.I.Y Injection. It's a friendly venue to pop into for the daily crepe and coffee offer too. **Map** 1 C1 **Metro** Nakheel

Bread Street Kitchen

European
04 426 2626

Atlantis The Palm, Nakhlat Jumeira

Emulating the warehouse style of the original, Gordon Ramsay's Bread Street Kitchen brings a slice of London to The Palm. The atmosphere is lively and vibrant. A weekly 'Brunch Confidential' also features live London style busker performances every Friday. **Map** 1 C1 **Metro** Nakheel

Going Out

Restaurants & Cafes

Brunswick Sports Club
Sheraton Mall of the Emirates, Al Barsha 1

International
056 404 0685

The first licensed venture by the Dubai restaurateurs behind Tom & Serg, Brunswick Sports Club serves food that harkens back to their Australian roots. The menu is rustic and portions are 'man sized'. The main attractions are the unique burgers and their suggested beer pairings. **Map** 3 E2 **Metro** Mall of the Emirates

Bu Qtair
Nr Burj Al Arab, Umm Suqeim 2

Seafood
055 705 2130

This casual seafood joint has a dedicated following despite its plastic plates and cutlery. The only offerings are the day's catch, and it's all prepared the same way – marinated in a masala sauce and fried. The price depends on the type of fish and the amount you order. In the evenings a line starts to form in anticipation of the 6pm opening as it's first come, first served. **Map** 3 E1 **Metro** FGB

Bubbleology
Boxpark, Al Wasl

Cafe
055 788 6406

This new cafe in Boxpark serves up tasty fruit-flavoured bubble tea. The name doesn't stem from the chewy tapioca balls found at the bottom but to the bubbles that form when the tea is shaken.
Map 1 G2 **Metro** Business Bay

Bundoo Khan Express
Al Rostamani Business Center, Al Safa 2

South Asian
04 388 4866

Bundoo Khan Express may only have five tables in its small, funky restaurant, but the famed Pakistani chain has a fun, fresh vibe. This is no fast food, greasy spoon-style diner – everything from the lassi to the naan is freshly and traditionally made. It's a cut above other 'express' eateries. **Map** 1 F2 **Metro** Noor Bank

Burger & Lobster
Seafood
Burj Daman, Zaa'beel 2 — 04 514 8838
There's no menu because they only serve – you guessed it – burgers and lobster. They keep it simple, relying solely on the superb quality of the ingredients. **Map** 2 D2 **Metro** World Trade Centre

Bushman's Restaurant & Bar
Australian
Anantara The Palm Resort & Spa, Nakhlat Jumeira — 04 567 8312
Should your taste buds crave hearty Australian food, Bushman's serves fresh seafood and prime cuts of meat, including sirloin of kangaroo. Allow the Salt Guru to recommend the perfect salt variety to complement your meal. **Map** 1 D2 **Metro** Nakheel

Bussola
European
The Westin Mina Seyahi, Marsa Dubai — 04 511 7136
Adventurous, delicious Sicilian-influenced pizzas served alfresco on a terrace by the sea – Arabia doesn't get much more Mediterranean than this. Upstairs the open air deck offers a relaxed atmosphere, with more formality downstairs. **Map** 3 B1 **Metro** Nakheel

The Butcher Shop & Grill
Steakhouse
Mall of the Emirates, Al Barsha 1 — 04 347 1167
This restaurant is all about steak, so pick your giant fillet, rump, T-bone, prime rib or rib-eye and tuck in. There's quality as well as quantity. This popular chain also has outlets located at The Walk, JBR and City Centre Mirdif. **Map** 3 E2 **Metro** Mall of the Emirates

Cafe Bateel

Middle Eastern

The Dubai Mall, Burj Khalifa   04 339 9716

A local favourite, Cafe Bateel offers all the charms of the Middle East in one cafe, with warm hospitality, amazing coffee and delicious desserts, such as date pudding with caramelised pecans and rhutab dates. **Map** 2 C3 **Metro** Burj Khalifa/Dubai Mall

Cafe Belge

European

The Ritz-Carlton DIFC, Zaa'beel 2   04 372 2323

Inspired by Belgium's golden era and located in the swanky Ritz-Carlton hotel, Cafe Belge embodies 1920s style and elegance. The menu features an impressive range of seafood and there's a decent selection of Belgian beers. **Map** 2 D2 **Metro** Financial Centre

Cafe Habana

South American

Souk Al Bahar, Burj Khalifa   04 422 2620

Cafe Habana boasts a menu that's small in size but big on flavour with all the South American staples thrown in, from huevos rancheros and nachos to quesadillas and burritos. The flair bar-tending and upbeat Cuban grooves add to the atmosphere.
Map 2 B3 **Metro** Burj Khalifa/Dubai Mall

Casa de Tapas

European

Dubai Creek Golf & Yacht Club, Port Saeed   04 416 1800

Inspired by the rustic Bodega-style venues found in the back streets of Madrid, but with a dash of chic upscale Dubai thrown in to its design, this creekside venue is classic Spanish lounge on the bottom, with rooftop bar Cielo a floor up. **Map** 4 D6
Metro GGICO

Going Out

Catch

American
04 357 1755

Fairmont Dubai, Trade Center 1

This American brand brings the taste of New York City to Dubai. The rugged look and feel of the interior may reflect Catch's industrial roots but its delectable seafood menu and superb service standards are all class. **Map** 2 E1 **Metro** World Trade Centre

Cavalli Cafe

European
04 551 9671

The Beach, Marsa Dubai

A chic venue offering the intimate charm of an Italian cafe blended with the style and design of renowned fashion designer Roberto Cavalli, the Cavalli Cafe offers a great choice for a quick coffee or a full meal. **Map** 3 A1 **Metro** Jumeirah Lakes Towers

Celebrities

European
04 399 9999

The Palace at One&Only Royal Mirage, Al Sufouh 2

Dine under crystal chandeliers at this elegant restaurant, which offers romantic views of softly lit gardens from tables peppered with rose petals and iridescent stones. The well-priced European menu contains dainty but filling dishes such as sea bass and baked rack of lamb. **Map** 3 A1 **Metro** Nakheel

The Cheesecake Factory

American
04 419 0223

The Dubai Mall, Burj Khalifa

Famed for its cheesecake, this American restaurant chain also serves up eye-poppingly large portions of savoury comfort food, from avocado rolls to the indulgent mac and cheese burger. And then there's the cheesecake – more than 40 different types.
Map 2 C3 **Metro** Burj Khalifa/Dubai Mall

El Chico
South American
Al Mamsha St, Marsa Dubai 04 705 9680

One of the most popular dining options on The Walk at JBR, this is proper Mexican overindulgence. The restaurant is unlicensed but its location along the buzzing JBR is great for people-watching.
Map 3 A1 **Metro** Jumeirah Lakes Towers

Choix
European
InterContinental Dubai Festival City, Al Kheeran 04 701 1136

Michelin-star chef Pierre Gagnaire's first standalone patisserie concept has made a name for itself with an extensive selection of beautifully-made French pastries, signature afternoon tea, camel milk entremets and coffees. The chic cafe also offers terrace views of the creek and Burj Khalifa. **Map** 1 J4 **Metro** Creek

Cipriani
European
Gate Village 10, Zaa'beel 2 04 347 0003

Cipriani's menu has deep Venetian roots, but it also includes more modern dishes incorporating Japanese and Italian elements. A lounge adjacent to the restaurant, called Socialista, will open soon.
Map 2 D2 **Metro** Emirates Towers

Claw BBQ
American
Souk Al Bahar, Burj Khalifa 04 432 2300

Claw BBQ guarantees an entertaining evening out. A casual bar-cum-diner vibe makes everyone feel comfortable, and the menu serves a gastronomic playground of American South delights. There's a terrace overlooking the Burj Khalifa and Dubai Fountain.
Map 2 B3 **Metro** Burj Khalifa/Dubai Mall

Coya
South American

Four Seasons Resort Dubai, Jumeira 2   04 316 9600

This Latin American concept is a contemporary take on traditional Peruvian cooking, with dishes served to share, family style. Coya also houses Pisco Lounge, Dubai's first pisco library, which has a seemingly-endless selection of the Peruvian brandy, as well as other exciting cocktails. **Map** 1 G2 **Metro** Business Bay

Crab Tavern
Seafood

Media One Hotel, Al Sufouh 2   04 427 1000

This cosy venue serves up succulent surf and turf whether you're ordering their special West Coast Bucket Boil or bar snacks. The bar has its own house draught beer, as well as an extensive cocktail menu, and some creative takes on milkshakes and root beer floats. **Map** 3 B2 **Metro** Nakheel

Creekside Restaurant
East Asian

Sheraton Dubai Creek, Riggat Al Buteen   04 207 1750

This upmarket Japanese eatery overlooks the creek and serves an extensive selection of Asian cuisine from sushi and miso soup, to stir fries and teriyaki. A teppanyaki grill allows the chefs to showcase their skills. **Map** 4 D3 **Metro** Union

Al Dahleez
Middle Eastern

Al Boom Tourist Village, Umm Hurair 2   04 324 3000

This cavernous shisha cafe with juices and Arabic grills is always packed. Al Dahleez serves some of the best shisha in Dubai, and boasts an extensive menu. Its bizarre, faux-cavern interior is a great place for a dose of Emirati authenticity. **Map** 4 C5 **Metro** Al Jadaf

Al Dawaar — International
Hyatt Regency Dubai, Al Corniche — 04 317 2222
Al Dawaar is a sophisticated buffet haunt. The slowly revolving restaurant offers interesting views. **Map** 4 D1 **Metro** Palm Deira

Le Dune Pizzeria — European
Bab Al Shams Desert Resort & Spa, Mugatrah — 04 809 6194
A cosy Italian with warm lighting and chunky wooden furniture, crossed with an Arabic-style grotto, Le Dune serves pizzas and pasta.

Going Out

Eataly
The Dubai Mall, Burj Khalifa

European
04 330 8899

On the lower ground floor of The Dubai Mall, Eataly is a great place for breakfast, lunch or Nutella, with a counter selling a range of purveyors for the popular chocolate-hazelnut spread. **Map** 2 C3 **Metro** Burj Khalifa/Dubai Mall

Eauzone
One&Only Royal Mirage, Al Sufouh 2

South-East Asian
04 399 9999

This beachside restaurant has a casual ambience by day and a more stylish feel after sunset. The Thai and Japanese fusion dishes are best accompanied by an unusual sorbet, such as chilli and raspberry, or some sake. **Map** 3 B1 **Metro** Nakheel

Emporio Armani Caffe
Mall of the Emirates, Al Barsha 1

European
04 341 0591

The decor is modern and chic and oozes fashionable sophistication, with black ceramic floors and low lighting that provides a feeling of intimacy and privacy. Try the famous Armani Dolci dessert and chocolate corner, or for a lighter offering there's a range of salads fit for a supermodel. **Map** 3 E2 **Metro** Mall of the Emirates

Enigma
Palazzo Versace Dubai, Al Jadaf

International
04 556 8888

Enigma – The Untold Story is the tagline, and a mystery indeed awaits. Not only will the restaurant change its menus four times a year, but the chef will also change four times a year. You'll have to wait to find out more until you're inside the restaurant as all menus are kept confidential until then. **Map** 1 J3 **Metro** Al Jadaf

Ewaan Lounge
Middle Eastern

The Palace Downtown Dubai, Burj Khalifa 04 888 3444

Surrounding the palm-lined pool in the Arabian-themed Palace Hotel, the private cabanas at this shisha joint sit directly beneath the towering Burj Khalifa. Customers can stretch out on Arabic seating while a musician plays the oud and attentive staff serve up shisha and tasty mezze. **Map** 2 B3 **Metro** Burj Khalifa/Dubai Mall

The Exchange Grill
Steakhouse

Fairmont Dubai, Trade Center 1 04 311 8316

This is a casual New York-style steakhouse. The menu specialises mainly in American beef such as Premium Gold Angus beef as well as County Hill Wagyu beef. There are also seafood options.
Map 2 E1 **Metro** World Trade Centre

Farriers
International

The Meydan Hotel, Nadd Al Shiba 1 04 381 3111

The Meydan's stylish restaurant Farriers has a bright, airy interior and a track-side terrace. The all-day dining buffet restaurant with live cooking stations is great for a casual meal. Its lively Friday brunch has free-flowing bubbly, live jazz and a kids' club. **Map** 1 G4

Fauchon
European

Mall of the Emirates, Al Barsha 1 04 399 0289

If you're hankering for a decent macaron to boost sugar levels while you shop, this is the spot. The gourmet chain is famed for its breads, viennoiseries, delicious preserves, quiches, classic teas, cheese, pastries, chocolates and confectioneries. **Map** 3 E2 **Metro** Mall of the Emirates

Fogueira Restaurant
South American
Ramada Plaza JBR, Marsa Dubai 04 439 8888

Located on the 35th level with stunning views of Dubai Marina and Palm Jumeirah, this Brazilian churrascaria offers authentic all-you-can-eat Brazilian barbecue. **Map** 3 A1 **Metro** Jumeirah Lakes Towers

Al Forsan
International
Bab Al Shams Desert Resort & Spa, Mugatrah 04 809 6194

An all-day dining restaurant with buffets for breakfast, lunch and dinner, Al Forsan has a separate bar and billiards area in addition to an outdoor terrace adjacent to one of the pool lawns and overlooking the desert dunes.

Fortnum & Mason
Cafe
Nr The Dubai Mall, Burj Khalifa 04 388 2627

Recreating the well known tea salon in London, Fortnum & Mason serves afternoon tea, or high tea served later in the day with hot dishes rather than sandwiches. Whatever time you visit, tea is a serious business so relax and take your time over this thoroughly British treat. **Map** 2 C3 **Metro** Burj Khalifa/Dubai Mall

Frankie's
European
Al Fattan Marine Tower, Marsa Dubai 04 399 4311

Grab a vodka Martini and pizza in the bar at this stylish joint, co-owned by Frankie Dettori and Marco Pierre White, or head into the main restaurant for classic Italian dishes and favourites such as duck ravioli. With its sultry interior, pianist and good quality Friday brunch, this is a classy, welcoming establishment. **Map** 3 A1 **Metro** Jumeirah Lakes Towers

Fratelli La Bufala
The Beach, Marsa Dubai

European
04 430 3497

The authentic ingredients and cuisine are straight from Italy, with buffalo mozzarella and buffalo meat at the core of its food offering. Service is quick and apparently their popular wood oven-baked pizzas are ready in 90 seconds! Fans love the fresh air and unobstructed beach views. **Map** 3 A1 **Metro** Jumeirah Lakes Towers

Frevo
Fairmont The Palm Dubai, Nakhlat Jumeira

South American
04 457 3457

This lively Brazilian steakhouse offers the authentic churrascaria experience where waiters bring skewers of succulent cuts of meat to your table. There's live music every night to put you in the carnival mood. **Map** 1 C2 **Metro** Nakheel

Fuego
Souk Al Bahar, Burj Khalifa

South American
04 449 0977

This modern eatery features a range of creative Mexican dishes served in a contemporary setting. One highlight is the lamb shank barbecoa, cooked and served in a banana leaf with prickly pear stems. **Map** 2 B3 **Metro** Burj Khalifa/Dubai Mall

Fume
Pier 7, Marsa Dubai

European
04 421 5669

The funky industrial interiors and vintage-style decor of Fume complement a menu of home-style food designed to reflect the city's multicultural population. The kitchen uses traditional cooking methods of hot and cold smoking, curing and slow cooking to prepare the dishes. **Map** 3 A1 **Metro** Jumeirah Lakes Towers

Garden
South American
JW Marriott Marquis Hotel, Business Bay   04 414 0000
Peruvian chef Edgar Hurtado is at the helm of a team dishing up ceviches, tiraditos, causas and quinotta. Creatively mixed drinks add to a fun culinary adventure set in a green and vibrantly decorated space. **Map** 2 A2 **Metro** Business Bay

Gaucho
Steakhouse
Gate Village 5, Zaa'beel 2   04 422 7898
This Argentinian-inspired steakhouse caters for carnivores with a soft spot for trendy settings and Latin culinary touches. The ultra-modern decor comes complete with rustic cowhide upholstery.
Map 2 D2 **Metro** Emirates Towers

Al Grissino Restaurant & Lounge
European
Emirates Financial Tower 1, Zaa'beel 2   04 352 4000
If you're looking to make dinner a more formal affair, Al Grissino offers a true taste of Italy in an elegant setting. There is also a unique glass dome bar – a cool place to have a cocktail and enjoy the sweeping views of DIFC. **Map** 2 D2 **Metro** Financial Centre

Al Hadheerah Restaurant
Middle Eastern
Bab Al Shams Desert Resort & Spa, Mugatrah   04 809 6194
Modelled on an ancient fort, Al Hadheerah restaurant features an array of stalls and tents with colourful displays of fruits and aromatic spice displays. The cuisine is served buffet style, with live cooking stations under the starry desert sky and features local dishes, prepared using traditional methods. Evening entertainment includes singing, dancing and animals.

Going Out

Restaurants & Cafes

Hakkasan
Emirates Towers, Trade Center 2

East Asian
04 384 8484

Renowned Hakkasan favourites are on the menu such as crispy duck salad and stewed Wagyu beef. Mains such as the Pipa duck and sweet and sour pomegranate chicken are best for sharing. It's expensive, but it's as good as dining gets in Dubai. **Map** 2 D2 **Metro** Emirates Towers

Al Hambra
Al Qasr, Al Sufouh 1

European
04 366 5866

A mariachi duo sets the mood at this excellent Spanish venue. The seafood paella is a must, but there are also delicious tapas and tasty vegetarian options. **Map** 3 E1 **Metro** Sharaf DG

Hoi An
Shangri-La Hotel Dubai, Trade Center 1

South-East Asian
04 405 2703

This colonial Vietnamese tea house in the Shangri-La Hotel on Sheikh Zayed Road offers an unforgettable dining experience. Explore a menu full of exotic dishes that are expertly described by enthusiastic, well-informed staff. **Map** 2 C1 **Metro** Financial Centre

Hong Loong
Sofitel Palm Jumeirah Resort & Spa, Nakhlat Jumeira

East Asian
04 455 6677

Offering a delectable dining experience in a beautiful setting that transports you immediately to China, specialities include traditional clay pot dishes. There's also delicious dim sum, seafood and meat dishes, along with veggie options and thought-provoking desserts. Staff are knowledgeable about the customs behind each dish. There's even a resident tea sommelier. **Map** 3 A1 **Metro** Nakheel

Imperium
European
04 453 0444

Jumeirah Zabeel Saray, Nakhlat Jumeira

Imperium has an impressive location in the opulent Jumeirah Zabeel Saray – expect chandeliers and gilded columns. It serves French-inspired dishes and a delicious selection of seafood.
Map 1 C1 **Metro** DAMAC

Indego by Vineet
South Asian
04 317 6000

Grosvenor House Dubai, Marsa Dubai

Touting the name of this Michelin-starred Indian chef, Indego's menu offers a range of dishes that expertly combine both traditional and contemporary ingredients to create a unique fine-dining experience. **Map** 3 B1 **Metro** DAMAC

Iris
International
04 444 1444

The Oberoi Hotel, Business Bay

Iris at The Oberoi is chic, mellow and welcoming. The open-air lounge boasts great views of the city's skyline while you enjoy inspired drinks and an exciting international menu. **Map** 2 A2 **Metro** Business Bay

The Ivy
International
04 319 8767

The Boulevard, Emirates Towers, Trade Center 2

If you've visited The Ivy's London sibling, you'll know exactly what to expect: ultra-fashionable interiors, impeccable service and, of course, great food. The restaurant serves predominantly British cuisine (think a high-end twist on traditional favourites like liver and crispy bacon and confit pork belly) but also international dishes. **Map** 2 D2 **Metro** Emirates Towers

iZ
Grand Hyatt Dubai, Umm Hurair 2
South Asian
04 317 2222

iZ's dark, contemporary interior is a beautifully designed space, complete with hardwood screens, sculptures and private rooms. The traditional tandoor dishes are presented tapas style – ideal for sampling several flavours. **Map** 4 B6 **Metro** Dubai Healthcare City

Izakaya
JW Marriott Marquis Hotel, Business Bay
East Asian
04 414 3000

Quirky Izakaya offers an upbeat and lively experience for all the family at this fun take on Japanese dining. Keep your eyes open for Wasabi Girl preparing fresh sushi and Saki Man who takes pride in turning socialising into 'sushilising'. **Map** 2 A2 **Metro** Business Bay

Jamie's Italian
Jumeirah Beach Hotel, Umm Suqeim 3
European
04 380 8890

Unlike many celebrity chefs before him, Jamie Oliver has opted not to chase the big bucks, but has instead gone for the mid-range and family markets. The restaurant is both chic and homely. The menu features some outstanding antipasti and a great selection of tasty traditional and innovative pasta dishes. **Map** 3 E1 **Metro** FGB

Jazz@PizzaExpress
Nr Movenpick Hotel JLT, Al Thanyah 5
European
04 441 6342

A pizza chain, but it is one with dignity, that also taps into the community music scene. The contemporary setting next to JLT's lake retains a cosy atmosphere, especially on Tuesday's open mic nights. Friday brunch combines a low key vibe with sultry jazz.
Map 3 A2 **Metro** Jumeirah Lakes Towers

Junsui
East Asian

Burj Al Arab, Umm Suqeim 3 04 301 7600

Another excuse to find ourselves at the iconic Burj Al Arab is this clean and contemporary pan-Asian buffet-style restaurant. They do everything from a classy Korean barbecue and the freshest sushi and sashimi, to dim sum and nasi goreng, and even a sensational Asian twist on high tea. **Map** 3 E1 **Metro** Mall of the Emirates

JW's Steakhouse
Steakhouse

JW Marriott Hotel Dubai, Al Muraqqabat 04 607 7977

At JW's Steakhouse you are greeted by the sight of chefs slicing huge chunks of meat in the open kitchen. Once you are shown to your stately leather armchair, a huge menu offers an impressive range of steak and seafood. **Map** 4 E4 **Metro** Abu Baker Al Siddique

Kaleidoscope
International

Atlantis The Palm, Nakhlat Jumeira 04 426 2626

This restaurant is popular for its action-packed buffet atmosphere, with live cooking stations and alternating themed nights serving Arabic, Indian, Mediterranean and other various international culinary specialities. **Map** 1 C1 **Metro** Nakheel

Karat
Cafe

The Address Dubai Mall, Burj Khalifa 04 888 3444

This is afternoon tea with serious style. Settle on a high-backed leather seat and choose from 26 teas before the four-course feast arrives. Devonshire cream scones are followed by finger sandwiches, miniature cakes, pastries and Arabic sweets.
Map 2 C2 **Metro** Burj Khalifa/Dubai Mall

Going Out

Restaurants & Cafes

Karma Kafe Restaurant Lounge

South Asian

Souk Al Bahar, Burj Khalifa 04 423 0909

Created by the masterminds behind Buddha Bar as an offshoot to the iconic nightlife powerhouse, Karma Kafe does well as the little, and affordable, sister with similarly lavish decor. Grab seats on the terrace for the best view. **Map** 2 B3 **Metro** Burj Khalifa/Dubai Mall

Katsuya by Starck

East Asian

The Dubai Mall, Burj Khalifa

A powerful collaboration between master sushi chef Katsuya Ueshi and French designer and architect Philippe Starck serving up Japanese classics at The Dubai Mall, the restaurant offers sleek surroundings for a mall eatery and an outside terrace with views of the Dubai Fountain. **Map** 2 C3 **Metro** Burj Khalifa/Dubai Mall

Khan Murjan Restaurant

Middle Eastern

Wafi, Umm Hurair 2 04 327 9795

Delicious hummus, hot breads straight out of the oven, and salads sprinkled with fresh pomegranate seeds delicately complement succulent meat grills and Middle Eastern specialities. **Map** 4 B5 **Metro** Dubai Healthcare City

Al Khayma

Middle Eastern

Dubai Marine Beach Resort & Spa, Jumeira 1 04 346 1111

The atmosphere at this popular Lebanese haunt is lively, and the tempting sofas are perfect for whiling away the hours over tasty Levantine bites. Try the veggie platter with dips before tucking into piping-hot barbecue grub and shish kebabs. Wash it all down with fresh juices or Lebanese wine. **Map** 1 H2 **Metro** Al Jafiliya

Kosebasi

Middle Eastern

Rimal 5, Marsa Dubai   04 439 3788

Kosebasi's friendly staff take you on a culinary tour of Anatolia right in the heart of JBR Walk. The Turkish mezze, breads and kebabs all have a hint of familiarity, but are surprisingly different to standard Arabic fare. **Map** 3 B1 **Metro** Jumeirah Lakes Towers

Kris With A View

South-East Asian

Park Regis Kris Kin Hotel, Al Karama   04 377 1111

Dining on the top floor of the Park Regis Hotel gives you a unique vantage point over the city. Enjoy dishes from across Asia, each prepared by a regional expert chef. Order dessert to be served at the adjacent wine bar, so you can enjoy live music and a great selection of wine. **Map** 4 B3 **Metro** BurJuman

Going Out

Levantine
Middle Eastern

Atlantis The Palm, Nakhlat Jumeira 04 426 2626

The splendour of Palm Jumeirah is captured in all its glory at Levantine, a Lebanese restaurant that boasts dazzling views of the water and surrounding landscape. Peruse the menu for fresh seafood, grilled meats and classic mezze. **Map** 1 C1 **Metro** Nakheel

The Lime Tree Cafe & Kitchen
Cafe

Nr Jumeirah Grand Mosque, Jumeira 1 04 349 8498

The Lime Tree Cafe & Kitchen is a great spot for breakfast or a casual lunch. The menu features plenty of roast vegetables, delicious salads and quiches. Don't leave without sharing an enormous slice of carrot cake, widely thought to be the best in Dubai. There are alfresco dining settings here, and at the Al Qouz and Sheikh Zayed Road branches. **Map** 1 H2 **Metro** World Trade Centre

Long Yin
East Asian

Le Meridien Dubai, Dubai International Airport 04 217 0000

Considered to be one of Dubai's best-loved Chinese restaurants, you'll be satisfied by the Cantonese and Szechuan fare at Long Yin. Explore a vast range of steamed and fried dim sum – or choose live seafood from the tank. **Map** 4 E6 **Metro** Airport Terminal 1

Luciano's
European

Habtoor Grand Beach Resort & Spa, Marsa Dubai 04 408 4202

Traditional and good-quality dishes from across Italy are served at this reasonably priced poolside restaurant. When the temperature permits, ask for a table outside underneath the fairy light-bedecked palm trees. **Map** 3 B1 **Metro** DAMAC

Al Mahara
Seafood

Burj Al Arab, Umm Suqeim 3 04 301 7600

Al Mahara is more than just a restaurant – it's an experience. Your visit starts with a simulated submarine ride 'under the sea', arriving at an elegant restaurant curled around a huge aquarium. The fine-dining menu is predominantly seafood – with gourmet delights such as Alaskan king crab and foie gras ravioli or poached Tsarskaya oysters – with prices to match. Gentlemen are required to wear a jacket. **Map** 3 E1 **Metro** Mall of the Emirates

Mahec
South Asian

Le Meridien Dubai, Dubai International Airport 04 217 0000

Get ready for a cross-country excursion through the valleys of Indian food, from street style chaat from the urban centres to tangy prawn curry from the beaches of Goa. **Map** 4 E6 **Metro** Airport Terminal 1

Maison Bagatelle
European

Shk Mohd Bin Rashid Blvd, Burj Khalifa 04 420 3442

Next to Souk Al Bahar, this fresh, vibrant and sophisticated cafe with reasonable prices and a Parisian vibe serves an array of breakfasts, salads, crepes and evening meals of an exceptional standard. **Map** 2 B3 **Metro** Burj Khalifa/Dubai Mall

The Majlis Dubai
Cafe

The Dubai Mall, Burj Khalifa

Something for foodie bucket lists on a trip to the Emirates: trying camel milk, which was part of a healthy staple diet among the Bedouin. On a shopping jaunt to The Dubai Mall, take a quirky coffee break at this sophisticated camel milk cafe. Not just for

Going Out

Restaurants & Cafes

discerning coffee drinkers, the menu offers everything from 'Camelattes' and camel milk chocolates, to local cold juices like karkadeh and an array of delicious European and modern Middle Eastern finger foods. **Map** 2 C3 **Metro** Burj Khalifa/Dubai Mall

Malecon   South American
Dubai Marine Beach Resort & Spa, Jumeira 1   04 346 1111

Graffiti-covered turquoise walls and low lighting create a sultry Cuban atmosphere that builds up during the evening, helped along by live music and salsa dancers. It's a great place to start or end the night with Cuban food and a superb drinks selection. **Map** 1 H2 **Metro** World Trade Centre

Al Mallah   Middle Eastern
2nd December St, Al Hudaiba   04 398 4723

Al Mallah offers great pavement dining with an excellent view of the world. It is perfect for people-watching in the busy area of Satwa, and for admiring the Ferraris that cruise by. The shawarmas and fruit juices are excellent and the cheese and zataar manoushi breads exceedingly tasty. **Map** 1 H2 **Metro** World Trade Centre

Manhattan Grill   Steakhouse
Grand Hyatt Dubai, Umm Hurair 2   04 317 2222

Try a New York style steakhouse that will please tummies and taste buds in equal measure. Considered one of the city's most popular steakhouses, this restaurant in the Grand Hyatt Dubai serves US prime beef and Wagyu, as well as surf n' turf additions and a range of seafood, lamb and chicken mains. **Map** 4 B6 **Metro** Dubai Healthcare City

Mannaland Korean Restaurant
East Asian
Al Mina St, Madinat Dubai Al Melaheyah   04 345 3200

A unique dining experience, this Korean restaurant in Satwa offers traditional floor seating and excellent, authentic food cooked at your table. This is the place to try kimchi – a dish made of fermented vegetables, said to be a superfood. **Map** 1 H2 **Metro** Al Jafiliya

Maya Modern Mexican Kitchen & Lounge
South American
Le Royal Meridien Beach Resort & Spa, Marsa Dubai   04 316 5550

Maya – from US chef Richard Sandoval – is a standout in Dubai. The food is a contemporary take on the dishes of rural Mexico. The crepas con cajeta is sumptuous and the terrace is perfect for margaritas. **Map** 3 B1 **Metro** DAMAC

The Meat Co
Steakhouse
Souk Al Bahar, Burj Khalifa   04 420 0737

Choose the country you'd like your steak to come from, the cut and how you want it prepared. While it isn't cheap, many consider this one of the best steak joints in the city, with a view of Burj Khalifa. There's also a branch at Souk Madinat Jumeirah. **Map** 2 B3 **Metro** Burj Khalifa/Dubai Mall

Mekong
South-East Asian
Anantara The Palm Resort & Spa, Nakhlat Jumeira   04 567 8304

Mekong restaurant presents a culinary journey infused with Thai, Vietnamese and Chinese food traditions. It features authentic south-eastern recipes served at rickshaw-style seating and oriental-style tables. **Map** 1 D1 **Metro** Dubai Internet City

Restaurants & Cafes

Mint Leaf of London
South Asian
Emirates Financial Tower 1, Zaa'beel 2   04 706 0900

If you love Indian cuisine, Mint Leaf of London should be on your list of restaurants to try. Perched on the 15th floor of Emirates Financial Tower in DIFC, the eatery boasts amazing views of Downtown Dubai and Burj Khalifa. Try the Kadai-spiced crispy soft shell crab, Adraki lamb chops or duck pepper fry. **Map** 2 D2 **Metro** Financial Centre

Mo's
American
City Walk, Al Wasl   04 344 3305

The name itself conjures up images of a friendly American diner – and as such Mo's matches expectations. It stands for huge helpings in laid-back surroundings at one of Dubai's most stylish outdoor shopping venues. **Map** 2 C1 **Metro** Burj Khalifa/Dubai Mall

Moana
Seafood
Sofitel Palm Jumeirah Resort & Spa, Nakhlat Jumeira   04 455 6677

Moana is a charming Polynesian-themed restaurant located away from the main hotel in a pagoda-style beachside setting. Dishes include seasonal oysters marinated in apple lime, baked crab legs and salt-crusted sea bass. **Map** 3 A1 **Metro** Nakheel

MORE Cafe
Cafe
Mall of the Emirates, Al Barsha 1   04 347 4696

MORE is a homely and popular cafe with an extensive breakfast, lunch and dinner menu. The huge portions of homemade, wholesome food will set you up for the full day. **Map** 3 E2 **Metro** Mall of the Emirates

Going Out

Restaurants & Cafes

Al Muntaha
European
Burj Al Arab, Umm Suqeim 3 04 301 7600
The breathtaking coastline view from the top of Burj Al Arab goes some way to excusing the grand yet eccentric decor. The Mediterranean menu, with its Atlantic lobster and sweetbread ravioli or wild sea bass three ways, offers a fresh twist on simple flavours and ingredients. **Map** 3 E1 **Metro** Mall of the Emirates

NA3NA3
Middle Eastern
The Address Dubai Mall, Burj Khalifa 04 438 8888
NA3NA3 is mainly known for its buffet spread, which promises a large selection of Middle Eastern and Arabic fare including juicy mixed grill meats, hot saj and Arabic breads straight out of the oven. **Map** 2 C2 **Metro** Burj Khalifa/Dubai Mall

Al Nafoorah
Middle Eastern
The Boulevard At Emirates Towers, Trade Center 2 04 366 5866
The menu at this highly rated Lebanese restaurant is extensive, with pages of mezze and mains to tantalise. After dinner, take a stroll round the Boulevard, or sit out and enjoy a shisha in front of the looming Emirates Towers. **Map** 2 D2 **Metro** Emirates Towers

Nando's
European
Saeed Tower 2, Trade Center 1 04 321 2000
Famous for its cheeky flame-grilled chicken, Nando's has branches across the city, including Nakhlat Jumeira, The Dubai Mall and Dubai Marina. Its Downtown Burj Khalifa restaurant overlooks the Dubai Fountain, and has a colourful alfresco dining area in which to enjoy its peri-peri specials. **Map** 2 D2 **Metro** Financial Centre

Nina
South Asian
04 399 9999
One&Only Royal Mirage, Al Sufouh 2
The refined menu includes roti and naan with savoury pickles and salads such as seared tuna with mustard cress and lime vinaigrette. The spinach kofta is exquisite, as are the tandoori prawns with lemon rice. **Map** 3 B1 **Metro** Nakheel

Nine7One
International
04 440 1407
The Oberoi Hotel, Business Bay
The large dining room is decked out with graffiti art and retro bicycles to transport diners to an urban street market. The menu features upscale street food from around the world and molecular desserts. **Map** 2 A2 **Metro** Business Bay

Nobu
East Asian
04 426 2626
Atlantis The Palm, Nakhlat Jumeira
Nobuyuki Matsuhisa, the godfather of sushi, has upped the ante for Japanese food aficionados with his Dubai offering. You'll love the exceptional quality, attention to detail and huge menu of sushi, sashimi and tempura. **Map** 1 C1 **Metro** Nakheel

Noire
International
04 311 8316
Fairmont Dubai, Trade Center 1
During the 90-minute dinner experience at Noire, waiters wearing night vision goggles serve a three-course meal, with paired refreshments, to 30 diners sitting in an entirely dark room. The goal? To heighten your four remaining senses. After finishing the meal, the lights are turned on for a culinary discussion with the chefs. **Map** 2 E1 **Metro** World Trade Centre

Going Out — Restaurants & Cafes

Nola

Armada BlueBay Hotel, Al Thanyah 5

American
04 399 8155

It is notoriously difficult to get a table at this New Orleans-inspired bar and restaurant. With live jazz, a massive central marble-topped bar and vintage decor, the atmosphere is warm and friendly, making it a great spot for a night out. **Map** 3 A2 **Metro** DAMAC

The Observatory

Dubai Marriott Harbour Hotel & Suites, Marsa Dubai

International
04 319 4795

It's all about the views at this atmospheric 52nd floor gastro-lounge. Spectacular 360° vistas over the marina and Palm Jumeirah accompany the menu. Come just before sunset then stay for evening cocktails. **Map** 3 B1 **Metro** DAMAC

Okku

The H Hotel Dubai, Trade Center 1

East Asian
04 501 8777

Electronic beats, dim lighting and a long, glossy black lounge make this a longstanding favourite, though it's not easy on the wallet. Okku has a thought-provoking Japanese fusion menu, with barbecue meat grills, black cod and Atlantic lobster with Asian spices. Dress to impress. **Map** 2 E1 **Metro** World Trade Centre

Olives

One&Only Royal Mirage, Al Sufouh 2

European
04 399 9999

There's an air of a riviera coastal cafe at Olives, with its dramatic archways, indoor foliage and white ceramic tiles overlooking the gardens and pool. Don't miss the braised lamb shank with roasted garlic salad and an orange rosemary jus – the chef's signature dish. **Map** 3 B1 **Metro** Nakheel

Operation: Falafel
The Beach, Marsa Dubai

Middle Eastern
04 424 3098

Operation: Falafel is on a mission to bring traditional Arabic street food into the 21st century. The casual venue also has outlets at Kite Beach and Boxpark. **Map** 3 A1 **Metro** Jumeirah Lakes Towers

Options by Sanjeev Kapoor
Dubai World Trade Centre, Trade Center 2

South Asian
04 329 3293

The brainchild of celebrity chef Sanjeev Kapoor, Options is a fine-dining experience offering a range of Indian salads, starters, mains and desserts. The sumptuous interior can be a bit overwhelming, but the carefully crafted menu doesn't disappoint. **Map** 2 E2 **Metro** World Trade Centre

Going Out

Ossiano

Seafood

Atlantis The Palm, Nakhlat Jumeira — 04 426 2626

Famed Spanish chef Santi Santamaria serves up delicate Catalan-inspired seafood dishes at this impeccable eatery. Glistening chandeliers and floor-to-ceiling views of the aquarium provide a formal but romantic setting. **Map** 1 C1 **Metro** Nakheel

Ossigeno

European

Le Royal Meridien Beach Resort & Spa, Marsa Dubai — 04 316 5550

Traditional Italian ingredients are fused with new flavours to create divine dishes. The emphasis is on sharing and there's a wide selection of antipasti as well as fish and meat dishes. **Map** 3 B1 **Metro** DAMAC

Pachanga

South American

Hilton Dubai Jumeirah Resort, Marsa Dubai — 04 318 2530

Pachanga's well-rounded Latin American menu hails from Mexico to Argentina. On Tuesdays, the restaurant celebrates with a Brazilian-style churrasco barbecue with succulent beef, chicken and lamb carved at the table. **Map** 3 A1 **Metro** Jumeirah Lakes Towers

Pai Thai

South-East Asian

Al Qasr, Al Sufouh 1 — 04 366 5866

You'll have a night to remember at the stunning Pai Thai, from the abra boat ride to the restaurant to the nouvelle Thai cuisine. The outdoor seating offers delightful views across the canals, and the menu provides some exciting twists on familiar favourites. Pai Thai is an ideal choice for a romantic dinner. **Map** 3 E1 **Metro** Sharaf DG

Ronda Locatelli

Going Out

Restaurants & Cafes

Paul

BurJuman, Mankhool

European
04 351 7009

Paul is a pleasant chain of cafes serving French pastries, cakes, desserts and light savoury dishes such as sandwiches, soups and salads. The cafes are modelled on a Parisian tea room and are a relaxing place to stop for afternoon tea. **Map** 4 C3 **Metro** BurJuman

Pax

Dusit Thani, Trade Center 2

European
04 343 3333

Pax does traditional Italian dishes in less than traditional sizes to give punters a pick 'n' mix of tastes. The style is called bocconcini (little delicacies), and with appetisers starting at Dhs.70, a hearty feed is not prohibitively expensive. **Map** 2 G6 **Metro** Financial Centre

Peppercrab

Grand Hyatt Dubai, Umm Hurair 2

South-East Asian
04 317 2222

Peppercrab offers the ultimate Singaporean gastronomic experience. You can watch the chef in action in the kitchen and even pack the children off to the kids' club. **Map** 4 B6 **Metro** Dubai Healthcare City

La Petite Maison

Gate Village 8, Zaa'beel 2

European
04 439 0505

This classy, unfussy restaurant is like a clean, white canvas on which the dining experience can paint itself. The French staff, dressed in bow ties and stripy aprons flit between tables serving typically Gallic dishes without the cliches. These are simple and delicious dishes with uncomplicated flavours, in which the high-quality fresh produce speaks volumes. **Map** 2 D2 **Metro** Emirates Towers

Picante

South American
04 397 7444

Four Points by Sheraton Bur Dubai, Al Hamriya

The wooden furniture and colourful ceramic tiles provide an authentic touch to this Portuguese restaurant. The menu is varied, with the chef featuring a range of traditional dishes, fish and seafood, steaks and vegetarian options. **Map** 4 C2 **Metro** Al Fahidi

Pierchic

Seafood
04 366 6730

Al Qasr, Al Sufouh 1

Situated at the end of a long wooden pier that juts into the Arabian Gulf, Pierchic offers unobstructed views of the Burj Al Arab. The

superior seafood is meticulously presented and the wine menu reads like a sommelier's wish list. The sea surrounds on all sides, making this a unique dining location. **Map** 3 E1 **Metro** Sharaf DG

Porterhouse
Steakhouse
Sofitel Palm Jumeirah Resort & Spa, Nakhlat Jumeira   04 455 6677
Indisputably romantic with a wonderful outdoor terrace overlooking Sofitel's pretty pools and palm trees, this is a place for steak aficionados looking to splash out on the best cuts from purebred Wagyu to Black Angus. **Map** 3 A1 **Metro** Nakheel

La Postreria
European
Souk Al Bahar, Burj Khalifa   04 442 1787
Although the restaurant is Mediterranean-themed, the menu spans the globe and includes a selection of shisha. There is also a delicatessen. **Map** 2 B3 **Metro** Burj Khalifa/Dubai Mall

Pots, Pans & Boards
International
The Beach, Marsa Dubai   04 456 1959
The first Tom Aikens restaurant in Dubai, Pots, Pans & Boards is tailored specifically to families and those looking for a relaxed, casual meal. Inspired by the warm, rustic kitchens of his childhood, this restaurant features long wooden tables and family-style service. **Map** 3 A1 **Metro** Jumeirah Lakes Towers

Prime Steakhouse
Steakhouse
The Meydan Hotel, Nadd Al Shiba 1   04 381 3111
On arrival, the oversized furniture – two-storey high doors and chandeliers – tell you this is a fine-dining restaurant. Here you'll

find premium cuts of Wagyu beef and other finest cuts from around the world. **Map** 1 G4

Puranmal
Vegetarian
Meena Bazaar, Al Souk Al Kabeer
04 351 3803

This 100% vegetarian restaurant offers all manner of Indian sweets and savouries that won't break the bank. From the Punjabi dishes of the north all the way down to specialities of the south, if it's vegetarian you'll find it at Puranmal. **Map** 1 J2

Qbara
Middle Eastern
Nr Raffles Dubai, Shk Rashid Rd Umm Hurair 2
04 709 2500

Designed by the award-winning, Tokyo-based Noriyoshi Muramatsu, the interior is bedecked with rich wood panelling, hand-carved in traditional Arabic designs. The food is traditional Arabic with a modern twist. **Map** 4 B5 **Metro** Dubai Healthcare City

Raffles Garden
Middle Eastern
Raffles Dubai, Umm Hurair 2
04 324 8888

This garden restaurant features open-air cabanas situated amongst the greenery on Wafi Mall's rooftop. Raffles Garden serves an array of Arabic delights, drinks and shisha and makes a nice escape from the city. **Map** 4 B5 **Metro** Dubai Healthcare City

Rare Restaurant
Steakhouse
Desert Palm, Warsan 2
04 323 8888

This tranquil tucked-away haven is a meat-lover's dream. Steaks, mostly 300 or 400 day grain-fed Australian beef, are the headline act, but grilled fish and seafood and corn-fed chicken will tempt the most ardent carnivores. The atmosphere is relaxed and refined. The wine list is lengthy, but manageable.

Ravi Restaurant
South Asian
2nd December St, Al Satwa　　04 331 5353
This much-loved diner offers a range of Pakistani favourites. The setting is basic, but that hasn't stopped Ravi's from gaining cult status among local expats. Most opt to sit outside with all of Satwa life on show. There's a second Ravi's near BurJuman mall. **Map** 1 H2 **Metro** World Trade Centre

Reem Al Bawadi
Middle Eastern
Nr Sunset Mall, Jumeira St, Jumeira 3　　04 348 4443
When it comes to a light Arabic mezze, mixed grill or fresh fruit juices and shisha, Reem Al Bawadi is one of the first places you should consider. You'll find branches all over the city. **Map** 1 E2 **Metro** Business Bay

Reflets Par Pierre Gagnaire
European
InterContinental Dubai Festival City, Al Kheeran　　04 701 1127
From the Michelin-starred grandfather of molecular gastronomy comes an imaginative dining experience incorporating French cuisine. The romantic waterfront setting is the perfect place to sample the superb wines. **Map** 1 J4 **Metro** Creek

Rhodes In Residence
European
Grosvenor House Dubai, Marsa Dubai　　04 317 6000
Rhodes In Residence is a stylish cafe, perfect for taking afternoon tea, and it is Rhodes W1 in the same location that offers more

substantial dishes. Afternoon tea includes top-notch treats such as quail's egg cress and mayonnaise sandwiches, or if traditional favourites such as lamb shank and shepherd's pie are what you're looking for, head to the English garden conservatory-style Rhodes W1. **Map** 3 B1 **Metro** DAMAC

Rhodes Twenty10
Steakhouse
Le Royal Meridien Beach Resort & Spa, Marsa Dubai 04 316 5550

If you just can't get enough of the celebrity chef, this restaurant describes itself as a culinary grill with a twist. Enjoy Euro-inspired cuisine with flavour influences from the Middle East. **Map** 3 B1 **Metro** DAMAC

Roberto's
European
Gate Village 1, Zaa'beel 2
04 386 0066

Fine-dining Italian restaurant Roberto's has a number of spots to indulge in delicious Mediterranean food with a contemporary twist. The main restaurant serves high-quality Italian dishes, from lobster pizza to freshly shucked oysters, and its I Crudi bar showcases a selection of raw seafood. A laidback lounge overlooks the Burj Khalifa. **Map** 2 D2 **Metro** Emirates Towers

Ronda Locatelli
European
Atlantis The Palm, Nakhlat Jumeira
04 426 2626

Giorgio Locatelli's cavernous restaurant can seat hundreds of diners in its raised alcoves or at tables surrounding a huge stone-built wood-fired oven. There's a charmingly rustic vibe and the casual menu offers a good range of authentic starters, pasta, mains and small dishes that are perfect for sharing. **Map** 1 C1 **Metro** Nakheel

Roseleaf Cafe

Cafe

Souk Al Bahar, Burj Khalifa 04 423 0903

After discovering the arty side of dusty Al Qouz, refresh in the Dubai Garden Centre, where this cosy cafe serves up home-cooked goodness, single-origin coffees and whole-leaf teas. The decor is cute and eclectic, with floral-patterned china teacups and plants hanging from the ceiling. **Map** 2 B3 **Metro** FGB

Saffron

South-East Asian

Atlantis The Palm, Nakhlat Jumeira 04 426 2626

This buffet-style Asian restaurant is popular not just for its remarkable spreads of seafood, but also for the welcoming family setting. Though Saffron is not hung up on formalities, the highly-attended themed dining means the crowd varies between casual and trendy. **Map** 1 C1 **Metro** Nakheel

Sahn Eddar

Cafe

Burj Al Arab, Umm Suqeim 3 04 301 7600

It may be an expensive cuppa, but this is the ultimate afternoon tea experience – as well as being the perfect way to see inside the Burj Al Arab, which otherwise requires a reservation in one of the hotel's restaurants or rooms. Your tea begins with a glass of bubbly and continues with course after course of dainty sandwiches and fine pastries. **Map** 3 E1 **Metro** Mall of the Emirates

Salero – Tapas & Bodega

European

Kempinski Hotel Mall of the Emirates, Al Barsha 1 04 409 5888

You may come for the tapas, but you'll end up staying for the warm, relaxed atmosphere. Salero serves up an array of authentic hot and

cold tapas, and has an impressive gin and tonic menu. **Map** 3 E2
Metro Mall of the Emirates

Salmontini Le Resto

Seafood
Mall of the Emirates, Al Barsha 1 — 04 341 0222

Salmontini's is the kind of casual chic restaurant where you'll always hear a buzz of conversation and laughter amid the clinking of glasses. You might not expect such ambience inside Mall of the Emirates, but its seafood-centric menu keeps people coming back for more. **Map** 3 E2 **Metro** Mall of the Emirates

SALT

American
Kite Beach, Umm Suqeim 1

A food truck located on the beach, SALT has a cordoned off seating area where you can enjoy the sand between your toes as you tuck into delicious burgers. **Map** 1 F24 **Metro** Noor Bank

Sapori di BICE

European
The Beach, Marsa Dubai — 04 551 6349

Part of the fine-dining BiCE network of restaurants, Sapori di BiCE is the casual, family-dining version. There are also locations at City Walk and The Palm, ensuring the restaurant is set within a fashionable and relaxed atmosphere. **Map** 3 A1
Metro Jumeirah Lakes Towers

Saravanaa Bhavan

South Asian
Abdul Aziz Mirza Bldg, Al Karama — 04 334 5252

This eatery takes its name from a much-loved hotel in Chennai, and here in Dubai, this unassuming joint is arguably the best of the

area's south Indian restaurants. It's the thalis that draw crowds. For around Dhs.10 you can get a plate packed with colour and flavours.
Map 4 C3 **Metro** ADCB

Scoopi
Jumeira St, Umm Suqeim 3

Dessert
04 279 0300

This parlour's smooth and creamy ice cream is frozen especially for you, so it will develop no ice crystals from sitting around in a freezer. Choose your flavour and the staff will pour your selected cream into the liquid nitrogen-freezing contraption that solidifies your desert into a silky scoop. If you happen to have a spare Dhs.2,999 to fritter away, try the Black Diamond, which adorns Madagascan vanilla ice cream with the world's most-expensive saffron, black truffle and gold leaf. **Map** 1 E2 **Metro** FGB

Seafire Steakhouse & Bar
Atlantis The Palm, Nakhlat Jumeira

Steakhouse
04 426 2626

Dinner at this friendly New York-style eatery starts with extravagant, delicious appetisers – just try to resist the succulent fillet or seafood grill. The Atlantis strip sirloin is one of the finest steaks you'll ever taste, and the sides are delicious. **Map** 1 C1 **Metro** Nakheel

Seagrill on 25 Restaurant & Lounge
Fairmont The Palm Dubai, Nakhlat Jumeira

Seafood
04 457 3457

Close enough to the beach that you can hear the waves lapping at the shore, Seagrill on 25 serves a range of seafood platters and fresh fish. There is also a dedicated caviar menu. The restaurant closes for the duration of Ramadan. **Map** 1 C1 **Metro** Nakheel

La Serre Bistro

Vida Downtown Dubai, Burj Khalifa

European
04 428 6969

Chef Izu Ani, who earned his fame at top Michelin-starred restaurants like London's The Square and La Bastide Saint Antoine in the South of France, dishes out an ambitious French-Mediterranean menu. In the downstairs Boulangerie, he serves truffle scrambled eggs and fresh baked breads for breakfast, and Provencal-style ratatouille topped with feta and whole-baked Camembert with country bread for lunch and dinner. Upstairs in the Bistro, it's a more formal affair. **Map** 2 B3
Metro Burj Khalifa/Dubai Mall

Going Out

Shabestan

Middle Eastern

Radisson Blu Hotel Deira Creek, Al Rigga
04 222 7171

Pause to admire the views of the Dubai Creek and its passing dhows before browsing the cooking stations around the restaurant which serve traditional Iranian rices, breads, stews and grilled meats. **Map** 4 D2 **Metro** Union

Shabu Shabu

East Asian

Al Hudaiba Bldg, Al Hudaiba
04 359 9224

While you can probably find better Japanese food in Dubai, this spot wins points for fun and affordability. Order the traditional Japanese hot pot and assemble your meal yourself. If you aren't familiar with the cuisine, the menu reads like a culinary guide to Asia, explaining each category of dishes and some of the history behind the food. **Map** 4 A2 **Metro** World Trade Centre

Shakespeare and Co.

Cafe

Al Saqr Business Tower, Trade Center 2
04 331 1757

With chic Victorian flair, an eclectic menu featuring cuisines from the US, Italy and the Middle East, and period-inspired decor, this ubiquitous chain offers more than just exquisite food and a relaxed atmosphere. Try the delicious smoothies, mocktails and hot and cold drinks and tuck into the home-made hand-wrapped chocolates and delicious French pastries. **Map** 3 D2 **Metro** Emirates Towers

Shang Palace

East Asian

Shangri-La Hotel Dubai, Trade Center 1
04 405 2703

Shang Palace's food is delicious and the attentive staff are available to guide you through the numerous options. With shark fin soup, live seafood and dim sum, this is certainly a place for something different. **Map** 3 C1 **Metro** Financial Centre

Shiba Restaurant & Bar
South-East Asian
The Meydan Hotel, Nadd Al Shiba 1
04 381 3111
A fusion of Indian, Chinese, Thai and Japanese cuisine, this restaurant brings Asian cooking styles together with some of the kitchen team's own innovations. The main restaurant has a sushi bar, two Japanese-style private dining rooms, and an outdoor terrace overlooking the racetrack. **Map** 1 G4

Shimmers
Seafood
Mina A'Salam, Al Sufouh 1
04 366 6730
If its beachfront fare you fancy, look no further than Shimmers. This open-air restaurant and lounge offers superb views of the Burj Al Arab and the turquoise Gulf. The menu features Mediterranean seafood. **Map** 3 E1 **Metro** Mall of the Emirates

Sicilia
European
Movenpick Hotel Ibn Battuta Gate, Jabal Ali 1
04 444 5613
This Italian restaurant serves up rustic home-style cooking with an apparent Sicilian slant. It's unpretentious and family friendly, offering wood-fired pizzas and classic pasta dishes in a homely setting. **Map** 1 B2 **Metro** Ibn Battuta

Signature By Sanjeev Kapoor
South Asian
Melia Dubai, Al Raffa
04 386 8111
The aptly named Signature bears all the hallmarks of its progressive and eclectic chef, with traditional Indian dishes given an innovative

makeover. Try modern delights such as tandoori wasabi lobster, basil pepper hammour tikka, honey mustard chicken chat puffs or paneer tikka with asparagus fritters and avocado mousse.
Map 4 B1 **Metro** Al Ghubaiba

Singapore Deli Restaurant
Nr Lamcy Plaza, Oud Metha

South-East Asian
04 396 6885

From bowls of steaming noodles to traditionally cooked nasi goreng, the authentic dishes and casual atmosphere draws a crowd of regular customers. **Map** 4 B4 **Metro** Oud Metha

Slider Station
The Galleria, Al Wasl

American
600 544005

Great for a quick bite, Slider Station's burger menu is extensive – and the best thing? You don't have to choose one. Pick three to have all your favourites. **Map** 1 G2 **Metro** Burj Khalifa/Dubai Mall

Smiling BKK
Wasl Square, Al Safa 1

South-East Asian
04 388 4411

This outstanding Thai pad near Safa Park is a rare thing: great food topped with good humour and superb service. The cheekily named dishes are reasonably priced, but with gossip mag pages for place mats and theme nights such as 'sing for your supper', it's the spirit that sets Smiling BKK apart. **Map** 1 F2 **Metro** Business Bay

Social by Heinz Beck
Waldorf Astoria Palm Jumeirah, Nakhlat Jumeira

European
04 818 2222

A fine-dining Italian restaurant, Social by Heinz Beck has the white tablecloths and wooden walls you'd expect from the Waldorf Astoria.

The menu by the Michelin-starred chef is small but perfectly formed, as are the plates. **Map** 1 D1 **Metro** Dubai Internet City

Spice Emporium Flavours of Thailand — South-East Asian
The Westin Mina Seyahi, Marsa Dubai — 04 399 4141

For a taste of top-notch Thai in a chic setting, Spice Emporium is top drawer. Its open kitchens serve up incredible curries, spicy salads and other traditional Thai dishes, best enjoyed family-style. **Map** 3 B14 **Metro** Nakheel

Splendido Restaurant — European
The Ritz-Carlton Dubai Hotel, Marsa Dubai — 04 399 4000

Clock the stylish decor and modern art and you may assume you have entered a New York-style grill – but this is an Italian restaurant, with a menu of traditional dishes given a modern twist. Head outside to the large patio for sea views. **Map** 3 A14 **Metro** DAMAC

Going Out

St Moritz Cafe

International
Mall of the Emirates, Al Barsha 1   04 409 4132

Keep warm apres-ski by sharing a chocolate fondant or the outrageous St Moritz Hot Chocolate at this Alpine resort-inspired cafe that looks onto the wintry slopes of Ski Dubai. **Map** 3 E2 **Metro** Mall of the Emirates

STAY By Yannick Alleno

European
One&Only The Palm Dubai, Nakhlat Jumeira   04 440 1030

The three Michelin-starred Yannick Alleno's contemporary French restaurant STAY puts emphasis on impeccably selected ingredients cooked to perfection. Seasons dictate the menu but signature dishes are constant. The Black Angus beef fillet 'cafe de Paris' is recommended. The open Pastry Library allows you to participate in the dessert making process. **Map** 1 C2 **Metro** DAMAC

El Sur

European
The Westin Mina Seyahi, Marsa Dubai   04 399 7700

Serving up contemporary Spanish fare, El Sur provides a relaxed meal on a Mediterranean-style terrace. Tapas includes traditional meats, breads, calamari, paella and prawns, all washed down with the restaurant's popular sangria. **Map** 3 B1 **Metro** Nakheel

Sushi

East Asian
Grand Hyatt Dubai, Umm Hurair 2   04 317 2222

Artfully prepared in the open kitchen of this petite venue, sushi and sashimi portions are served up delightfully and your bill is determined by the number of pieces you feel like indulging in. **Map** 4 B6 **Metro** Dubai Healthcare City

Table 9

European
04 212 7551

Hilton Dubai Creek, Riggat Al Buteen

Table 9 is a British serving of fine dining. The menu offers a mix of traditional favourites including chicken stuffed with foie gras and sea bass with egg, broccoli and hollandaise sauce. **Map** 4 D6 **Metro** Al Rigga

Taste of Italy by Heinz Beck

European
04 343 8292

The Galleria, Al Wasl

The casual-dining alternative to Social by Heinz Beck puts a home-cooked spin on the Michelin-starred chef's creations. You'll find a range of pizza and gelato on the menu, alongside poached lobster and breaded veal chop. **Map** 1 G2 **Metro** Burj Khalifa/Dubai Mall

The Thai Kitchen

South-East Asian
04 317 2221

Park Hyatt Dubai, Port Saeed

A decent range of Thai delicacies with rich, authentic flavours is served in this stylish and modern restaurant. Portions are perfect for sharing and the Friday brunch is a delight – more refined than most. **Map** 4 D5 **Metro** GGICO

Thiptara

South-East Asian
04 888 3444

The Palace Downtown Dubai, Burj Khalifa

With stunning views of the Burj Khalifa and The Dubai Fountain, it makes sense that Thiptara in Thai translates to 'magic at the water'. The restaurant specialises in Royal Thai cuisine, with an emphasis on Bangkok-style seafood. You'll be dazzled by the attention to detail in the atmosphere, service and cuisine here. **Map** 2 B3 **Metro** Burj Khalifa/Dubai Mall

Tokyo@thetowers
The Boulevard at Emirates Towers, Trade Center 2

East Asian
04 366 5866

Discover a corner of Tokyo in Dubai. You could opt to sit at the sushi bar to enjoy a meal of sushi, sashimi and tempura, but the real show is at the teppanyaki grill tables. Sit back, as a highly skilled chef cooks up a storm. **Map** 2 D2 **Metro** Emirates Towers

Tomo
Raffles Dubai, Umm Hurair 2

East Asian
04 357 7888

This award-winning home-grown Japanese restaurant is said to offer foodies the finest, most authentic interpretation of Japanese cuisine in the UAE, and the proof is in the Japanese nationals that frequent it. They've got it all, from mouth-watering sashimi to memorable black sesame mochi ice cream. Grab a table on the terrace and you'll be blown away by the broad-sweeping views of the Dubai skyline. **Map** 4 B5 **Metro** Dubai Healthcare City

Tong Thai
JW Marriott Marquis Hotel, Business Bay

South-East Asian
04 414 3000

This award-winning restaurant specialises in all kinds of Thai cuisine, from unique regional dishes, to authentic classics, to celebrated street food. It's a very trendy, modern space, with dark lighting and bright neon flashes of light, and decor features like hanging intricate temple bells. **Map** 2 A2 **Metro** Business Bay

Toro Toro
Grosvenor House Dubai, Marsa Dubai

South American
04 399 8888

The exclusive atmosphere of low lighting, lush furnishings and a playlist of Latin-inspired house music is complemented by thought-provoking drinks and mouthwatering tapas-style dishes that cross from land to sea. **Map** 3 B1 **Metro** DAMAC

Tortuga — South American
Mina A'Salam, Al Sufouh 1 — 04 366 6730

With chefs flown in straight from Mexico, colourful, casual Tortuga wants guests to experience the real 'mi casa es su casa' warmth of Mexican cuisine and hospitality. This is a fun spot to feast ahead of a lively night out. **Map** 1 R4 **Metro** Mall of the Emirates

Tribes — African
Mall of the Emirates, Al Barsha 1 — 04 395 0663

The menu at this African eatery is as vast as the continent and features dishes from Morocco to South Africa. The friendly staff also have some notable musical talent to really ramp up the atmosphere. **Map** 3 E1 **Metro** Mall of the Emirates

Going Out

Troyka

Ascot Hotel, Al Raffa

Russian
04 352 0900

Troyka conjures up a little of Russia's old world charm. The Tuesday night buffet is all-inclusive and comprises time-honoured Russian delicacies. A band plays every night followed by an extravagant, live Vegas-style cabaret. **Map** 4 B2 **Metro** Al Fahidi

Umai

The Oberoi Hotel, Business Bay

East Asian
04 444 1407

Sleek and elegant Umai has a comprehensive menu including a large selection of sushi, teppanyaki and yakitori delights, as well as dim sum, noodles, stir-fries, spring rolls and more. The service is excellent and the food gorgeously presented. **Map** 2 A2 **Metro** Business Bay

Vivaldi by Alfredo Russo

Sheraton Dubai Creek, Riggat Al Buteen

European
04 207 1750

Boasting amazing views of Dubai Creek, this stylish restaurant is brought to Dubai by Italian master chef Alfredo Russo. You can enjoy a feast of appetisers, pasta dishes, pizzas and main courses. Vivaldi also has a climate-controlled terrace to enjoy the views, even during summer. **Map** 4 D3 **Metro** Union

Wafi Gourmet

Wafi, Umm Hurair 2

Middle Eastern
04 324 4433

Deliciously prepared traditional Lebanese dishes, along with pastries, sweets, ice cream, exotic juices and hot drinks, make Wafi Gourmet a great sustenance stop when on a shopping spree. **Map** 4 B5 **Metro** Dubai Healthcare City

Warehouse
European
Le Meridien Dubai, Dubai International Airport   04 702 2455
Warehouse is a stylish and unusual addition to the old-school side of the creek because it houses several different themes: there is a beer garden on the ground floor serving fish and chips and the like, while up the spiral staircase you'll find a dual-personality restaurant – half fine dining and half sushi – with an extensive wine list. There is also a nightclub. **Map** 4 E6 **Metro** Airport Terminal 1

Wavebreaker
International
Hilton Dubai Jumeirah Resort, Marsa Dubai   04 399 1111
This beach bar serves snacks, light meals, barbecue grills and a variety of cocktails and mocktails. Enjoy juicy burgers, jumbo prawns or even lobster. At sunset, it's quiet, cool and the beach view is stunning. **Map** 2 A1 **Metro** Jumeirah Lakes Towers

White Orchid
South-East Asian
JA Jebel Ali Golf Resort, Mena Jabal Ali   04 814 5604
This fusion restaurant has consistently great reviews, not just for its outstanding service and approach to honest, uncomplicated Asian food, but also for its beautiful and relaxed ambiance, and stunning views from the terrace.

Wox
South-East Asian
Grand Hyatt Dubai, Umm Hurair 2   04 317 2222
Grand Hyatt's Asian offering is said to be reminiscent of hawker stands in South-East Asia, with fresh and flavourful soups, noodles and wok dishes hailing from Cambodia, Vietnam, Singapore and beyond. **Map** 4 B6 **Metro** Dubai Healthcare City

Xiao Wei Yang Hotpot
East Asian
Rolla Residence, Al Raffa   04 266 5558

If you like Chinese comfort food, and love not breaking the bank when you indulge in it, then this is a must-do in Deira. The menu is pretty basic; the main focus here is on the incredible hotpots – a steaming stew bowl with thinly sliced meats, seafood and mushrooms or egg dumplings. **Map** 4 B2 **Metro** Al Fahidi

XVA Cafe
Cafe
XVA Art Hotel, Al Souk Al Kabeer   04 353 5383

Tucked away amongst the narrow winding stone pathways of the Al Fahidi Historical Neighbourhood, this cute hotel and art gallery is dreamily quiet. Its tree-shaded courtyard cafe serves Middle Eastern-inspired classics and comfort food. **Map** 4 C2 **Metro** Al Fahidi

Yalumba
International
Le Meridien Dubai, Dubai International Airport   04 217 0000

Famous for its raucous Friday bubbly buffets, this Australian-influenced restaurant doesn't limit itself to steak. Head there for the Thursday night buffet with unlimited champagne, sushi, stir-fry, seafood, steak and more desserts than you can possibly manage.
Map 4 E6 **Metro** Airport Terminal 1

Yuan
East Asian
Atlantis The Palm, Nakhlat Jumeira   04 426 2626

This exclusive venue's Friday brunch is a particular highlight. It takes the Chinese culinary tradition of Yum Cha, a leisurely meal of dim sum and aromatic tea, and kicks it up a notch. **Map** 1 C1 **Metro** Nakheel

Going Out

Zaroob
Middle Eastern
Jumeirah Tower, Trade Center 2 — 04 327 6060
This eatery has fun decor. The Levantine street fare is scrumptious, and comes hot and fast. **Map** 2 D2 **Metro** Financial Centre

Zheng He's
East Asian
Mina A'Salam, Al Sufouh 1 — 04 366 6730
This waterside spot in Madinat Jumeirah gives a superb take on Chinese delicacies. **Map** 3 E1 **Metro** Mall of the Emirates

Zuma
East Asian
Gate Village 6, Zaa'beel 2 — 04 425 5660
Zuma has gained a firm following as one of Dubai's best restaurants. The food that arrives from the open kitchen and sushi bar is presented in classic Japanese style – it is all about simplicity and flair here, with prices to match. **Map** 2 D2 **Metro** Financial Centre

BARS, PUBS & CLUBS

Sky-high cocktail lounges, beachside bars and enough clubs to keep you dancing for a year all jostle for your evening attention.

360° Bar Lounge & Club
Rooftop Bar
Jumeirah Beach Hotel, Umm Suqeim 3 — 04 406 8999
This two-tiered circular rooftop bar boasts all-round views of the Arabian Gulf and Burj Al Arab. House DJs spin at the weekends, and late afternoon loungers give way to scruffily chic stylistas sipping cocktails as the tempo rises. **Map** 3 E1 **Metro** FGB

40 Kong
Rooftop Bar
The H Hotel Dubai, Trade Center 1 — 04 355 8896
Situated in the middle of Dubai's busiest business district, this rooftop lounge offers a welcome escape from the hustle and bustle below. Its position on the 40th floor offers stunning panoramic views of the city. **Map** 2 E1 **Metro** World Trade Centre

Armani/Prive
Nightclub
Armani Hotel Dubai, Burj Khalifa — 04 888 3308
The first nightclub to be personally crafted by Giorgio Armani, and located in the world's tallest building, Armani/Prive is one of the city's top spots for clubbing. **Map** 2 B2 **Metro** Burj Khalifa/Dubai Mall

Bahri Bar
Cocktail Bar
Mina A'Salam, Al Sufouh 1 04 366 6730
The spacious terrace has fantastic views, and inside, lavish but comfortable furnishings create an intimate atmosphere to enjoy its selection of cocktails. **Map** 3 E1 **Metro** Mall of the Emirates

Barasti
Beach Bar
Le Meridien Mina Seyahi, Marsa Dubai 04 399 3333
Head to this lively venue in flip-flops or dolled up to the nines. Barasti boasts a tasty menu, beach access, sea views, big screens, live music and a friendly crowd that makes for a good night out.

Going Out

Entry is free all day, so you can spend the day on the beach and then head to the bar. **Map** 3 B1 **Metro** Nakheel

Belgian Beer Cafe
Pub
Crowne Plaza Dubai Festival City, Al Kheeran 04 701 2222
This is one of the best beer-drinking spots in town. On top of all manner of European amber nectar delights, there's good food, especially the moules frites. Other branches are located at Madinat Jumeirah and Grand Millennium, TECOM. **Map** 4 J3 **Metro** Creek

Biggles Pub
Pub
Millennium Airport Hotel, Al Garhoud 04 702 8833
Biggles Pub is the place to go if you're yearning for a bit of that comfortable, down-to-earth pub culture that seems to have been all but forgotten. Rich, dark wood gives this pub a warm familiar feel. It's a great place to watch the match. **Map** 4 D6 **Metro** GGICO

Buddha Bar
Bar
Grosvenor House Dubai, Marsa Dubai 04 317 6000
Half restaurant, half bar, this stylish nightspot never fails to impress with moody lighting, a huge Buddha statue and marina views. If you like sake, Buddha Bar has an extensive and exquisite selection to choose from. **Map** 3 B1 **Metro** DAMAC

Cabana
Rooftop Bar
The Address Dubai Mall, Burj Khalifa 04 888 3444
This Miami-cool pool bar sits beneath the Burj Khalifa. Lounge by the pool, or enjoy your cocktail and the chilled-out soundtrack from the privacy of a cabana. **Map** 2 C2 **Metro** Burj Khalifa/Dubai Mall

Cargo
Bar
Pier 7, Marsa Dubai
04 361 8129
Cargo is a bar and restaurant that serves up pan-Asian 'street food' and eclectic cocktails. The interior is contemporary and industrial, with exposed pipes and light fittings – but if you're here during the cooler months, you'll want to snag a seat on the huge terrace overlooking Dubai Marina. **Map** 3 A1 **Metro** Jumeirah Lakes Towers

Cavalli Club
Nightclub
Fairmont Dubai, Trade Center 1
04 332 9260
Roberto Cavalli's leopard print and Swarovski encrusted nightspot is one of the city's places to be seen if you're part of the 'it' crowd. Make sure you dress to impress and book a table to be granted entry. **Map** 2 E1 **Metro** World Trade Centre

Cirque Le Soir
Nightclub
Fairmont Dubai, Trade Center 1
056 115 4507
With the words 'freak show' marked on the walls, expect a night of outlandish entertainment. While dancing the night away, enjoy stunts and stage shows from stilt walkers, contortionists, jugglers, drummers, burlesque dancers, sword swallowers, magicians and fire eaters. **Map** 2 E1 **Metro** World Trade Centre

Cocktail Kitchen
Cocktail Bar
Armada BlueBay Hotel, Al Thanyah 5
056 828 0727
This too-cool cocktail bar and kitchen is famed for experienced mixologists and their artistic flair, as well as its daily Dhs.19 happy hour. Even the food is cocktail-inspired ('Bloody Mary Beef' or 'Duck on A Side Car'). **Map** 3 A2 **Metro** DAMAC

Bars, Pubs & Clubs

Crossroads Cocktail Bar
Cocktail Bar
Raffles Dubai, Umm Hurair 2 — 04 324 8888

Home of the Dubai Sling, a mix of coriander, chilli, fig and lemon, Crossroads has extremely knowledgeable staff, well-executed bar snacks and a dizzying choice of drinks. You won't even mind paying above-average prices for the experience. **Map** 4 B5
Metro Dubai Healthcare City

THE DEK On 8
Rooftop Bar
Media One Hotel, Al Sufouh 2 — 04 427 1000

Sip champagne and sample cocktails as you laze on white sofa beds and take in the stunning views of Marsa Dubai. The venue now hosts an indie rock night once or twice a month on Thursdays.
Map 3 B2 **Metro** Nakheel

Dhow & Anchor
Pub
Jumeirah Beach Hotel, Umm Suqeim 3 — 04 406 8999

This popular restaurant offers a modern twist on British cuisine in a stylish, yet casual pub setting. Dhow & Anchor's bar is a popular spot, particularly during happy hour – try the outdoor terrace and enjoy glimpses of the Burj Al Arab. **Map** 3 E1 **Metro** FGB

Double Decker
Pub
Al Murooj Rotana, Trade Center 2 — 04 321 1111

Double Decker is famed as the venue to go to when you feel like a raucous night out and a king-sized hangover the next day. You won't find Dubai's elite 'it' crowd here. Adorned with London transport memorabilia, this two-storey bar serves upmarket pub grub. **Map** 2 C2 **Metro** Burj Khalifa/Dubai Mall

Clockwise from top left: Double Decker, Cabana, Cavalli Club

Dubai **Visitors'** Guide

Going Out

The Dubliner's
Pub
Le Meridien Dubai, Dubai International Airport 04 702 2307
Cosy and lively, this Irish pub has a weekly quiz, good music and plenty of screens for watching sports. The menu is full of fresh, tasty and reasonably priced dishes. Save room for the Bailey's cheesecake. **Map** 4 E6 **Metro** Airport Terminal 1

Embassy Dubai
Nightclub
Grosvenor House Dubai, Marsa Dubai 04 317 6000
This is a nightclub, restaurant and champagne and vodka bar. The decor is opulent, with stunning views of Marsa Dubai. Fine-dining appetisers include oysters, caviar (at Dhs.2,000 for 50g) and foie gras. It's not cheap – dinner is Dhs.500-600 per person without alcohol – but you won't be disappointed. **Map** 3 B1 **Metro** DAMAC

FAI
Bar
The Palace Downtown Dubai, Burj Khalifa 04 888 3444
FAI is a chic lounge set in the gardens of The Palace Hotel and overlooking Burj Lake. Inside, the elegant sofas are comfortable and great for sipping drinks. Meanwhile, outside on the veranda, which is adorned with burning torches, you can feast your eyes on the magical Dubai Fountain. **Map** 2 B3 **Metro** Burj Khalifa/Dubai Mall

Fibber Magee's
Pub
Saeed Tower 1, Trade Center 1 04 332 2400
If you enjoy a good night out with friends, a few drinks and a hearty home-cooked meal then head to Fibber Magee's. The atmosphere is instantly warm and friendly and you're guaranteed to have a fun time. The bar stocks an excellent selection of Irish drinks, and the

cosy bar offers entertainment in the form of an Irish band, quiz nights and sporting fixtures. **Map** 2 D2 **Metro** World Trade Centre

Girders
JA Ocean View Hotel, Marsa Dubai

Pub
04 814 5590

As a welcoming, traditional British pub with a Gaelic-themed menu, this is a place to come to enjoy the pub quiz, sporting action, weekend live music and a daily happy hour between 6pm and 10pm. In the winter, the upstairs Girders Garden has barbecue stations and a big screen. **Map** 3 A1 **Metro** Jumeirah Lakes Towers

Gold on 27
Burj Al Arab, Umm Suqeim 3

Cocktail Bar
04 301 7600

Gold on 27 is a recent addition to Dubai's nightlife, housed inside one of the most famous hotels in the city. Expect nothing but the best inside this opulent and gold bedecked interior where everything from the stools to the floor is fashioned in gold. Creative cocktails using unusual ingredients, including saffron, goat's cheese, truffle and even charcoal, are the signature of the venue. As you might expect, prices do reflect the extravagant environment with mixed drinks starting at around Dhs.100 each. **Map** 3 E1 **Metro** Mall of the Emirates

The Gramercy
DIFC Gate 3, Zaa'beel 2

Pub
04 437 7511

The Gramercy is a comfortable bar and restaurant which serves hearty gastro-pub cuisine, as well as an array of premium drinks. This is more than a relaxing place to eat; there is a wonderful jazz band in the background. **Map** 2 D2 **Metro** Emirates Towers

The Grape Escape

Wine Bar

Hilton Dubai The Walk, Marsa Dubai   04 399 1111

This quiet bar, tucked away in the Hilton Dubai The Walk serves a wide range of cheese and charcuterie alongside fine wines. Its flight of three wine-tasting option for Dhs.95 is good value.
Map 3 A1 **Metro** Jumeirah Lakes Towers

Harry Ghatto's

Karaoke

The Boulevard at Emirates Towers, Trade Center 2   04 366 5866

Dubai's most renowned karaoke bar, a night at Harry Ghatto's is sure to be entertaining. To keep you going through the night, there's also a delicious Japanese menu, which includes sushi, sashimi and teriyaki. **Map** 2 D2 **Metro** Emirates Towers

The Irish Village

Pub

31A St Al Garhoud   04 282 4750

This laidback Irish pub offers both indoor and alfresco seating, managing to create an authentic pub experience complete with a sprawling beer garden. There's a good selection of pub grub and it also hosts concerts and events. **Map** 4 D6 **Metro** GGICO

The Jetty Lounge

Beach Bar

One&Only Royal Mirage, Al Sufouh 2   04 399 9999

This beachside bar manages to strike a great balance between stylish and relaxed. Located in the exclusive One&Only Royal Mirage, just steps from the hotel's private beach, the loungy setting is perfect for sundowners: plop onto comfy seats, kick back and indulge in tasty snacks. You can also take a ferry to the hotel's sister property, One&Only The Palm. **Map** 3 B14 **Metro** Nakheel

Going Out

Bars, Pubs & Clubs

Koubba Bar
Cocktail Bar
Al Qasr, Al Sufouh 1 04 366 6730
Stunning views of Dubai await you from the terrace of this sumptuous cocktail bar. Check out the Armoury Lounge, where you can indulge in Cuban cigars. **Map** 3 E1 **Metro** Sharaf DG

Left Bank
Cocktail Bar
Souk Madinat Jumeirah, Al Sufouh 1 04 368 4501
This bar serves stylish food and cocktails in laidback surroundings. In winter, the waterside terrace is a relaxing spot to share a tea-themed cocktail (served in a teapot) with friends. Inside the intimate decor features sofas and low, warm lighting. **Map** 3 E1 **Metro** Mall of the Emirates

Loca
Wine Bar
Dubai Marine Beach Resort & Spa, Jumeira 1 04 346 1111
The stainless steel and brick facade gives Loca its underground appeal. Follow your drink from keg to glass through a stream of industrial pipework. The taps at the bar will test your knowledge of South American drinks. There is another branch in Souk Al Bahar. **Map** 1 H2 **Metro** World Trade Centre

Lock Stock & Barrel
Sports Bar
Grand Millennium Dubai, Al Thanyah 1 04 514 9195
Inspired by trendy, industrial music venues around the world, Lock Stock & Barrel focuses on live music and sports. It features an American food menu and a buy-one-get-one-free happy hour every day of the week. The decor is unpretentious and relaxed. **Map** 3 C2 **Metro** Dubai Internet City

Magnum
Nightclub
Ramada Jumeirah Hotel, Al Hudaiba 04 702 7072
From Edward Maya and Avicii to Ritchie Hawtin and Sven Vath, Magnum has all your favourite beats covered six days a week. Tuesday is ladies' night, go breakdancing on Fridays and get 50% off selected beverages on Saturdays. **Map** 1 H2 **Metro** Al Jafiliya

McGettigan's Irish Pub
Pub
Bonnington JLT, Al Thanyah 5 04 356 0560
This fairly cavernous bar is pretty rowdy all week. There are plenty of stools, tables and nooks for drinkers and diners, with a menu that focuses on inexpensive but hearty fare over haute cuisine. Big matches are shown, the quiz is a hoot and there's regular live entertainment. **Map** 3 A2 **Metro** Jumeirah Lakes Towers

Movida
Nightclub
Nassima Royal Hotel, Trade Center 1 04 386 6844
Mingle with the 'in' crowd and rub shoulders with some of the world's A-list celebrities in this award-winning nightspot. The state-of-the-art sound system, LED lighting and a choice of five dance floors will have you dancing until the early hours. **Map** 2 E1 **Metro** World Trade Centre

The Music Room
Cocktail Bar
Majestic Hotel Tower Dubai, Mankhool 04 359 8888
If you have a taste for some live music, you can count on The Music Room to satisfy your cravings. Whether it's a local battle of the bands, a theme night or headline act, there is always something going on here. **Map** 4 B2 **Metro** Al Fahidi

Going Out

Bars, Pubs & Clubs

Going Out — Bars, Pubs & Clubs

Nasimi Beach
Beach Bar
Atlantis The Palm, Nakhlat Jumeira · 04 426 2626
Next to Atlantis hotel, Nasimi Beach has a relaxed vibe. The restaurant's menu features expertly prepared seafood and meat dishes and, as evening becomes night, superstar DJs take to the decks and the glamour levels soar. While not cheap, it's a great Dubai experience. **Map** 1 C1 **Metro** Nakheel

Nelson's
Pub
Media Rotana, Al Thanyah 1 · 04 435 0000
Pitch up to this unpretentious bar if you want to watch football, tuck into traditional English dishes and enjoy some British banter. Punters can settle into large armchairs, prop themselves up on bar stools or cluster around the TVs. **Map** 3 C2 **Metro** Dubai Internet City

Nezesaussi Grill
Pub
Manzil Downtown Dubai, Burj Khalifa · 04 428 5972
Celebrating the sport and cuisine of the tri-nations, the restaurant pays ode to its passions with rugby paraphernalia and 13 big screens. You'll get great beer and food here with a menu of meaty mains including South African sausages, New Zealand lamb and Australian steaks. **Map** 2 B3 **Metro** Burj Khalifa/Dubai Mall

Oscar's Vine Society
Wine Bar
Crowne Plaza Dubai, Trade Center 1 · 04 331 1111
Wine cask tables, dim lighting and a warm welcome set the mood at Oscar's for indulging in full-bodied reds and ripe cheeses. Special dining promotions throughout the week offer good value for great French dishes. **Map** 2 D1 **Metro** Emirates Towers

Pacha Ibiza

Nightclub

Souk Madinat Jumeirah, Al Sufouh 1　　　　　　　　04 567 0000

With all of the nightclub trappings you'd expect – internationally known DJs, incredibly good looking hosts and plenty of room for dancing – Pacha Ibiza in Dubai also features a full dinner show with dancers and acrobats. **Map** 3 E1 **Metro** Mall of the Emirates

Purobeach Urban Oasis

Pool Bar

Conrad Dubai, Trade Center 1　　　　　　　　04 444 7111

Located within Dubai's Conrad Hotel, this poolside retreat is a city sanctuary surrounded by lush landscaped gardens. Open every evening until 8pm, this urban oasis is ideal for sipping drinks at sunset and listening to music playing into the evening. **Map** 2 D1 **Metro** World Trade Centre

Q43

Bar

Media One Hotel, Al Sufouh 2　　　　　　　　04 443 5403

Q43 is a busy bar offering great sea views from the 43rd floor of Media One Hotel's office tower. In the early evening, it's a laid-back lounge with pool tables but it soon livens up when the late-night crowd fills up the dance floor. **Map** 3 B2 **Metro** Nakheel

QD's

Cocktail Bar

Dubai Creek Golf & Yacht Club, Port Saeed　　　　　　　　04 295 6000

Sitting so close to the water's edge that you can almost dip your toes into the creek, you can watch the passing abras as the sun sets over Sheikh Zayed Road from this charming and atmospheric locale. Elegant bar snacks accompany an excellent cocktail list and a live band keeps the crowd entertained. **Map** 4 D5 **Metro** GGICO

Going Out

Bars, Pubs & Clubs

Going Out

Bars, Pubs & Clubs

Qube Sports Bar
Pub
The Meydan Hotel, Nadd Al Shiba 1 — 04 381 3111
The 'Qube' refers to a giant structure made up of big projection screens in the middle of this sports bar, which is decked in dark wood and red leather, and has a further eight plasma screens and two pool tables. It serves burgers and bar snacks. **Map** 1 G4

Rock Bottom
Nightclub
Regent Palace Hotel, Al Karama — 04 396 3888
Your experience at Rock Bottom, a real Dubai institution, depends on your time – or condition – of arrival. The sweaty, heaving, hedonistic home of the legendary Bullfrog cocktail has a unique appeal, which it has replicated well at a second venue in TECOM. The music is refreshingly rocky, with some anthems thrown in for good measure. **Map** 4 C3 **Metro** BurJuman

Rodeo Drive
Cocktail Bar
The Stables Bar & Restaurant, Trade Center 1 — 04 501 3512
The centrepiece of this American gastro-pub is a mechanical bull (free for all as long as you sing a waiver), and there are separate levels of the room dedicated to every college student's favourite game (do ping pong balls and plastic cups ring a bell?). **Map** 2 D1 **Metro** World Trade Centre

The Rooftop Terrace & Sports Lounge
Rooftop Bar
One&Only Royal Mirage, Al Sufouh 2 — 04 399 9999
Rooftop is a hangout for the beautiful people, so expect to pay high prices for your tall drinks. That aside, the views of The Palm are superb. **Map** 3 B1 **Metro** Nakheel

Al Sarab Rooftop Lounge

Sama Lounge — Rooftop Bar
Ramada Plaza JBR, Marsa Dubai — 04 439 8888

Relax under the stars, and enjoy Arabic mezze, mixed grill and a wide selection of shisha and drinks overlooking The Palm Jumeirah and Jumeira Beach. **Map** 3 A1 **Metro** Jumeirah Lakes Towers

Al Sarab Rooftop Lounge — Rooftop Bar
Bab Al Shams Desert Resort & Spa, Mugatrah — 04 809 6194

With panoramic desert views, this two-storey Arabian rooftop lounge is a great place to watch a desert sunset with a cocktail.

Going Out

Going Out

Bars, Pubs & Clubs

The Scene
Pub
Pier 7, Marsa Dubai   04 422 2328
This unapologetically British restaurant is the brain child of celebrity chef and TV personality Simon Rimmer. They're serious about great food, interesting beers and cocktails. There's also a terrace overlooking the marina. **Map** 3 A1 **Metro** Jumeirah Lakes Towers

Sho Cho
Cocktail Bar
Dubai Marine Beach Resort & Spa, Jumeira 1   04 346 1111
The huge terrace, not to mention the sunshine holiday vibe, is what attracts the beautiful clientele to this Japanese restaurant. The mix of house and trance music and a gorgeous view of the shoreline makes this a must. **Map** 1 H2 **Metro** World Trade Centre

Siddharta Lounge By Buddha Bar
Rooftop Bar
Grosvenor House Dubai, Marsa Dubai   04 317 6000
Soak up some rays at this slick white venue with a pool terrace. In the evening there's a chilled lounge vibe, which ramps up a notch when the DJ starts to play. The menu is innovative, as are the cocktails. **Map** 3 B1 **Metro** DAMAC

Skyview Bar
Cocktail Bar
Burj Al Arab, Umm Suqeim 3   04 301 7600
Located in the iconic Burj Al Arab hotel, this bar has attitude, and those who enter must be prepared to spend a fair chunk of cash. A cocktail can easily run into triple figures and you have to book well in advance. There's a minimum spend of Dhs.320 per person just to get in. The views are amazing, as you would expect. You can also take afternoon tea here. **Map** 3 E1 **Metro** Mall of the Emirates

Societe
Nightclub
Marina Byblos Hotel, Marsa Dubai 050 357 1126
You may wander into this nightspot and feel like you've crashed a wedding thanks to the unashamedly cheesy music from the 70s, 80s and 90s (as well as current tunes), but you won't feel like you shouldn't be there. Refreshingly unpretentious, this club attracts anyone who wants to have a good, old-fashioned boogie.
Map 3 A2 **Metro** Jumeirah Lakes Towers

Speakeasy Bar & Restaurant
Pub
Ramada Plaza JBR, Marsa Dubai 04 439 8888
Reflecting on the traditions of speakeasies from the 1920s prohibition era, this American bar offers a wide selection of drinks, cigars, burgers, grills and entertainment including theme nights, DJs, live bands and darts. **Map** 3 A1 **Metro** Jumeirah Lakes Towers

Stereo Arcade
Nightclub
DoubleTree by Hilton Jumeirah Beach, Marsa Dubai 04 558 6062
Hipsters, retro gaming enthusiasts and alternative music lovers cannot get enough of this Dubai version of a uniquely cooler-than-cool dive bar. It's half retro club, half rock pub, with an old school video arcade in the middle featuring classics like Pac Man and Street Fighter. **Map** 3 A1 **Metro** Jumeirah Lakes Towers

Story Rooftop Lounge
Cocktail Bar
Holiday Inn Express Dubai Internet City, Al Sufouh 2 055 773 0010
This arty urban hangout with two rooftop terraces offers sweeping coastal views. The bar is chic, yet bohemian, with funky, abstract Latin-American murals. **Map** 3 C2 **Metro** Dubai Internet City

Going Out

Bars, Pubs & Clubs

Trader Vic's
Cocktail Bar
Souk Madinat Jumeirah, Al Sufouh 1 — 04 366 5646
The famously exotic cocktails, served in ceramic skulls and seashells pack a serious punch – no wonder people love to dance here and the party keeps going until late! **Map** 3 E1 **Metro** Mall of the Emirates

The Underground Pub
Pub
Habtoor Grand Beach Resort & Spa, Marsa Dubai — 04 408 4257
The Underground Pub models itself on an English pub and resonates to the vibrant beat of London – just the ticket for a good night out. **Map** 3 B1 **Metro** DAMAC

Urban Bar & Kitchen
Pub
Movenpick Hotel JLT, Al Thanyah 5 — 04 438 0000
UBK is a great social hangout at any time of the day. There's a warm welcoming ambience in the lounge and in the beer garden.
Map 3 A2 **Metro** Jumeirah Lakes Towers

Vista Lounge
Rooftop Bar
InterContinental Dubai Festival City, Al Kheeran — 04 701 1127
With fabulous views over the creek from the relaxed terrace, this is a romantically lit piano and cocktail bar. **Map** 1 J4 **Metro** Creek

La Vita
Cocktail Bar
Palazzo Versace Dubai, Al Jadaf — 04 556 8860
Located inside the new, ultra-luxurious Palazzo Versace, this bar is great for a little glamour. You can enjoy boutique wines by the glass, creative cocktails and craft beers from a terrace overlooking Dubai Creek. **Map** 1 J3 **Metro** Al Jadaf

White Dubai
Nightclub
The Meydan Hotel, Nadd Al Shiba 1   04 381 3111
This achingly cool club is the Dubai version of its immensely popular sister-club in Beirut and is the place to be seen. It's a must for lovers of electronic and house music thanks to great guest performers and DJ line-ups. **Map** 1 G4

XL Beach Club
Nightclub
Habtoor Grand Beach Resort & Spa, Marsa Dubai   04 399 5000
With ample style and more than a pinch of decadence, XL Beach Club doesn't get going till late, but this is partying under the stars at its finest. Private cabanas and a shimmering pool set the scene, and superstar DJs, stylish crowds, an eye-popping drinks list and lively vibes complete the picture. **Map** 3 B1 **Metro** DAMAC

Zero Gravity
Nightclub
Jumeirah Beach Residence, Marsa Dubai   04 399 0009
This Skydive Dubai-based hangout is rightfully described as a 'day to night oasis'. It's a beach club, a garden, a sports bar, a sexy lounge with viewing deck, and a restaurant. All of this takes on a club vibe the lower the sun drops. **Map** 3 B1 **Metro** DAMAC

Zinc
Nightclub
Crowne Plaza Dubai, Trade Center 1   04 331 1111
The soundtrack to Zinc is modern, funky R&B, house and hip-hop, with Housexy (Ministry of Sound) and Kinky Malinki ferrying over their rostas of UK DJs. Design-wise, there are shiny flatscreens, lounge areas and glitzy mirrored walls, as well as a big dancefloor. **Map** 2 D1 **Metro** Emirates Towers

Index

A

Abaya	13
Abra	61
Abu Dhabi	130
Abu Dhabi Desert Challenge	152
Accidents & Emergencies	43
The Act	224
The Address Dubai Mall	63
The Address Dubai Marina	70
Adrenaline Junkies	30
Adventure Zone By Adventure HQ	92
AED (Arab Emirate Dirham)	39
Aeroplane Tours	138
African Food	238
Al Ahmadiya School & Heritage House	83
Al Ain	132
Al Ain Palace Museum	132
Al Ain Zoo	132
Airlines	35
Airport Bus	36
Airport Transfer	35
Ajman	136
Alcohol	218
All-Terrain Vehicles	154
Alserkal Avenue	31, 94
American Food	238
American Hospital Dubai	43
...ADVERT	ix
Anantara Dubai The Palm	63
Annual Events	49
Aquaventure	28, 32, 160
Arabian Ranches Golf Club	150
Arabian Saluki	159
Arabia's Wildlife Centre	137
Arabic Coffee	9
Arabic Language	40
Arafat Day	48
Architecture	32
Armani Cafe	30
Armani Hotel	62, 63
Art	31, 182
Art Dubai	50
Artisans Of The Emirates (ARTE)	189
Art Sawa	94
Art Source	182
At.mosphere, Burj Khalifa	19
ATMs	39
At The Top, Burj Khalifa	19
Australian Food	238

B

Bab Al Shams Desert Resort & Spa	72
Al Badia Golf Club	150
Baggage Services	34
Balloon	138
Banned Medications	39
Bargaining	180
Bars	310
Bastakiah Nights	221
The Beach at JBR	107
The Beach Waterpark	146, 196
Beaches	29, 146
Belgian Beer Cafe	110
Best Of Dubai	30
Big Red	154
Big Spenders	30
Boating	147
Boat Tours	138
Bollywood Parks Dubai	126
Bookshops	46
Al Boom Diving	149
Al Boom Tourist Village	148
The Boulevard At Emirates Towers	198
Bounce	94
Boxpark	114, 196
Brunch	219
Burj Al Arab	23, 32, 64, 121
Burj Khalifa	19, 32, 63
Burjuman	30, 198

Burkha	13
Bus	55, 138
Bussola	258

C

Cabaret	224
Cafe	238
Camel Museum	80
Camel Racetrack	50
Camel Racing	159
Camel Rides	21
Canal	16, 114
Careem	44
Car Hire	58
Car Rental Agencies	56
Carpets	184
Catamarans	147
Cavalli Club	62, 313
Cayan Tower	32
Central Souk, Sharjah	184
Century Village	111
Children's City	83
Christie's	182
Cigarettes	37
Cinema	222
City Centre	
...Al Shindagha	199
...Deira	198
...Mirdif	199
City Sightseeing Dubai	24, 55, 138
...ADVERT	139
City Walk	115, 200
Climate	38
Clothing	37
Codeine	37
Coffee Museum	80
Coins Museum	80
Comedy	223
Commemoration Day	48
Counterfeit Goods	191
The Courtyard	95
Creek Park	84
Creekside Souks	84
Crime & Safety	42
Crossroads Of Civilisations Museum	80
Cruising	147
Culture	6, 9, 31
Cycling	56

D

D3 (Dubai Design District)	182
Al Dawaar	246
Daylight Saving	38
Department Stores	210
Desert	21
Desert Driving	154
Designers	30, 62, 198, 212
Dhows	147
...Cruise	24
...Dhow Wharfage	31
...Al Gaffal Dhow Race	51
Dirham	39
Disabilities	43
Dishdash	13
Diving	32, 134, 148
DJs	218
Dos & Don'ts	37
Downtown Dubai	27, 98
DP World Tour Championship	149
Dragonboats	110
Dragon Mart	200
Dreamland Aqua Park	160
Drink Driving	37
Driving	58
Driving Range	151
Drugs	37
Drunken Behaviour	37
Dubai Aquarium & Underwater Zoo	30, 190
...ADVERT	101
Dubai Art Season	83
Dubai Autodrome	30, 152
Dubai Butterfly Garden	129
Dubai Canal	16, 114
Dubai Canvas	50
Dubai Creek	82
Dubai Creek Golf & Yacht Club	150

330

Dubai Visitors' Guide

Index

Dubai Dolphinarium	84	Dubai Transport Museum	81	The Farmer's Market		Beach Resort & Spa	70
...ADVERT	v, x	Dubai World Cup	50, 159	On The Terrace	190	Hafit Tombs	133
Dubai Ferry	61	Dubai Youth Hostel	71	Fashion Avenue	30	Hajar Mountains	134, 136
Dubai Festival City	200	DUCTAC	224	Fast-Food	32	Hammam	164
Dubai Food		Dunes	21	Fasting	12	Hatta	30, 135
Festival	50, 221	...Dune Bashing	30, 154	Federation	7	Helicopter Tours	138
Dubai Fountain	27, 100, 158	...Dune Buggies	30	Feeder Bus	54	Heritage	20
Dubai Garden Centre	92			Ferrari World		Heritage &	
Dubai Ice Rink	156	**E**		Abu Dhabi	152	Diving Villages	26, 86
Dubai International		East Asian Food	238	Festival City	110	Heritage Island	81
Airport	16, 34, 43	East Coast	134	Festival Waterfront		Heritage Sites	
Dubai International		Economic Diversification	15	Centre	110	& Museums	81
Art Centre	115	Eid Al Adha	48	Fine Dining	32	Hijri Year	48
Dubai International		Eid Al Fitr	48	Fishing	147	Hilton Dubai Creek	71
Film Festival	51, 222	Electricity & Water	38	Fish Market	22	Hilton Dubai Jumeirah	
Dubai International		Electronics Souk	190	Five Pillars of Islam	10	Resort	65
Kite Fest	50	The Els Club Dubai	151	Flight Information	34	Hindi	40
Dubai International		Emirates	34	Flyboarding	162	History	6
Writers' Centre	85	Emirates Airline Dubai		Flydubai	34	Hong Loong	268
Dubailand	16, 126	Jazz Festival	49, 223	Food & Drink	9, 32	Horse Museum	81
The Dubai Mall	25, 27, 30, 98, 202	Emirates Airline Dubai		Food Tours	221	Hospitality	9
		Rugby Sevens	51, 155	Formula 1 Etihad		Hospitals	43
...ADVERT	203	Emirates Golf Club	151	Airways Grand Prix	152	Hostels	71
Dubai Marina Mall	204	Emirates Palace	130	Four Seasons DIFC	69	Hotels	62
Dubai Marina Yacht Club	70	Emirati Culture	20	Friday Market	190	Houbara Bustard	133
Dubai Maritime Museum	80	Emirati Food	221	Frying Pan Adventures	221	Hypermarkets	212
Dubai Marriott Harbour		Emirati Nationals	15				
Hotel & Suites	70	The Empty Quarter	182	**G**		**I**	
Dubai Miracle Garden	127	Entertainment	218	Al Gaffal Dhow Race	51	Ibn Battuta Mall	206
Dubai Modern		Essential Information	2	Galleries	31, 182	Ice Land Water Park	160
Art Museum	80	European Food	239, 240	Garhoud	110	ifly dubai	158
Dubai Moving		Explorer Art	182	Getting Around	52	Iftar	12
Image Museum	80	Exploring	74	Al Ghurbia	133	IMG Worlds Of	
Dubai Municipality		Expo 2020	14	Al Ghurair Centre	206	Adventure	126
Museum	80			Global Village	127	Imported Food	213
Dubai Museum	26, 31, 86	**F**		Going Out	216	Independent &	
Dubai Offline Map App	44	Al Fahidi Historical	26, 31	Gold	185	Noteworthy Shops	214
Dubai Outlet Mall	204	Neighbourhood	51, 71, 82	Gold & Diamond Park	214	Index Tower	32
Dubai Parks & Resorts	126	Fairmont Dubai	69	Gold Souk	22, 185, 191	Insurance	58
Dubai Police Museum	81	Fake Goods	183	Golf	149	International Fund For	
Dubai Safari Park	126	Falafel	10	Golf Academy	150	Houbara Conservation	133
Dubai Shopping Festival	49	Falcon & Heritage		Grosvenor House	64	...ADVERT	xi, 57
Dubai's Museums &		Sports Centre	81	Guesthouses	71	Irish Village	111, 223
Heritage Sites	80	Falconry	159			Islam	10
Dubai Summer Surprises	51	Falcon Shows	21	**H**		Islamic Calendar	48
Dubai Tram	54	Al Fanar	110, 221	The Habtoor Grand		Islamic New Year	48

askexplorer.com 331

J

JA Jebel Ali	
Golf Resort	73, 151
Thejamjar	31
Jazz Festival	49, 223
Jebel Ali Racecourse	159
Jumeira	114
...Archaeological Site	81
Jumeirah Beach Hotel	65
Jumeirah Beach Park	115
Jumeirah Beach Residence	106
Jumeirah Creekside Hotel	70
Jumeirah Emirates Towers	69, 102
Jumeirah Mosque	12, 20, 116
Jumeirah Zabeel Saray	65, 70
JW Marriott Marquis	69

K

Kahwa	9
Karama	220
Karama Complex	191
Kartdrome	154
Karting	30
Kempinski Hotel Mall Of The Emirates	69
Khandura	13
Khanjars	185
Khan Murjan	183, 192
Khasab Travel & Tours	148
Khor Dubai	82
Khouzi	10
Kidzania	102
Kite Beach	29, 116, 146, 161
Kitesurfing	161

L

Lailat Al Mi'raj	48
Language	40
The Laughter Factory	223

Legoland Waterpark	160
Level Shoe District	30
Live Music	223
Liwa Oasis	134
Local Cuisine	10
Local Knowledge	38
Lost Chambers Aquarium	28
Lost Property	34

M

Mackenzie Art	182
...ADVERT	vi
Madinat Jumeirah	66
Al Maha Desert Resort & Spa	72
The Majlis Gallery	88
Majlis Ghorfat Umm Al Sheif	116
Al Maktoum Family	6
Al Maktoum Hospital Museum	81
Al Maktoum International Airport	16, 34
Malayalam	40
Mall Of The Emirates	30, 206
Mamzar Beach Park	88, 147
Marina Market	192
Marina Walk	107
Markets	188
Al Marmoom ...Camel Racetrack	159
...Heritage Festival	50
Marsa Dubai	70, 106
Massage	164
Mawlid Al Nabee	48
Media & Further Reading	46
Medication	37
Mercato Shopping Mall	207
Meridien Dubai	71
Metro	42
Meydan Racecourse	50, 159
Middle Eastern Food	242
Mobile Apps	44
Mobile Telecoms	44

Modern Dubai	14
Modhesh World	51
Money	39
Monorail	54
Al Montazah	160
Montgomerie Golf Club	151
Mosques	10, 12, 20, 115, 116, 130
Motionegate Dubai	126
Motocross	152
Motorsports	152
Musandam	135, 148
Museum Of The Future	81
Museum Of The Poet Al Oqaili	81
Museums & Heritage Sites	81
Muslims	10

N

Nail Bars	173
Nakhlat Jumeira	120
National Dress	13
New Developments	16, 77, 81, 126, 178
New Dubai: JBR & Marsa Dubai	106
Newspapers & Magazines	46
Nightclubs	220
Nightlife	32, 218
Night-Time Golfing	151
Nobu	28
Nol Card	54
Norman Foster	32
Northern Emirates	136

O

Oasis	132
Off-Roading	136, 154
Old Dubai	82
Omega Dubai Desert Classic	149
One&Only Royal Mirage	66
One&Only The Palm	70

P

The Palace Downtown	66
Palazzo Versace	62, 71
The Palm	28
Palm Monorail	54
Parasailing	30
Park Hyatt Dubai	67
Parking	58
Partying	32
Pashminas	185
Pavilion Dive Centre	149
Pearling	6
Penguins	18
People & Economy	14
Places To Stay	62
Plant Street	117
Plugs	38
Police	42
Population	14
Pork	10
Prayers	10
Prozac	37
Public Holidays & Annual Events	48
Pubs & Clubs	310

Q

Al Qouz	92
Quad Bikes	154
Quad Biking	30

R

Radio	47
Radisson Blu Hotel	71
Raffles Dubai	67
Rainfall	38
Ramadan	12, 49
Ras Al Khaimah	136
Religion	10
RIPE Food & Craft Market	192
Ritz-Carlton	67, 69
Le Royal Meridien	66
Rub Al Khali (Empty Quarter)	134
Rugby	155

332   Dubai Visitors' Guide

Rugs	184
Rules & Regulations	34
Russian Food	242

S

Saadiyat Island	132
Safa Park	117
Safaris	133, 138
Sailing	32, 161
Saks Fifth Avenue	212
Sandboarding	21, 30
Satwa	220
Schengen Visa	36
Seafood	242
Sea Kayaking	161
Sega Republic	102
...ADVERT	IFC
Shangri-La	69
Sharjah	137
Sharjah Golf & Shooting Club	137
...ADVERT	ii, iii
Shawarma	10, 32, 220
Sheikh Mohammed Centre For Cultural Understanding	12, 20 31, 88
Sheikh Saeed Al Maktoum House	89
Sheikh Zayed Grand Mosque	130
Sheraton Dubai Creek Hotel & Towers	70
Sheraton Dubai Mall Of The Emirates	68
Sheylas	13
Shipping	181
Shisha	185, 221
Shopping	25, 30, 176
Shopping Malls	196
Signature Towers	32
SIKKA Art Fair	51, 182
SIM Card	44
Size Conversions	180
Skatepark	95
Skating & Skiing	156
Ski Dubai	18, 30, 121, 156

...ADVERT	157
Skydive	30, 158
Skydive Dubai	158
Skyview Bar	23
Snoopy Island	134
Sofitel Downtown	69
Souk Al Bahar	27, 193
Souk Madinat Jumeirah	122, 193
Souks	22, 31, 188
South American Food	243
South Asian Food	243
South-East Asian Food	244
Souvenirs	31, 185
Spas	164
Special Needs	43
Spice Souk	194
Sports	142
Steakhouses	245
Street Names	60
Street Cafes	32
Street Food	220
Al Sufouh	120
Al Sufouh Beach	122
Summer Temperatures	38
Sunset Beach	29
Supermarkets & Hypermarkets	212

T

Tagalog	40
Tailoring	186
Taxi	35, 58
Telephone & Internet	44
Television	46
Temazepam	37
Textile Souk	22, 194
Theatre	224
The Third Line	31
Timezone	38
Tipping	39
Tourism	15
Tours & Sightseeing	138
Trade	7

Traditional Sports	159
Transit Visa	37
The Trucial States	6

U

UAE National Day	48
Uber	44
Umm Al Quwain	136
Umm Suqeim Beach	147
UESCO World Heritage	82
Union House	117
Urdu	40

V

Vegetarian	219, 245
Visa On Arrival	36
Visas & Customs	36
Visiting Dubai	34
Voltage	38

W

Wadi Adventure	160
Wadis	154
Wafi	209
The Walk At JBR	107, 208
Walking	60
Water	39
Water Bus	61
Water Parks	32, 122, 160
Watersports	32, 106, 137, 161
The Westin Dubai Mina	68
Wheelchair Access	43
Wildlife	133, 137
Wild Wadi Water Park	32 122, 161
...ADVERT	vii
Windsurfing	161
Windtower	26, 83
World Records	15

X

Xline by XDubai	103, 158
XVA Art Hotel & Gallery	31, 71 89

Y

Yachts	147
Yas Island	132
Yas Mall	132
Yas Waterworld	160

Z

Zabeel Park	89
Zaha Hadid	32
Zip Line	103, 158
Zomato	44
Zoo Skatepark	95

Explorer Products

Residents' & Visitors' Guides

Photography Books

Children's & Cultural Books

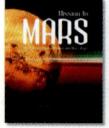

Dubai **Visitors'** Guide

Check out ask**explorer**.com/shop

Maps & Street Atlases

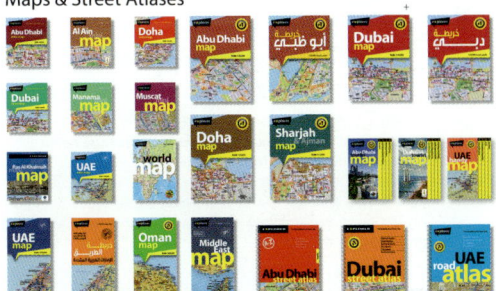

Adventure Guides

Calendars

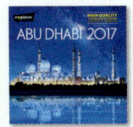

Apps & eBooks
+ Also available as applications.
* Now available in eBook format.
Visit askexplorer.com/shop

explorer

PUBLISHING | MAPPING | CONTENT
محـتـوى | خـرائـط | نـشـر

Dubai Visitors' Guide
9th Edition

Explorer Team
Chief Content Officer & Founder Alistair MacKenzie **Sr. Corporate Editor** Julie Hayes
Editor Emily Snyder **Data managed by** Maria Luisa Reyes, Lara Santizo, Jacqueline Reyes
Designed by Ieyad Charaf, M. Shakkeer, Niyasuthin Batcha **Maps by** Zainudheen Madathil
Photography & Gallery Manager Pamela Grist **Photographs by** Hardy Mendrofa, Pete Maloney, Gary McGovern, Bart Wojcinski, Victor Romero, Henry Hilos **Sales Manager** Bryan Anes **Director of Retail** Ivan Rodrigues

EXPLORER
Explorer is the leading publishing, mapping and content provider in the GCC, boasting a wide range of bestselling retail products and an impressive corporate solutions portfolio, engaging visitors, residents and companies across the Middle East for the past 20 years.

Publishing
Explorer creates engaging content, delivered in a diverse range of consumer and corporate print and digital products.

Mapping
We offer the most innovative and fully client-integrated mapping solutions in the Middle East.

Content
Explorer develops unique content for clients and licenses a huge breadth of consumer content in various formats and languages.

20 YEARS exploring **THE UAE**

PO Box 34275, Dubai, UAE | T +971 4 340 8805 | info@askexplorer.com
askexplorer.com | f ♥ ▶ 8+ ◉ in ⓟ /askexplorer

How can we help you?

MEDIA SALES
sales@askexplorer.com
Contact us for details of our advertising rates, corporate bulk sales, online marketing packages, content licensing and customised wall maps.

RETAIL SALES
retail@askexplorer.com
Check out Explorer retail sales options, distribution services and e-shop orders.

CORPORATE SALES
corporate@askexplorer.com
For all your corporate needs, Explorer services include mapping solutions, corporate gifts, bespoke publications, customised books and a wide range of digital options.

GENERAL ENQUIRIES
info@askexplorer.com
Call us on +971 4 340 8805 as we'd love to hear your thoughts and answer any questions you might have about this book or any Explorer products.

CAREERS
jobs@askexplorer.com
Send us your CV if you are talented, adventurous, knowledgeable, curious, passionate, creative and, above all, fun.

Rate us
We'd love to hear your views on this guide: what you enjoyed, as well as your suggestions. Please share your thoughts with us at *askexplorer.com/feedback*

Win with Explorer
Win exciting prizes by entering Explorer's various online competitions. *askexplorer.com/competitions*

Like us!
Stay up to date with activities, tips and information about the GCC by following us.

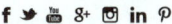

Are you an author?
If you're interested in contributing, or dream of becoming an author yourself, send your ideas. *askexplorer.com/corporate*

Useful Numbers

Dubai Municipality	04 221 5555/800 900
Tourist Security Department	800 4438
Dubai Police (Emergency)	999
Fire Department	997
Ambulance	999/998
American Hospital	04 336 7777
Medcare Hospital	04 407 9111
Life Pharmacy (24 Hour)	04 344 1122
UAE Country Code	+971
Dubai Area Code	04
Directory Enquiries	181/199
International Operator Assistance	100
Weather Updates	04 216 2218

Airport Info

Emirates	600 55 55 55
flydubai	04 231 1000
Dubai International Airport:	
Help Desk	04 224 5555
Flight Information	04 216 6666
Baggage Services	04 224 5383
Al Maktoum International Airport:	
Headquarters	04 814 1111

Taxi Companies

Arabia Taxi	04 285 5111
Dubai Taxi Corporation	04 208 0808
Cars Taxi Services	04 269 3344
Metro Taxis	04 267 3222
National Taxi	04 339 0002